Pg-52 - Def. of Hard Chance

Acknowledgements

I would like to express grateful appreciation to the reporting staffs of the *Sydney Morning Herald* and its sister publications for the reports that served as a foundation for portions of this book. Also, much thanks goes to writer Bryan Burrough for his early and clear account of the Sydney-Hobart race published in *Vanity Fair* magazine. My thanks also goes to the CYCA and Network Ten PTY LTD for their important contributions. And to Karin Ronnow I extend my deepest appreciation for her many unflagging efforts from start to finish.

Kim Leighton

Kim Leighton

A HARD CHANCE

The Sydney-Hobart Race Disaster

WILLOW CREEK PRESS

Minocqua, Wisconsin

Published in 1999 by Willow Creek Press
P.O. Box 147, Minocqua, Wisconsin 54548

For information on other Willow Creek Titles,
call 1-800-850-9453

Library of Congress Cataloging-in-Publication Data

Leighton, Kim.
   A hard chance : the Sydney-Hobart race disaster / by Kim Leighton.
     p. cm.
   ISBN 1-572-23282-X
    1. Sydney-Hobart Race (54th : 1998)--History. 2. Storms--Tasman Sea--
History. 3. Search and rescue operations--Tasman Sea--History. I. Title.

GV832 .L45 1999
797.1'4'0916478--dc21
                                   99-039554
                                       CIP

Printed in the United States

Dedication

A Hard Chance is dedicated to the memory of the six sailors who died in the 1998 Sydney to Hobart and to the indomitable Australian spirit of adventure.

Contents

A Hard Chance: *A term used by old-time sailors to describe a bash into heavy weather.*

Foreword

I n the closing days of the 20th century, despite many technological advances, modern sail boats still sink. But because communications are so immediate and rescue aircraft so swift, loss of life has become the exception rather than the rule.

But even such a safety net was not enough to prevent the deaths of six sailors in Australia's 1998 Sydney to Hobart race. Yet it could have been unimaginably worse.

Forty-eight others in the event, which is known as the Everest of ocean racing, were plucked from certain death by helicopter crews who put their own lives in danger. Additionally, eight were rescued by military ships and fishing boats in what became the largest rescue ever mounted by Australia.

In the 130-year history of ocean racing, the 1998 Sydney to Hobart ranks as Australia's worst disaster and the sport's second-deadliest. Only the 1979 Fastnet race off Great Britain took a larger toll in human life. In both, the killer was a monster storm.

On the day after Christmas 1998, 115 boats and more than 1,135 crew members set sail from Sydney Harbor under a bright sun and in perfect sailing conditions for a 630-nautical-mile race south. Their destination was the capitol of Tasmania, the port city of Hobart. The entire fleet sailed into an ambush the first night that for the next 24 hours mangled boats, injured crew and gripped a nation. The racers were prepared for a rough ride, but not for a malevolent storm with 80-foot spiking waves and winds of 90 miles per hour.

Only 44 of the 115 original boats finished the race. Five were sunk, while four others were dismasted, most after tumbling from the tops of waves the size of seven- and eight-story buildings. Five boats were rolled laterally through 360 degrees. And in addition to the many rescued by helicopters, 25 other crewmen were washed overboard and recovered by their own crew. Of the 71 boats to pull out of the race, 41 were forced out with storm damage; the rest sailed for the nearest port and shelter from the storm.

But statistics don't impart the horror of seeing a fellow crewman and longtime friend shot like a missile across the cabin to a bloody collision with a bulkhead. Nor do they even hint at the panic of being trapped under water in collapsed rigging, knowing that it's your last breath. And statistics are silent when it comes to the utter loneliness and unspeakable despair of being cast adrift at midnight to die alone in a tempest.

This is a true story about sailors and the sea. But it is also the story of thoroughly modern urban men and women trying to keep a tacit link to the natural world, and their nobility when it turns against them. Ultimately, it is an ancient story played out on a modern stage.

Until little more than 100 years ago, world exploration, commerce, cultural exchange and conquest were borne by wooden ships and canvas sail. In the process, untold thousands of ships and crew have met their end in violent storms.

Boats under sail remain the workhorses of Third World and some developing nations. But it is largely the First World nations where sailing technology continues to be developed. And almost all developments arise from recreational sailing — racing in particular.

It is likely that no racing skipper thinks of himself or herself as the custodian of the world's knowledge of sailing. They sail because it is a passion, one they share with others around the world. In the sharing lies the heartbeat that keeps sailing alive. Competitive sailing began in Great Britain and spread to Australia and the United States. But unlike the U.S.

and the U.K., sailing in Australia, where 90 percent of its people live near the coast, is far more egalitarian. In races such as the Sydney to Hobart, for every tycoon and multi-million dollar superyacht, there are 10 owner/skippers of moderate means who have made sacrifices to sail their smaller boats in the race.

Wealthy or not, each skipper wants to win the race. Some, like the overall winner of the 1998 event, consider it a holy grail, a quest of such significance that it is passed down through generations. The Sydney to Hobart remains one of blue-water racing's few premier amateur events. But corporate sponsorship and safety zealots are threatening the "Hobart." And it would be tragic to lose the Everest of amateur ocean racing to either — a loss that would extend far beyond the world of ocean racing.

Defending the Sydney to Hobart shortly after one of his countrymen was killed in the event, Britain's Robin Knox-Johnston, the first man to sail around the world non-stop, solo, said: "For many of us, a life without mental and physical challenges would be a life without color or stimulus. We react in differing ways according to our characters — some people climb mountains, some try to balloon around the world. And those who feel the call of the sea, search for the hardest races. It is because they want to stand a little taller than their friends who have not competed in such a tough event. They also want the satisfaction of knowing that they have achieved something special. The greater risk adds the spice, makes the adrenaline course, the eyes brighter, the senses fully alert. Yes, it is dangerous, but it brings real meaning to living. If society wants to bar mankind from such stimulation, then the whole human species might as well be castrated."

Kim Leighton
June 30, 1999

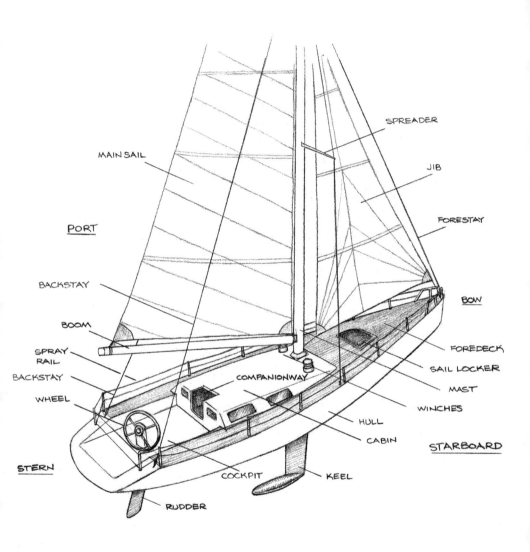

SPREADER

MAIN SAIL

JIB

PORT

FORESTAY

BACKSTAY

BOW

BOOM

SPRAY
RAIL

FOREDECK

BACKSTAY

SAIL LOCKER

WHEEL

COMPANIONWAY

MAST

WINCHES

HULL

CABIN

STARBOARD

STERN

COCKPIT

KEEL

RUDDER

A brief look at the outer components that make up a typical sailboat like the ones in the Sydney Hobart race

The "Run-Up" to the 54ᵗʰ Sydney to Hobart

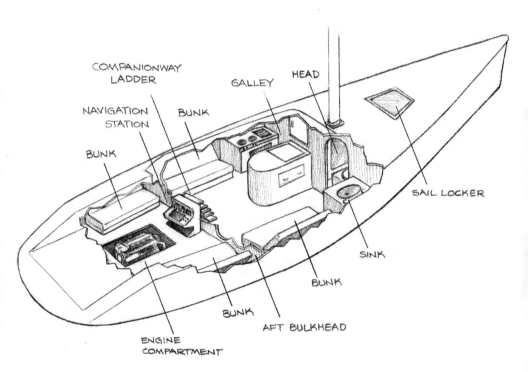

COMPANIONWAY
LADDER

GALLEY   HEAD

NAVIGATION
STATION   BUNK

BUNK

SAIL LOCKER

SINK

BUNK

BUNK   AFT BULKHEAD

ENGINE
COMPARTMENT

A brief look at the inner components that make up a typical sailboat like the ones in the Sydney Hobart race

CYCA Investigation into Tragic Sydney to Hobart
21-Jan-99 12:00 AM

The Cruising Yacht Club of Australia (CYCA) today issued the following press release regarding its review of the 1998 Telstra 54th Sydney to Hobart Yacht Race in which six yachtsmen died and seven yachts were abandoned by their crews when a severe storm hit the 115 boat fleet in Bass Strait on December 27-28, 1998:

During the storm, winds were reported from the west and southwest at up to 78 knots, with breaking seas of 10 metre height in the area about 50 to 60 nautical miles south-east of Gabo Island off the south-eastern tip of mainland Australia. Of the 115 yachts which started in the race, only 44 finished the 630 nautical mile course.

This initiated the biggest search and rescue operation in the history of the ocean classic, with a total of 55 yachtsmen being rescued, 50 of them by helicopters in some heroic operations by the pilots and crew.

CYCA Commodore Hugo van Kretschmar said that it would be several months before the 1998 Sydney Hobart Race Review Committee's work would be completed and findings announced. "While we are moving as fast as we can, thoroughness, not speed, is what's important now," he said. "We are working closely with the Coroner and respecting his wishes and keeping the details of our Review confidential.

"In the fullness of time our finding and recommendations will be a matter of public record, but until that time it is critical that the Committee get on with the job."

Mr. van Kretschmar dismissed suggestions that the Club would not conduct an objective review on the basis all yachties have a vested interest in the outcome. "Our only interest is to reduce risk and improve safety for not only ocean racing but also every single person who ventures to sea in a boat," he said.

The Committee has already established a Frame of Reference and issued an initial Questionnaire to the 1998 Sydney-Hobart Race fleet. The Frame of Reference includes:

- Race Background
- Weather
- Communications
- The ability of yachts and equipment to withstand the conditions
- The ability of Skippers and Crews to withstand the conditions
- Search and Rescue

It is expected to be some weeks before these questionnaires are completed and the results tabled to provide the Committee with a detailed understanding of exactly what the issues are. "Some aspects of our Review are self evident, and we are addressing them immediately, others are not and will only become clear from the results of the questionnaire and review submissions from other interested parties," Mr. van Kretschmar said.

Overleaf: *With metropolitan Sydney in the background, Sydney to Hobart boats maneuver behind the starting line in the minutes before the race.*

Sydney, Australia, Dec. 26, 1998 — Three hundred thousand people — fully 10 percent of Australia's oldest and largest city — are gathered in groups large and small on the promontories of Sydney Harbor. It is Boxing Day, a national holiday celebrated throughout the British Commonwealth, from which Australia has been independent since 1901. For the crowds jamming the harbor, piers and headlands, and the 115 sailing yachts and their crews which number 1,000, assembling on the starting line, it is a higher holiday. It is the start of the 54th annual Sydney to Hobart yacht race.

Begun as a cruise under sail from Sydney, down the coast of New South Wales and ending at the port city of Hobart in Tasmania, the Sydney to Hobart has steadily gained stature and status. It now ranks with such ocean-racing icons as the America's Cup, the English Whitbread and the Irish Fastnet as a world-class ocean race. Due to currents, sea depth and Antarctic weather influences, the Sydney to Hobart eclipses its companion blue-water classics. The 630-nautical-mile Sydney to Hobart is the Everest of yacht racing.

But for the throngs gathered under the midmorning sun that pushes the temperature to the 90s for the 1 p.m. start of the race, it is a festive occasion. Christmas Day is a fond memory and the New Year celebration that will usher in the last year of the century and the countdown to the 2000 Olympics in Sydney is just days away. Punctuating the excitement, nine news and film helicopters — "flying dirt bikes," as some Australians call helicopters — buzz the fleet, each vying for an optimum camera angle. Still others, in an impromptu regatta of power yachts, jet skis and daysailers, shadow the thoroughbreds to the line. And seemingly not to be outdone, landlocked fans send aloft a multi-hued garland of kites that weave and bob in the breeze in colorful counterpoint to the racing fleet's stark white sails.

On board the boats in the international field of entries, sailors — men and women from the ages of 12 to 74 — make final preparations for the start. Local favorite *Brindabella*, a 75-foot "maxi" skippered by Australian George Snow with a crew of 21 is in the hunt for her second consecutive win. *Brindabella* is a serious ocean racer built for the purpose. She's built for speed.

Brindabella's main rival is *Sayonara*, a huge maxi at 80 feet. Skippered by American Larry Ellison and with a crew of 23, *Sayonara* has been kept under wraps in the days leading up to the race, which has prompted wide-ranging press speculation in the *Sydney Morning Herald* and other area newspapers. Like *Brindabella, Sayonara* was designed as an ocean racer, spartan, light and strong, with few concessions to creature comfort. Like her design, *Sayonara's* crew was selected by Ellison, the billionaire owner of Oracle Software, from among the very best in ocean racing. Ellison and *Sayonara* are here to win.

But the Sydney to Hobart, true to its origin, is not comprised just of yachts and skippers with a laser-like focus on crossing the finish line first. Some, like the crew of the *Winston Churchill*, are content to compete within their class and handicap. At 49 feet, the venerable cutter named for wartime Britain's prime minister, with his blessing, is setting out on her 17th Sydney to Hobart. One of the few wooden boats in the race, the *Winston Churchill* sailed the first Sydney to Hobart in 1945. While serious competitors, Sydney Skipper Richard Winning and his crew of eight revere the aging cutter and tip their hats more to history than to line honors.

Still others, such as 19-year-old Liz Wardley of Port Moresby, Victoria, are competing for the experience and with an eye on line honors in future Sydney to Hobarts. A champion catamaran racer in the 16-foot class, Skipper Wardley's keen sense of competition and her seamanship skills at the helm of her 39-foot *Dixie Chicken* could surprise everyone. If not, she'll be a force to reckon with in future races.

And there are many others with professional crews, the will to win and the skill to pull it off. Yachts tack back and forth in the harbor, limbering up, sporting such fanciful names as *Marchioness, Adagio, Kingurra,*

Midnight Rambler, Tevake, Scarborough of Cerebrus and *Sword of Orion*. Too, there are boats that bear international corporate names, because in corporate culture the Sydney to Hobart is prime time.

At the gun, the yachts leap for the starting line several hundred yards distant, 115 mainsails and jibs coming to perfect trim for the 3-mile run to the Sydney Heads. And not without purpose. Besides the trophy for reaching the heads first, with the wind at 15 knots from the northwest, the boat that clears the heads, turns south and unfurls its spinnaker, a large parachute-like sail designed for running with the wind, has an early advantage. It's a spectacle of grace and skill as the yachts heel sharply to leeward, their crews sitting side by side on the windward deck to counterbalance their boats. The helicopters hover and dart about like summer dragonflies while an armada of spectator boats follow the fleet to the Heads and beyond.

Six hundred and thirty nautical miles distant, in Hobart, preparations are under way for the arrival of the racers and the start of Tasmania's mardi gras, a New Year's party celebrating the Sydney to Hobart yacht race and, close on its heels, the Melbourne to Hobart yacht race.

Meanwhile, off the coast of southeast Australia a storm of massive magnitude is brewing and taking its bearings.

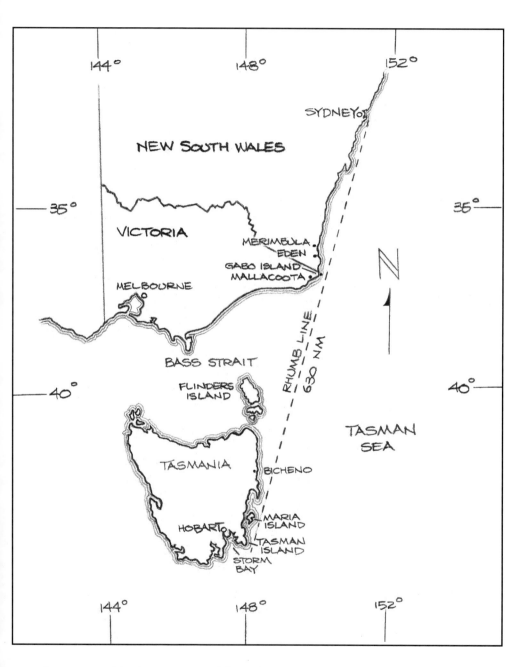

The 630 nautical mile race course of the Sydney to Hobart.

"But in the same way that the Kentucky Derby transcends being a mere horse race, the Sydney to Hobart takes on a life of its own. It is not a weekend regatta subject to postponement in the event of inclement weather."

—Kim Leighton

A Southerly "Bomb" Takes Shape

ecember 1998 was a chaotic weather month for Australia. Early in the month, a pair of hurricanes, or cyclones as they are called west of the international date line, Billy and Thelma, struck the sparsely populated northwest coast. The strongest, Thelma, born in the Timor Sea off Indonesia, packed winds of 155 miles an hour and gusts in excess of 180 miles an hour. It is unusual for such Category 5 hurricanes to make landfall anywhere in the world, but when one does, it is devastating, especially in populous areas. One, Hurricane Camille, struck the United States coast in Mississippi in 1969, killing 256 people and causing $1.4 billion in damage.

In Tasmania, the Australian island state off the coast of Victoria and the end of the Sydney to Hobart yacht race, record-breaking high temperatures were recorded in December.

On December 26 and 27, gale winds of up to 54 miles an hour with gusts up to 90 miles an hour toppled trees and leveled buildings in several inland communities on the southeast coast of Australia, in Victoria. A rapidly developing deep depression over eastern Bass Strait, the 100 miles of ocean between Victoria and Tasmania, was the culprit. Just before the cold front swept through Victoria, unseasonably warm weather lured thousands of beach-goers to the Victorian coast. Lifeguards had their busiest single day ever, rescuing 44 swimmers from unusually strong rip tides.

But when the low front swept through, it brought snow and biting temperatures. Thousands of people from Melbourne headed west for Australia's "Swiss Alps" the day after Christmas to ski and toboggan on a day when the temperature is typically in the mid-80s. Ski lifts that usually carry mountain bikers to their alpine riding trails during Australia's summer were locked in a thick coating of ice and could not be operated. Farther inland, the developing low front caused huge dust storms and wind-blown forest fires.

For the 115 yachts racing from Sydney to Hobart, it was the handwriting on the wall.

The Tasman Sea off the coast of New South Wales and Bass Strait have long been a challenge for sailors. For one, the area lies in the 40th latitude, what sailors call the "roaring forties" for the constant west wind. Too, Bass Strait is shallow, at one-fifth the depth of the adjacent Tasman Sea. This has the effect of greatly amplifying the surface activity of the strait. Developing storm waves that in deeper water build and extend well below the surface are forced by Bass Strait's lack of depth to extend above the surface. The term "mountainous seas" truly applies.

And then the East Australian Current, a branch of the South Equatorial Current between Australia and South America, is a factor. This current is essentially a massive river within the ocean that moves from north to south at up to five miles an hour along the coast of New South Wales, breaks at Tasmania and sweeps east to New Zealand. When the wind and the current off the coast of New South Wales move in somewhat the same direction, sailing can be pleasant if not exhilarating. When the wind and the current come from opposite directions, sailing the same area can be deadly.

Additionally, where the Tasman Sea and Bass Strait meet, on Tasmania's northeastern tip amid barrier islands, the East Australian Current, unimpeded for thousands of miles, is countered by the West Wind Drift, a huge corridor of jetstream between southern Australia and Antarctica. As this jetstream passes south of Tasmania, it bifurcates through Bass Strait and, squeezed between Tasmania and the mainland, increases in velocity. Driven by the West Wind Drift, the waters of Bass Strait essentially collide with the southerly current of the Tasman Sea, making the area a longstanding navigational hazard. Indeed, the undersea flanks of the rugged Tasmanian coast are littered with ships of all types that were caught in the area's complex winds, currents and fast-rising storms from the Antarctic.

This powerful cocktail of natural forces is what makes the Sydney to Hobart yacht race the Everest of ocean racing. Yet while the Sydney to Hobart has always been challenging, it has seldom been lethal. It has, however, had its moments.

Powerful squalls during the 1956 event prompted what was at the time Australia's largest search and rescue. Eighty-mile-an-hour winds dismasted many boats. One yacht, the 36-foot *Renene,* was blown well off the racecourse and lost its radio and engine. The crew tied itself to the mast until the boat was found — three days later.

A proposal to have a corvette, an escort boat, sail with the racing fleet and assist with emergencies was roundly rejected. The highly individualistic skippers of the Sydney to Hobart refused to be chaperoned, "nursemaided," as they called it.

More than 20 years later, in 1977, a vicious storm hit the Hobart fleet and an unprecedented 50 boats withdrew from the race. In the 35 preceding Sydney to Hobart races the greatest number of withdrawals had been 15. The number of boats quitting the race in 1977 was portentous. Two years later, the Fastnet race in the Irish Sea became the world's great-

est ocean-racing disaster. Only 85 boats of the fleet of 303 finished the
storm-racked race, and 15 sailors were killed. Safety regulations for
Australian yacht races were tightened in reaction to the fatal Fastnet race.

In the 1988 Sydney to Hobart, 29 storm-battered boats pulled out of
the race with broken masts and injured crewmen. One crewman was hit
by a boom and died in the hospital weeks later. It was the first death in
the 46-year history of the blue-water event. But a year later, another man
was killed in the race when a collapsing mast struck him on the head.
Then, in the 1993 Sydney to Hobart, a 20-year-old man died of a heart
attack. Sixty-six boats pulled out of the 1993 race and its harsh conditions, a new record for withdrawals. In the 1995 event, a 39-year-old man
was washed overboard in the storm and lost at sea.

By 1998, the Sydney to Hobart had claimed five lives during its 54-
year history, which had fielded more than 4,300 boats and 34,000 crewmen. This remarkable safety record is in large part due to the seamanship
skills of Sydney to Hobart participants, mostly Australian, and the expert-
ise of Australian rescue authorities.

But there were different forces at work during the 1998 race. Chief
among them was the weather. The racers and organizers were given an
equivocal warning by the New South Wales Meteorology Bureau of a
developing storm a day before the race began. Many veterans of the race,
accustomed to the weather vagaries of Bass Strait and confused by the
equivocal forecast, interpreted it as a "southerly buster," a squall, not a
"bomb," as the strait's treacherous low-pressure systems are called. But in
the same way that the Kentucky Derby transcends being a mere horse
race, the Sydney to Hobart takes on a life of its own. It is not a weekend
regatta subject to postponement in the event of inclement weather.
Indeed, the compelling forces that bring the boats to the starting line are
imbued from the moment the boat begins taking shape on the marine
architect's drawing board. And those forces themselves are sired by the rare

breed who aspire to win world-class ocean races. The lead-up to a race such as the Sydney to Hobart is long, costly, complex and deliberate, beginning, in most cases, years before the event.

Fundamentally, a world-class boat is modern alchemy, a blending of hull and keel design and composition with rigging, sail plans and fittings. But to make it fly requires a skipper and crew with the experience and will to wring the utmost from its thoroughbred heart. For such a sailing yacht and crew, a major ocean race such as the Sydney to Hobart is a unique and important test of overall performance. The Sydney to Hobart is one race among many as the crew campaigns the boat in other races, under other conditions. Each race is unique and adds to the crew's cumulative experience and is therefore not to be missed.

That is not to say that safety is overlooked in a vigorous sailing campaign. Safety in modern yacht racing is mandated by a host of international rules and regulations that are augmented and enforced by the sponsoring yacht club. But the highest maritime safety law is defined by an ancient rule of the sea that remains in full force today: A captain is the master of his vessel. That means the captain's knowledge and experience prevail. It's the reason behind the noble gesture of a captain going down with his ship, which was commonplace well into the 20th century. And the maritime axiom continues to work because its underlying principle is direct accountability: action, reaction; cause and effect. In practice it means that informed decisions are the *lingua franca* of life aboard ship. Faulty decisions can and often do have a price in human lives.

Too, there are societal and economic factors that drive ocean racing. While Australia has a seafaring history inherited from Great Britain, yacht racing is largely an expression of the refreshing irrepressibility of its people. Somewhat fateful in their approach to life, Australians have forged a vibrant, multi-tiered economy that affords them free time. And Australians take their free time seriously and work hard at having fun. As in most countries, ownership of a world-class racing yacht is reserved for the wealthy. And on some social levels in Australia "yachties," as they're called, are dismissed as the idle rich and their yacht clubs are perceived as the domains of the privileged. But when it comes to yacht racing, there are few other major metropolitan areas in the world that turn out 300,000 local residents to herald the start of a race. Although not as popular as Australian football, yacht racing gets far more than grudging support.

As its popularity has grown, the Sydney to Hobart has evolved into a multi-million dollar event sponsored by some of the world's largest corporations: Telstra, Nokia, ABN Amro Merchant Bank, CSR, Canon, Foxtel, Computerland, Maglieri Wines, Mercedes and Trust Bank. In that regard, the Sydney to Hobart is no different than other blue-water ocean races. There is a corporate esprit de corps that infuses the event.

Against such a backdrop, the 1998 Sydney to Hobart was a maritime juggernaut on a collision course with a force of unparalleled strength and fury.

The 55 foot cutter Winston Churchill *and her crew in one of the last photographs taken of the boat*

The Start: *A Magnificent Day to Sail*

S ayonara and her crew of 23 seasoned yachtsmen arrived in Sydney with a mission: to win line honors. To win line honors in a yacht race simply means being the first boat to cross the finish line. There are overall honors and winners based on handicap by the size of a boat. But for the maxis, the boats of 70 feet and larger, the big prize, *Sayonara's* objective, was line honors.

Sayonara represented the quintessential alchemic blend of the right boat and the right crew. Shortly after her American Farr-designed hull was laid in 1995 in New Zealand, *Sayonara* captured line honors in the Sydney to Hobart. Two years later, Australia's *Brindabella*, also a maxi, took line honors in the Hobart. For the 1998 Sydney to Hobart, Ellison, *Sayonara's* owner, had hired a crew of professional racing sailors chosen from among Olympic medalists and the New Zealand national ocean-racing team. More experienced now, and fresh from a significant Maxi Worlds win at Newport, Rhode Island, Ellison had returned to Australia with his eye on the prize.

Despite its name, *Sayonara* was a Sydney to Hobart entry from the United States. Ellison is the 52-year-old billionaire chief executive officer of Oracle software and *Sayonara's* home port is San Francisco. Billed as one of the most advanced maxi racing yachts in the world, *Sayonara* was designed, built, fitted and rigged for speed in every detail. From her honeycomb carbon-fiber hull, to her graphite-composite mast and boom, to her titanium winches and fittings, to her high-tech synthetic sails, *Sayonara,* at 80 feet, is a remarkable balance of strength and light weight.

A year after Ellison sailed in the 1995 Sydney to Hobart aboard *Sayonara,* his chief rival in the business world, German software mogul Hasso Plattner, not only won the race but set a new record. In 1998, Plattner kept his maxi *Morning Glory* out of the race. Ellison had a bit of hard-edged fun in the Sydney press about *Morning Glory's* absence at Plattner's expense. But without *Morning Glory, Brindabella* was *Sayonara's* chief rival.

Brindabella was a 75-foot Australian Jutson design fresh from her own recent round of good racing results and refitted with a new carbon-fiber mast. She had returned to the 1998 Sydney to Hobart as the defending champion. *Brindabella's* skipper, Sydney financial executive George Snow, and his crew of 22 were after line honors for the second consecutive year. She sailed out of the Cruising Yacht Club of Australia (CYCA), which annually fields 70 percent of the Sydney to Hobart entrants. Unlike Ellison, Snow, like most Australian competitors, crewed *Brindabella* with amateurs, friends and relatives who shared his keen interest in ocean racing and with whom he had sailed for several years. But the crew of *Brindabella* was amateur only in that its members were not paid to crew. Most of the crew members had Hobarts under their belts and many had sailed the event a dozen times or more.

A third maxi, *Wild Thing,* was also in the hunt for line honors. A 70-footer of Australian design, *Wild Thing* was considered the favorite in the race. Her skipper and owner Grant Wharington of Victoria had taken the unusual approach of buying the spare racing mast and sails of *One Australia,* the country's America's Cup entry, and designing the smallest boat possible to sail under the huge rig. What Australian yacht designer

The American maxi Sayonara sets her sights on Hobart.

Andy Dovell came up with was a sleek, fast sloop with the potential to fly through the oceans of the South Pacific. With the downwind conditions forecast for the Hobart, conditions in which *Wild Thing* excelled, the Cruising Yacht Club listed her as "the one to beat," even though this was her first major contest since she was launched three months earlier.

Also in the field of boats were such notables as *Nokia, Fudge, Ausmaid, Marchioness* and *Ragamuffin*. Each was a svelte thoroughbred and each could win the race. Some ran downwind best; some ran best upwind. All but *Wild Thing* had a proven track record, and nothing within the skippers' control was left to chance. But as each knew, chance plays a role in ocean racing. A broken mast, a disabled rudder, an injured crew member can happen under the best of circumstances. The 1998 Hobart was far from the best of circumstances and chance would affect all in the 115-boat fleet — none for the better.

To race in the Sydney-Hobart, a boat must be at least 30 feet long and carry a crew of six. It does not take six sailors to operate a 30-foot sail boat. But since it is a non-stop race of 630 nautical miles that can take as long as five days to complete, two full crews are required on all boats, regardless of size. One crew rests while the other crew sails. The watches are set by the skipper and can last from three to six hours, depending on the rigors of the race.

It is the smaller boats that account for 90 percent of the entrants in the Hobart year in and year out. And like their Australian brethren on the maxis, the smaller boats are crewed by amateur sailors who often are friends and relatives of the owner. And like the crews of the Australian maxis, the crews of the smaller boats participate out of love of the sport and have extensive ocean-racing experience, especially in the Hobart.

Two such smaller boats in the 1998 Hobart were *AFR Midnight Rambler* and *Aspect Computing*. Both boats were somewhat unusual in that they had financial sponsorships, which most of the maxis have and which most of the smaller boats do not. *AFR Midnight Rambler*, co-owned and skippered by Sydney accountant Ed Psaltis, was sponsored by the Australian Financial Review. Psaltis, 39, and his partner Bob Thomas bought the boat in early December, only weeks before the race. *Midnight Rambler*, a 1994-vintage Hickman, was designed and built specifically for the Hobart. Psaltis had competed in six Hobarts in a 30-footer, also named *Midnight Rambler*. Nonetheless, his unfamiliarity with the new boat made the prospect of a top finish an attainable but lofty goal.

"We had the boat trucked up from Melbourne and got it ready to race. It was a real rush. We all knew that we had a good boat and that this could be our best Hobart. But given our preparation time, we thought we'd just do our best," he said behind the hint of a smile.

David Pescud, skipper of *Aspect Computing*, is a big bear of a man with a red beard and mustache that set off a pair of eyes that can be mischievous one moment and piercing the next. When he tries to recall a telephone number during an interview, he apologizes in frustration. "I'm dyslexic," he says. "I can't remember the bloody thing. Hell, I can't remember my address." Since 1994, though, Pescud has headed up the "Sailors With disAbilities" program, the only one like it in the world.

Each year Pescud crews 60-foot *Aspect Computing* with six physically or mentally handicapped sailors and six "ABs," or able-bodied, for the Sydney to Hobart race. With few exceptions, all crew members earn their berths. For the 1998 Hobart, the 1984-vintage sloop's crew included two dyslexics, a stroke victim, a blind man and a woman with multiple sclerosis. *Aspect Computing* also carried the Hobart fleet's youngest crewman, 12-year-old Travis Foley, who is dyslexic. *Aspect's* best finish had been a respectable division third place in 1995. But Pescud knew that credibility for his boat, for his crew and for his unique organization lay in remarkable finishes, not respectable finishes. By 1998 he had made improvements to the boat, which was designed as a serious racer. Too, he had what he considered a race-honed crew. *Aspect Computing* was, by Pescud's description, a "gun boat," a serious contender.

Unlike any other international ocean race, the Sydney to Hobart sends all boats off the starting line at the same time. Hitting the starting line at full speed is the ideal start. But with 115 experienced crews and yachts all trying to do that and then maneuver for an ideal starboard tack to the Sydney Heads, the competition is fierce.

The start of the Sydney to Hobart usually brings all boats to the harbor at least two hours before the starting gun. Skippers and crew are getting the feel of the day's sailing conditions. Some are sailing out past the heads and back. Twenty minutes before the race begins, key decisions are made about which sails to use from among the boat's wardrobe of specialized sails — primarily mainsails and spinnakers.

Ten minutes before the race begins, the starter boat raises signal flags and fires a pre-start warning cannon. Now each boat begins to reveal its starting-line tactic, which must follow a couple of inflexible rules. A false start — crossing the line before the starting gun — means a boat has to return and start again. There is a danger of being forced over the starting line early. At full speed and with boats close on either side heading for the starting line, a tactician who misjudges has nowhere for his boat to go except across the line — a false start. The option is to start in the second row of boats, which puts a boat in the wind shadow of the first-row boats. The result is often a slower start. Equally important is the right-of-way rule. A boat tacking to port must yield to a boat on a starboard tack. That means that when two boats are approaching the same point at opposite angles on their zigzag tacking paths, the boat on the right has to reduce speed and pass behind the boat on the left. Since the wind was out of the northeast at 15 knots the day of the race, the preferred start was a starboard tack up the right (south) side of the harbor.

Five minutes before the start of the Sydney to Hobart, the starter boat fires a second gun and again raises its flags. At this point the crews trim sails and get in position to begin the high-speed run for the starting line.

With seconds to go before the start the bowman checks his stopwatch and signals the distance to the starting line to the boat's helmsman and tactician. The precision approach to the starting line is akin to drag racing. Dragsters rev their engines at top speed as the lights change from yellow to green and attempt to cross the line the first millisecond the light turns green. If the bowman's calculations are correct and the sail trimmers, the driver and the tactician do everything just right, the boat hits the starting line at full speed right at the starting gun, fired at exactly 1 p.m. by Australian Eastern Standard Time.

Despite the careful preparations for the race, *Sayonara* was hobbled just before the starting gun when a starboard jib winch broke down. Winches are indispensable pieces of hand-operated equipment on a sailboat that allow the trimming or inboard tightening of the mainsail and the jib, the triangular sail just forward of the mainsail. When sailing into an oncoming wind or to windward, a properly trimmed sail means speed. A boat that is "on the wind" or positioned to take maximum advantage of an oncoming wind will have its sails trimmed tightly to the lateral centerline of the boat. On the wind and with sails trimmed, the boat will heel over at a significant angle and fly through the water. In all but the smallest sailboats, though, it is far beyond human strength to trim a sail without the help of a powerful winch. Thus *Sayonara* was hindered, though far from crippled. She was off the line fast and well. But it was the first in a series of incidents and of sufficient magnitude for Ellison to call the start of the race "ominous."

As omens go, another starting-line incident involved the maxi ketch *Nokia*, the largest boat in the fleet, which grazed Sydney-based *Sword of Orion* and *Bright Morning Star*. And while the ordeal that lay ahead was fearsome for most, *Sword of Orion's* fate was to be much worse.

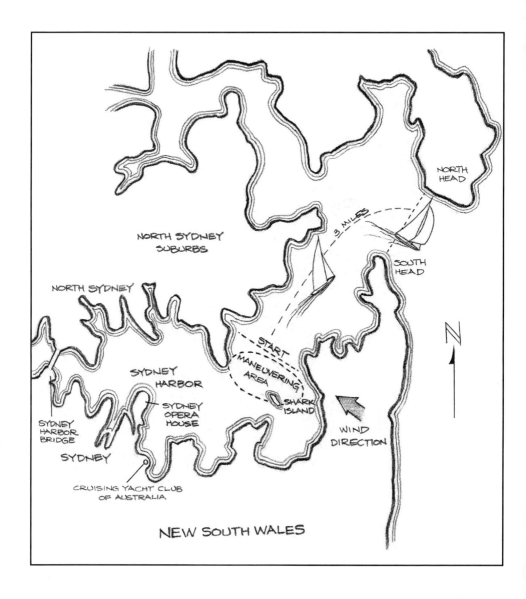

NORTH
HEAD

NORTH SYDNEY
SUBURBS

3 MILES

SOUTH
HEAD

NORTH SYDNEY

START

MANEUVERING
AREA

SYDNEY
HARBOR

SYDNEY
OPERA
HOUSE

SHARK
ISLAND

N

SYDNEY
HARBOR
BRIDGE

WIND
DIRECTION

SYDNEY

CRUISING YACHT CLUB
OF AUSTRALIA

NEW SOUTH WALES

Detail of the start of the Sydney to Hobart

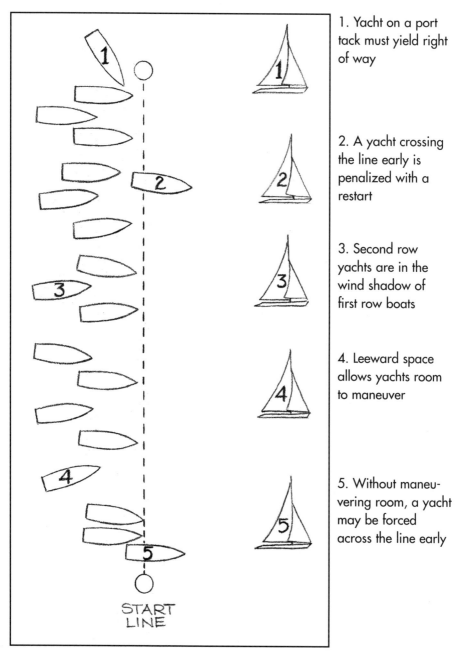

1. Yacht on a port tack must yield right of way

2. A yacht crossing the line early is penalized with a restart

3. Second row yachts are in the wind shadow of first row boats

4. Leeward space allows yachts room to maneuver

5. Without maneuvering room, a yacht may be forced across the line early

START LINE

Starting Line principles

Defending champion *Brindabella* got a good start, though not the one the crew wanted. "What we thought about at the start was that we were slower upwind than *Sayonara* and if we could get ahead that first day and try to hold her out we would have a good chance to win the race," said Geoff Cropley, *Brindabella's* chief sail trimmer. "We knew she had a very good bunch of professional sailors crewing her and that it was going to be a tough race. We came off the line nicely, but there was a bit of a shift in the wind and we had to tack into a bit of an alleyway. When we tacked she took first on our starboard and went up the right side of the harbor, where we had to go up the left side of the harbor to get clear. As a result, *Sayonara* led us out of the harbor, not by much — I think by about five or six lengths. It's about three miles up the harbor and around two turning markers you've got to go around. All of that was pretty uneventful. There were no mishaps or anything like that. So the harbor race was fun."

Wild Thing also got a good start, though *Sayonara* edged her out too. "We got quite a good start," said *Wild Thing's* sailing master Scott Gilbert. "Our problem was that *Sayonara* was on top of us and they actually rolled over the top of us soon after the start, to windward. *Brindabella* was just to the leeward of us. We had a pretty good race with the two boats going out through the heads. And in the end *Sayonara* and *Brindabella* beat us out of the heads by two or three boat lengths. It's always good to be first out of the heads, but it doesn't determine the outcome of the race."

Most of the maxis got off the starting line and away before the big maxi *Nokia* struck *Sword of Orion* and others. But not the smaller boats, which were affected in a chain reaction that threatened to become a pile-up. *Aspect Computing* was one of those.

"We had a really good start and we were very happy about it four minutes out, which helped us get into it," said Pescud. "We had four people who were racing their first Hobart and they were really excited. So you're trying to keep them down, and two of them were critical on the boat, two headsail trimmers. So you're just trying to hold them down and just get into the race. And it's important to get a good start in the Hobart. You want to get out in front quick and it sets the boat up so that you're not playing catch-up before you're away. We didn't need any boats in our way. It was a 15- to 18-knot nor'easter, just a run for us, and *Aspect* is very fast when running. So we thought we'd get out to the heads among the top 15 boats and in those conditions we'd run them down. In those conditions we should have been in the top 10 pretty fast and sitting on the back end of the big guns, the maxis. Unfortunately one of the maxis, *Nokia*, came across and got in an altercation with other boats. We got the backwash of it.

"What happened was everybody went roaring off. *Sword Of Orion* came up and hit the weather. *Nokia* came screaming down on starboard tack, head to weather. *Sword* backed their headsail and shot onto port tack. So now they've got no rights [of way] at all. *Nokia's* coming hammering in on top of them. We're trailing in high up [going almost directly into the wind], but *Nokia* can't point as high as *Aspect*. So they're going to go to this point and we're going to [cross paths without incident]. All of a sudden *Nokia* threw onto port [tack]. And, shit, we're screaming at them to get back on starboard. So we've got to hit the brakes and dive around. And everybody's then sort of in this dive-around mode, which put us on the port side of the harbor. And we were stuck on the port side. The starboard side is the side to go out on. But we got out there in pretty fine shape."

In defense of the Hobart fleet's largest boat, *Nokia* crewman Andrew Short said the fault for the starting-line mishap lay with *Sword Of Orion*. "*Sword Of Orion* came in behind us and got below us and then got into trouble by getting in the wind shadow of our mainsail. We're almost twice as big as she is. We tacked over onto port and had the rest of the fleet coming down on us on starboard."

The collision will likely be the subject of study among race tacticians. But no protest was filed. And like *Sword Of Orion's* skipper, Rob Kothe said: "In the context of things it really became an unimportant matter."

For Ed Psaltis and his new and diminutive 35-footer, *Midnight Rambler*, the start could almost have served as a miniature shakedown cruise. It was, he said, a good one.

At least for the moment the Hobart racing fleet was enjoying classic sailing weather and conditions. Once at the heads, to port lay Australia's Great Barrier Reef, warm weather and smooth sailing. To starboard lay the finish line 630 nautical miles down Australia's east coast, across Bass Strait, down the east coast of Tasmania and up the Derwent River. Most of the fleet had rounded the Sydney Heads within 30 minutes of the 1 p.m. start and were sailing south in a following breeze for Hobart. Conditions were so good that the maxi crews were entertaining thoughts of breaking *Morning Glory*'s 1996 race record of two days, 14 hours and seven minutes, especially Ellison's *Sayonara*. The downwind conditions reminded many of the 1974 Hobart — a "dream run," veteran Hobart sailors call it — when the race was a spinnaker run all the way to Hobart. That was the year *Kialoa*, a 79-foot sloop from California, set a race record that held for 21 years until *Morning Glory* bested it by 29 minutes in 1996.

Sayonara rounded the heads at the sea marker a mile outside the harbor, set its largest, lightest parachute spinnaker and turned south on a 180-degree rhumb line for Hobart. With the wind following from the northeast at 15 knots and a blue sky overhead, the sleek sailing yacht, it's huge spinnaker billowed and emblazoned *Sayonara* in Japanese script, led the 115-boat fleet. With Ellison at the helm, *Sayonara*'s crew members could take a moment to enjoy the fruits of their efforts, but only a moment.

"We were going for about 45 minutes, with a pretty good lead on *Brindabella*, and we blew out our 3/4-ounce 'chute [spinnaker]," Ellison said. "Maybe I was driving the boat a little hot to get a little more boat speed. I'm not sure. It might have been a gust, might have been a flaw in the sail."

Sayonara replaces a blown spinnaker minutes out of the Sydney Heads.

With *Brindabella* closing, *Sayonara's* crew replaced the ruined spinnaker with a spinnaker made of fabric twice as heavy, one Ellison called "unbreakable." Back under way with the replacement spinnaker and *Brindabella,* a lighter boat that does extremely well in following winds, closing, it was again a chance to savor the moment of unalloyed head-to-head competition. "We were in a good boat race with *Brindabella,* enjoying ourselves," Ellison recalled. "It was a fabulous, fabulous day to be sailing."

Brindabella *under full sail and spinnaker, during the first hours of the race*

"What happened there," said *Brindabella's* Cropley, "was that they put up a lot of cloth in that 'chute. But they recovered very quickly. They had another one up in less than a minute and a half. We made a gain on them. As soon as we settled down and got the boat running with the wind we started to pull around her. It was one of the best parts of the race for us. We started to pass her and *Sayonara* heated up. We came along side and we were gunnel-to-gunnel. We were so close that crew were reaching out from both boats to touch hands. Eventually we passed her and I took a photo of *Sayonara* dead astern of *Brindabella*."

An hour into the race and shortly after passing *Sayonara*, *Brindabella* was on a course "outside" and was spotted by an ABC (Australian Broadcasting Company) helicopter in the lead.

Going "outside" or farther offshore is one of the reasons *Brindabella* was able to maintain her early lead. She was taking advantage of the East Coast Current, a 4- to 5-knot current that runs north to south along the coast of New South Wales. That much current added to the speed of a boat over a distance of 450 miles is significant and many Hobart competitors often use it to their advantage. Those who did in the 1998 Hobart would pay a steep price.

Wild Thing, which is a faster boat heading into the wind than with it, was holding her own, sailing under a huge mainsail and spinnaker on her enormous America's Cup mast. "We heard that *Sayonara* had broken a spinnaker, which wasn't too disappointing," her sailing master said, illustrating the keen nature of the Sydney to Hobart competition.

"Down the coast of New South Wales it was beautiful conditions," *Wild Thing's* Gilbert recalled. "It couldn't have been better. You were thinking that if conditions stay like this, in two days we'll be in Hobart having a party."

That party is the rousing end of the Sydney to Hobart, one that its competitors look forward to each year. "It's a chance to get together with your

Australian maxi Brindabella, *with her crew on the rail, flies down the New South Wales coast shortly after the start*

Wild Thing *at the start of the race*

mates and talk over the race and just have a good time with people you haven't seen for a while," said Gilbert, a Hobart native. He added that the party for the Hobart fleet includes the crews of the Melbourne to Hobart race, which finishes at approximately the same time as the Sydney to Hobart race — in time for Hobart's huge and popular New Year's celebration.

A mere five miles in the wake of the maxis, the Sailors With disAbilitie's boat, *Aspect Computing*, was living up to its "gun boat" status.

"Everyone knows when they see *Aspect's* yellow sails to look out because were going to get you. Which is exactly what happened. We threw a spinnaker up and started chewing through boats. And that's how we ran, just screaming through the afternoon, doing 22 to 23 knots over the ground. We were passed by only one boat, a maxi. And I found out later that we were within sight of *Sayonara* and *Brindabella*. I couldn't make them out except for blurs, but a friend of mine, the sailing master on *Nokia*, which was just ahead of us, later told me."

The 1998 Sydney to Hobart may have represented the best and worst of what it has ever offered in its 54-year history. The best was that first afternoon.

"It really was fantastic," said Stan Zemanek, skipper of the maxi *Foxtel Titan Ford*. "There is nothing better than to have a good stiff breeze behind you, have your spinnaker up and just power the boat down. I had the time of my life behind the wheel. I can't describe the feeling to anybody who hasn't been on a boat this size. You just go from one sea to another sea. The crew's working the breeze, working the spinnaker and I'm working the wheel. We're working together and it's just a great feeling of how these boats get the maximum speed they possibly can."

"The run down the coast was quite sensational," said *Sword of Orion* skipper Kothe. "I think the whole fleet was having a good time. The speed over the bottom was 23 knots. And *Sword of Orion* likes those conditions. We're good at that. And we were screaming down the coast. Glyn Charles, particularly, hadn't had that sort of experience in his home [British] waters. And he did a lot of helming on the way down. It was a ball for awhile."

"We had three people who were doing their first Hobart, two 15-year-old boys and a lady in her 30s. Watching them was an experience, their emotions and their awe," said skipper Roger Hickman of *Atara*.

With all of the boats out of the heads and on the race course, the Royal Australian Navy's sail training ship *Young Endeavour* set off to shadow the fleet to Hobart. Carrying veteran volunteers from the Cruising Yacht Club of Australia, *Young Endeavour's* role was radio support and safety, two functions in which it would soon be fully engaged.

The jubilation of running at extraordinary speeds was to come quickly to an end as the low-pressure system predicted by the Melbourne Meteorology Bureau began to make its presence known. It was about 7 p.m. on Saturday, December 26, five days after Australia's summer solstice — the longest day of the year — when the winds started to build quickly, though they remained from the northeast.

"We then blew out an ounce-and-a-half unbreakable spinnaker, which was really a surprise. This does not happen very often," Ellison said.

As the winds built, *Sayonara* was running (sailing on a following wind) at 26 nautical miles an hour, or 28.5 miles per hour over land, which is extremely fast for a large boat under sail. The winds, averaging 40 knots, were not steady, though. They were, said Ellison, "puffy, gusty," the kind of winds that require extraordinary skill when running, perhaps exquisite skill when racing. Such intermittent winds call for rudder and often sail adjustments between each puff. During a puff, the boat heels over with the force of the wind, requiring the helmsman to head off the wind. This maneuver, which orients the stern almost directly into the following wind, minimizes heeling and slows the boat by putting the sails at an angle that takes less advantage of the wind. Conversely, between puffs and gusts, turning the bow slightly up, or toward the direction of the following wind, takes maximum advantage of the wind and speeds the boat up. A balance of the two fundamentals as required by the wind is employed to keep the boat at a constant speed. Ellison and his crew were employing such skills while *Sayonara* was clipping along at 26 knots.

"The boat was flying along and the seas were still fairly smooth," Ellison said, describing the gusty conditions. "The wind wasn't a normal 35 knots. You'd just get 'boom, boom,' and it would really hammer you."

Sayonara was taking such a pounding when her third heavy spinnaker blew out. Replaced with a "mini," a true spinnaker but much smaller, she was under way only briefly when the unthinkable happened. A spinnaker pole, the connecting rod between the bottom of the spinnaker and the mast, broke. And it didn't simply break. *Sayonara's* carbon-fiber spinnaker pole is capped with a metal fitting that screws some two feet deep into the center of the pole. This metal fitting was ripped intact from the pole, sans its coarse, large threads. The heavy-duty spinnaker pole was replaced by a lightweight spare. It is skipper Ellison's first glimmer of understanding of the true nature of the 1998 Sydney to Hobart.

"I just have never been in anything like it at all," he said of the gusts that caused the triple spinnaker blowout and the loss of the spinnaker pole. "You sensed that something screwy was going on." But, Ellison added, "It was still very manageable." And *Sayonara* was managing the situation handily, running well ahead of the race record.

What had been a sparkling summer day was deteriorating quickly. Ahead of the Hobart fleet bolts of lightning arced between cloud and sea. Intermittent wind-driven rain fell in a curtain on the northern edge of the building front, which was moving northeast. And the sky darkened as clouds the color of a bad bruise collected on the periphery of the low.

"It started to get dark around 7:30," recalled *Atara's* skipper Hickman. "The lightning was flashing. The crew was getting nervous about the southerly. And the apprehension among the younger people, the first-timers, was quite alarming."

Sally Gordon, *Atara's* navigator, added: "There's certainly some apprehension about the buster [low front]. How's it going to be and that sort of thing. And your gut twinges a bit thinking that it's going to be pretty wild."

The low-pressure system into which the fleet was sailing was beginning to bare its teeth. The massive system rotating clockwise over Bass Strait caused a fast wind shift of nearly 180 degrees. This remarkable 30-minute wind shift caused two immediate problems for the fleet. The most immediate was to make the many incremental adjustments from sailing with the wind to sailing into the wind, or to windward, as the 40-knot wind shifted from the northeast to the southwest. Secondly, once the boats were reoriented to windward they faced the problem of hull and rigging damage as they ascended and dropped from steep waves with "no backs." By way of illustration, this is roughly equivalent to driving a car up and off an 8-story ramp – repeatedly. Off eastern Australia such waves are greatly amplified when the southerly 4-knot current meets gale- and hurricane-force winds from the opposite direction. The effect during the 1998 Sydney to Hobart was waves as high as 80 feet with no backs: eight-story ramps from which 25,000-pound sailboats fell.

For the fastest boats, the maxis, it was around 10 p.m. Saturday that the 1998 Sydney to Hobart began its metamorphosis from an ocean race into a battle for survival, a battle that six sailors lost. Seventy-one boats of the Hobart fleet would not finish the race. For all 115 boats and their crews it was the start of what would become hour after hour of beating to windward into wild seas, what old-time mariners called "a hard chance."

"I went off my shift around 9 o'clock," said *Foxtel* skipper Zemanek. "By the time I came back on at midnight it was blowing clappers. We were getting 40 knots of wind across the deck. It was just peeing down with rain. And the conditions on deck were just miserable. The big seas were there. The crew did a sterling job. The only way they could move around on deck was on their backsides or on their stomachs. And I could see the tension on the crew's faces. They knew they were in for a hard time."

Atara's Hickman said, "When we pulled the trisail down, one of the crew looked at me and said, 'Hickman, you've got a lot on here.' And that just captured the moment. We had a lot on. Everybody had a lot on."

Within hours of the radical wind shift, a half-dozen Hobart boats had turned back for Sydney or had begun discussing the idea of retiring from the race. Among them, the 66-foot French maxi *Elysion Blue*, sailing out of Italy with a world-class crew, was taking a pounding and her skipper was having second thoughts.

"Around 10 p.m. things began to get a little strange," recalled Mike Toppa, a sail trimmer on *Elysion Blue*. With 26 years of offshore racing experience, Toppa, 43, of Ft. Lauderdale, Fla., was sailing in his first Sydney to Hobart. "We started to gibe as the wind shifted and we blew a spinnaker, which we replaced with a number three jib. A half hour later we were sailing to windward in 10- to 15-foot seas.

"By 1 a.m. the wind was blowing at 45 knots and the waves were tight and steep, with no backs. That was making life pretty uncomfortable. Waves were washing over the deck and people were getting bounced out of their bunks. And the boat began developing leaks from the constant crashing off waves. We were monitoring the various weather channels and it was obvious that the storm was going to get a lot worse, with 60-knot winds and severe conditions."

Two hours later Yvon Berrehar, *Elysion Blue's* skipper, made the decision to withdraw. The boat, four miles off shore to take full advantage of the 4-knot southerly current, had been bearing closer to shore in the interim. But now the decision was reached. For sailor/athletes such as Toppa and crew members Jacques Vincent, a Whitbread winner, Ross Field, who broke the Around Alone speed record, Kevin Burnham, an Olympic silver medalist, and others, retirement from a race does not come easy.

"We would have made it," Toppa said, his competitive spirit clashing with reason and reality. "It would have been tough, but we would have made it."

By sunup *Elysion Blue* was safely within the protected waters of Sydney Harbor, along with a dozen other racing yachts whose captains had made the same sound decision.

"It was then that we started hearing the horror stories on the radio about the boats that were still out there," Toppa recalled. "There's no question that [retiring] was the right thing to do."

Aboard *Sayonara* the wind was shifting quickly from north to south and the crew made adjustments from running to jibing, or zigzagging downwind to maintain boat speed. At the same time crewmen were struggling to replace the broken spinnaker pole in the tumult of wind, waves and darkness. In this flurry of activity the mainsail got caught on a backstay, a cable securing the mast, and the leech cord and a batten, critical points when reefing or shortening the sail in high wind, were damaged. But the wind shift from northeast to southwest was so quick that spinnakers, jibing and spinnaker poles became moot. *Sayonara* was now sailing on the wind, to windward, approximately 250 miles into the race. Her position was approximately halfway to the port town of Eden, just north of the New South Wales/Victoria border, the last protected harbor before Bass Strait. Eden, at the head of Twofold Bay, is also where the Tasman Sea starts to yield to the treacherous winds and currents of Bass Strait.

Sydney to Hobart veterans often joke about the race and its conditions, calling it the Sydney to Eden. Eden is a coastal community some 25 miles north of "the corner," the point at which the Australian coast veers southwest along Bass Strait. The home port of about 100 commercial tuna boats large and small, Eden's protected harbor has offered sanctuary to storm-tossed Sydney to Hobart boats and crews for years. And Eden's mercurial economy makes the port and its rustic fishermens' pubs safe havens to which visiting yachtsmen are welcomed.

"It's one of the best sheltered ports on the east coast of Australia," said sailing master Scott Gilbert. "If you're pleasure sailing from Sydney to Hobart you always stop in Eden. It's friendly and the people there are great. They always look forward to Christmas because of the number of Sydney to Hobart yachts pulling in. Sometimes it's as many as 70. That's where the race finishes for a lot of people."

Eden is the last mainland harbor for Sydney to Hobart racers. Bypassing Eden means a commitment to crossing often treacherous Bass Strait for the next safe harbor, Hobart — the finish line — on the south coast of Tasmania, some 175 miles distant.

Through the first night, the weather and the sailing conditions would go from bad to worse. Scores of boats would head for the nearest port — any port. But primarily they returned to Sydney or sought shelter in Bateman's Bay, about 150 miles south of Sydney, still north of Eden. For skippers unaccustomed to such conditions, especially the sharp waves of the Tasman Sea, the developing storm threatened their crews, their rigs and their boats. By the cardinal principles of the sea and sail, crewmen are not to be lost or injured, sails and masts are not to be lost or damaged, and hulls are not to be split and boats sunk. Among Australian Hobart veterans, retiring is not considered a lack of fortitude, but a commendable racing tactic. Indeed, several boats in the 1998 Hobart and races before it weathered the worst of the storm in port and then finished the race. But by inference it is not valid to conclude that those who continued did so recklessly.

Skipper David Pescud, like many other Hobart veterans, said of the conditions: "I've not raced anywhere else in the world so I don't know how other people race or what conditions they get into. But as far as the Hobart, it was just another day at the office."

Weather forecasting became a major issue in the 1998 Hobart. But all skippers and crew knew that there was a front developing on the course. From there, forecasts and opinions vary widely. Almost without exception, though, skippers agree that the "buster" or "bomb," as Australians call a rapidly developing low-pressure system, was far worse than predicted. And most were proceeding with the advice that the storm would move west, away from Bass Strait, by the time they reached the notorious stretch of water.

"At the first sked [position report] we got a weather update. Nothing in the forecast indicated that we were going to get anything more than 55 knots of wind," said crewman Peter Meikle of *Kingurra*.

"The breeze increased to 25 or 30 knots very quickly and there was a lot of thunderstorms. So I went below to the weather station and got the weather faxes for the 8:30 p.m. feed," said Brian Northcote, the navigator aboard *Sharp Hawk V.* "It showed the secondary low sitting there in Bass Strait was slowing down, which was the first indicator for a bit of concern."

Being the fastest boats in the 1998 Hobart was a blade that cut both ways for the leaders, *Sayonara* and *Brindabella*. Their great speed meant that they would be the first to experience what lay in store to the south.

Aboard *Sayonara* after midnight, visibility in the dark and fog was reduced to zero. No star, horizon or land form could be seen on which to keep a bearing. So besides her instruments, which have a two-second lag time, skipper Ellison and helmsman Brad Butterworth were driving *Sayonara* blind. The wind, now at 60 knots, made it impossible to keep the boat on the wind. Too, the huge wave troughs engulfing *Sayonara* were shadowing her sails from the wind she needed to propel her up the face or through the wall of the next wave. When she came out of each trough, the storm-force winds shot the boat dangerously forward into the next set of erratic and inconsistent waves.

To make matters worse, most of the crew, including Ellison who is an aircraft stunt pilot, were violently seasick, most of them for the first time in their lives. Seasickness is a rare affliction for a world-class sailing crew. It is not only debilitating, but its accompanying symptom of appetite loss posed a distinct danger for the crew of *Sayonara*. All crew positions require mental acuity and significant physical strength and agility to stand the long watches and accomplish required tasks. Therefore, boats are provisioned with good food and lots of it. Seasickness was so prevalent on *Sayonara*, though, that food, and in many cases water, was avoided for most of the race.

"We were at our limits as we were entering Bass Strait in these terrible conditions," Ellison recalled.

It was under such conditions only hours earlier that the wind, influenced by the storm, switched direction, increased rapidly and caught *Sayonara* unprepared, her huge mainsail still hoisted. The simple solution was to reef, or shorten, the mainsail. But for those under sail on the Tasman Sea during the early hours of December 27, 1988, there were no simple solutions. Reefing is done by lowering the sail from the masthead and tying or rolling the slackened amount of sail at the foot or bottom of the sail around the boom. The boom is the horizontal bar attached to the bottom of the mast. Reefing is done in pre-determined amounts at the sail's reefing points. Reefing is necessary because as the wind velocity increases, incrementally smaller amounts of sail are required to maintain forward motion of the boat. Full sail in a high wind is an invitation to a knockdown (turning the boat on its side or worse).

Reefing sail is a routine procedure, except in the dark with the wind howling at 60 knots in a murderous sea and with the mainsail damaged and jammed near its topmost position.

That was precisely the situation aboard *Sayonara*. Partially reefed, the mainsail was flogging dangerously in the high wind, threatening to tear itself to shreds. The problem was that a metal track running the entire length of the mast on which the mainsail is raised and lowered was separating from the mast. The separation was preventing the big sail from going up or down. The mainsail was jammed in a high wind. It was an emergency.

Crewman T.A. McCann used an allen wrench to remove parts of the bent mainsail track while another crewman, Joe Wilson, reefed the flogging mainsail. The process took an agonizing half hour, and McCann, bloodied and bruised, was repeatedly slammed into the mast by *Sayonara's* wild pitching. It was finally brought down, and a cluster of crewman literally sat on the heavily damaged mainsail to keep it from blowing away. Allen immediately joined crewman Robby Naismith to save the carbon-fiber boom, which was bending and threatening to break.

"I couldn't believe it," skipper Ellison said. "It was the worst sea I'd ever been in up to that moment, and those guys were drilling holes in the boom and attaching a steel plate to the boom at night in those kinds of conditions. I found that impressive."

Now *Sayonara* was under sail with only a #5 jib, a small sail forward of the mainsail. A jib tends to move a sailboat sideways rather than forward. And without forward movement, directional stability and steerage, the boat's ability to respond to her rudder, decreases. Like a bicycle, a sailing boat is most stable when it is moving forward. And, like a bicycle, a sail boat can only change direction in response to rudder movements (steerage) when it is moving forward. Under the storm jib *Sayonara* was making more leeway than headway and was losing steerage in the tempestuous seas. Without steerage in high seas, a boat is in danger of broaching, lying broadside to the wind and waves. Broaching is usually the prelude to laying over, which puts the mast, sails and rigging in the water. Boats that broached in the 1998 Sydney to Hobart were doomed.

"We had to get the trisail up," said Ellison.

And it took all hands on deck to do so. Thirty arduous minutes later the tiny replacement for the mainsail was rigged.

On deck, exhausted, sick and thirsty, sailors cleared their goggles of sea spray and driving rain, though the only thing in the blackness was the next lightning bolt. All refrained from talking except when absolutely necessary, lest their words be drowned in the howling of the rigging or snatched by the wind itself. But it was better than below decks, where rest was fitful for imaginations unencumbered by routine and on the ragged edge of night.

"We felt like sending out a radio call and say, 'Everyone go home. This is just insane. This is absolutely insane. This is not what sailboat racing is supposed to be about.' It was very, very bad. But we didn't really understand what was going on."

—Larry Ellison, skipper *Sayonara*

Day Two: *A Hard Chance*

The grudging dawn on the morning of December 27 was a long time coming for the remaining Hobart fleet. Crews had battled the increasing wind and building waves through the long night. Three-hour deck watches went on interminably as bowmen, helmsmen, sail trimmers, grinders, navigators and tacticians did their critical jobs in bulky wet-weather gear and safety harnesses in the dark. Most boats were sailing under deeply reefed mainsail or a storm jib at dawn. The overnight sail changes were done by degrees: as the wind built, sails were shortened and shortened. For the 1,000 crewmen sailing the Hobart, reefing and changing sail is routine, and they are very quick and good at the task. But under storm conditions such routine tasks become dangerous feats. Cumbersome clothes, safety lines, driving rain, a pitching deck, the darkness and the wind screaming a dissonant *a capella* in the rigging transformed the routine to the hellish. Too, rampant seasickness and an inability to eat or drink had begun to complicate an already complex situation.

By dawn on Sunday most of the big boats — the maxis — were in Bass Strait or very near it. The rest of the fleet was three to four hours behind and would not get into what was described as the "washing machine" until late morning or early afternoon. All of the boats' various experiences — none pleasant — would depend on when they reached Bass Strait. Equally important would be whether they sailed "outside" to take advantage of the current or "inside," hugging the coast of New South Wales.

Because maximum speed is the objective of racing a maxi in an ocean race, nearly all of the big boats stayed "outside" to take advantage of the 4-knot south-flowing current. Among the many smaller boats, with few exceptions, skippers and tacticians also did what they had done in earlier Hobarts. About two-thirds of them stayed inside. The rest opted for the current assist on the outside.

At least in the planning stages, few skippers altered their courses in anticipation of the storm. But most, like Ed Psaltis of 35-foot *Midnight Rambler*, factored the storm into their course and race strategy.

"The current was running quite hard farther offshore and quite a few boats took the temptation to go farther out to sea to take advantage of the current," said Psaltis. "And the southwest change [storm] was forecast, which was coming from the other side of the course [east]. And we said, 'Forget about the current. We're going to get a bit of it. And with the change coming there would be a big advantage to being the top boat closest to the change, because we could pull away with the freshening winds and go fast right on our course.' So that was our race strategy. And in hindsight it did work this year. In other years it hasn't worked. It has been better to go outside [east]. But this year the boats that went outside got caught on the wrong side of a southwest change that lasted two days in the end. And what they were doing was trying to get in [to the shelter of Eden], where we were already in."

As a dubious reward for her speed and the skill of her crew, the American maxi *Sayonara* was the first to reach Bass Strait on Sunday morning. Many of her crew, like T.A. McCann, were injured and bruised.

Aboard Nokia with the seas building and the wind blowing at 70 knots

But they had made it through the first night and were, unexpectedly, beating to windward at some 16 knots into a beautiful morning.

The respite is the first time Ellison and his crew had a chance to think beyond the boundaries of survival, beyond the small world of *Sayonara*.

Brindabella and her crew had taken a beating overnight, too. The fast spinnaker run down the coast ended almost precisely at midnight, when the Australian maxi experienced the 180-degree wind shift from the northeast to the southwest and then the first lashings of "the bomb." Her crew was experienced at sailing in such adverse conditions. What they were not accustomed to was the pounding the big boat took as it launched off the huge waves the storm was generating.

The waves that developed in Bass Strait on December 27-28 require unique circumstances that exist in only a few places in the world, of which Bass Strait is perhaps the classic example. The basic ingredients for creating "sharp" waves, those with a steep leading edge and an even steeper trailing edge or "back," are shallow sea in a restricted area. A classic example is the surf at almost any beach in the world. Waves build and break on the beach because moving sea water, restricted by the increasing lack of depth as it approaches the beach, has no place to go except up — piled high in a wave. If the beach is in a cove, the geography further restricts the incoming wave, resulting in the sea water piling higher yet. If there is a significant undertow or backwash that counters each wave, that current forces the incoming wave even higher. Finally, if the incoming waves are driven by high wind against vertical (depth) and horizontal (land) restrictions and an opposing current, they can grow to truly awesome heights.

All these elements exist in Bass Strait. The 175-mile-wide strait is shallow. The land boundaries Bass Strait flows through — mainland Australia and the island of Tasmania — restrict the ocean. The current running north to south down the east coast of Australia collides with the waters of Bass Strait, which are driven by the prevailing west winds in the "roaring forties."

Negotiating gargantuan waves that the storm in Bass Strait was generating is not something a sailor can learn from a textbook. Experienced heavy-water sailors say that each big wave is unique and must be negotiated according to its size, shape and stability at the top. The top is significant because if it is breaking, it cannot support the weight of a boat. Therefore a boat that reaches the wave crest when it breaks must go through the wave, which means tons of water over the deck and a momentary loss of steerage. Conversely, a wave that is not breaking — even if it reaches great height — allows an easier passage over the top, steerage is uninterrupted and rudder adjustments can be made for the high-speed run down the back of the wave. If the wave has no back, it's a free fall.

Huge waves with no backs were what *Brindabella* and *Sayonara* faced as they raced to the leading edge of the storm between midnight and Sunday morning.

"I vividly recall *Brindabella* launching off the back of several steep waves," said sail trimmer Geoff Cropley. "And I remember counting 'one, two' and then, *wham!*, she hits and shudders and all the rigging flutters. She's got a Kevlar hull and wasn't damaged. But when she launches off a wave into a 25-foot free fall it's pretty uncomfortable."

Despite the storm they sped into, *Brindabella* and *Sayonara* had dueled through the night for the lead. And like the American maxi, *Brindabella* had damaged a mainsail in high winds overnight. As the mainsail was reefed under the building winds, it was not tied down properly and got chafed, Cropley said.

Instead of the maelstrom they expected Sunday morning, the two Hobart lead boats unexpectedly found themselves in a 15-knot breeze under a blue summer sky. Both were some 20 nautical miles ahead of *Morning Glory's* position when she set the record in 1996. The nearest boats to the pair of leaders were *Wild Thing* and *Fudge,* both of which trailed by only a few miles on a course 20 miles to the west. The rest of the fleet was strung out for 60 miles between Eden and Bateman's Bay to the north, sailing an average of 30 miles offshore.

For Ellison and crew the unusually fine weather was a chance to make repairs to *Sayonara*, treat cuts and bruises among the crew and reflect on the previous night. Ellison thought about the boats that were headed into what *Sayonara* had just come through.

"It dawns on us all that if we're having this much trouble as we get into this part of the race course, what about the 40-footers?" Ellison recalled. "I can't even imagine. What are they going to do? *Sayonara* is an 80-foot yacht, perfectly maintained, with probably the world's best professional crew and we're at the limits of our ability to keep everything together and keep this boat racing. It was inconceivable what's going to happen to the small boats when they get there. We felt like sending out a radio call and say, 'Everyone go home. This is just insane. This is absolutely insane. This is not what sailboat racing is supposed to be about.' It was very, very bad. But we didn't really understand what was going on.'"

Ellison's concern for the smaller boats of the Hobart fleet was certainly justified. But as a racing division, it was the big boats, the maxis, that took the worst beating overnight. Two strong contenders for line honors, *Wild Thing* and *Marchioness*, were forced to pull out of the race with rig damage. Four smaller boats, *ABN AMRO Challenge, Sledgehammer, Sydney* and *King Billy*, were forced out with hull and rudder damage. Victorian yacht *Challenge Again*, skippered by veteran yachtsman Lou Abrahams, lost a man overboard but recovered him and continued the race. It was the first of 26 man-overboard incidents in the race.

Sydney-based *ABN AMRO Challenge* took such a beating when she encountered the storm that her rudder was completely torn off and her 46-foot hull cracked open 14 hours into the race. When it happened she was among the top 12 boats leading the race and had been considered a strong contender as the overall winner. Owner Ray "Hollywood" Roberts had raced her superbly in the 1997 Hobart. For the 1998 race he had assembled a top-flight crew that was not looking for second place.

At 3 a.m. on December 27, *Challenge* was taking on water 30 miles off Bateman's Bay. Hours earlier, Roberts, unaware of how badly his boat had been damaged, had declined assistance from the racing yacht *Alexander of Creswell.* At 11 a.m., *Challenge* was in serious trouble, and Shoalhaven Marine Rescue, one of Australia's many volunteer rescue associations, took action. After apprising "Telstra Control," the call sign for the race's radio-relay ship *Young Endeavour* of its willingness to assist *Challenge,* Shoalhaven Rescue contacted Royal Volunteer Coastal Patrol, Bateman's Bay. RCVP immediately sent its vessel, *Bay Rescue,* to *Challenge's* aid. At dawn the next day, a relieved Ray Roberts and the crew of the battered *Challenge* reached the safety of Bateman's Bay at the end of *Bay Rescue's* towing cable. It was the first rescue in what would become a massive rescue operation in which Australia's volunteer rescue associations would play a large — but largely overlooked — role.

King Billy, a classic 38-footer made from Tasmanian King Billy pine in 1992, suffered hull damage overnight and radioed in two hours after *Challenge* that she, too, was taking on water and was heading for Sydney. A comfortable cruising yacht rather than a spartan ocean racer, *King Billy* had seen her share of ocean races, including the 1995 Hobart. In the 1998 Hobart her crew was "expecting a comfortable ride south."

Sledgehammer, a 40-footer, and 60-foot *Sydney*, both New South Wales entries, damaged their rudders in the roller-coaster ride south early Sunday morning and were forced to pull out. *Sledgehammer* was the first in a series of 1998 production boats designed by noted Australian yacht designers Murray, Burns and Dovell (designers of ill-fated *Wild Thing*). Built to compete with 40-foot production boats of American design by Bruce Farr, *Sledgehammer* was being closely watched. She, like *Sydney*, was among the 20 lead boats in the 1998 Hobart when she lost her rudder.

Wild Thing's skipper Grant Wharington said that pulling out of the race was disappointing because they were hot on the heels of the race leaders.

"We were very close to *Brindabella*," Wharington said. "I think they were three miles ahead of us at the time and they were a little further in shore but we set ourselves up where we wanted to be a little further out to sea. The boat was travelling really nicely. It's very disappointing."

Wharington's disappointment did not hint at the rough night his new yacht with the enormous America's Cup mast and sails had just come through.

Keeping pace with *Sayonara* and *Brindabella*, 70-foot *Wild Thing* was sailing to windward at 20 knots in 40 knots of wind by 2 a.m. on December 27. She had gone far outside to take advantage of the southerly current and was doing 23 knots over the ground, said her sailing master Scott Gilbert. At those speeds *Wild Thing* was launching off towering waves and crashing into the troughs, surfing down the backs of the waves when she was lucky.

"At one point we did a deep nosedive off a wave," Gilbert said. "When she came back up the #4 headsail was gone and it had taken all the stanchions with it. One of the guys who was hanging onto the sail was taken overboard with it but he had his harness on and we got him back aboard quickly."

Falling off the steep waves and hammering to the sea surface hour after hour also caused *Wild Thing's* steering cables to jump off the boat's steering gears. Without steerage in such conditions, the boat was in extreme danger. "We had to pull all the sails in while we repaired the steering mechanism," said Gilbert.

No sooner was *Wild Thing* back under way when, according to Gilbert, "We heard a couple of quite loud bangs and so we had a look around. But we didn't see anything. By morning we had 40 to 50 knots of wind. And it was then that we decided to look around the boat to see what happened to it during the blow. I was sitting below decks and looked up through a hatch and could see a split in the mast from the gooseneck (the bottom) to the second spreaders (two thirds the length of the mast). It was really starting to blow by then and the seas were building quickly. We could not put any stress on the mast, so we just put up a storm jib and headed back to Eden. We were 10 miles south of Eden and a long way off shore. We were probably the boat farthest off shore."

Wild Thing was actually 70 miles off shore. Only the Tasmanian yacht *Allusive* went farther east. *Wild Thing* had charted its outside race line hoping to skirt the slow-moving storm to the west. The split mast cost her skipper and crew not only the race but 27 hours of painstaking work limping the crippled maxi to the shelter of Eden's Twofold Bay.

The maxi *Marchioness* "copped it," as Hobart sailors call sailing into a storm, a short time after *Wild Thing* was disabled. Even with her crew's combined experience of 150 Sydney to Hobarts, a new keel and rudder and brand new sails, *Marchioness* was not equal to the conditions that knocked her out of the race. Sailing closest to the coast of all the maxis, *Marchioness* had leaders *Brindabella* and *Sayonara* in her sights when she got into trouble Sunday night.

The crew radioed *Young Endeavour,* saying that the boat's spinnaker pole had snapped, causing severe broaching. The sail and half the pole went under the boat, which took an hour and a half to retrieve. During the retrieval, one crew member went overboard but was saved by his safety harness. Another was lifted off the deck by a flying mainsail, which caught him in the mouth and broke several teeth. With the additional loss of her mast supports, navigator Dave Lawson said continuing the race was not an option.

"They were forecasting some pretty wild weather in Bass Strait," Lawson told press and radio reporters from his disabled yacht. "The seas that we were in when we decided to pull out weren't very nice and we realized we could endanger the mast on the boat and if that had come down we realized we could have hurt some of the crew as well."

Also early Sunday morning, the top brass of the Cruising Yacht Club of Australia, the race's sponsor, withdrew from the Sydney to Hobart. CYCA Commodore Hugo van Kretschmar radioed in shortly after 2 p.m. that he was pulling his boat, *Assassin,* out of the race and heading for the shelter of Eden.

For skippers and crews of the boats forced out of the race by weather, seasickness, injuries or boat damage, hopes were dashed and years of preparation seemingly went for nought. They were the lucky ones.

By midmorning Sunday *Sayonara* was under full sail again in a fresh breeze and calmer seas. The mainsail had undergone a five-hour repair on deck, and the damaged track on which to hoist it had been put back into service.

"We were under the mainsail and the #1 jib and it was sunny and beautiful," recalled the skipper. "So I go below and say, 'This is fabulous. Let me check the weather out.'"

Sayonara is equipped with a state-of-the art weather station that displays satellite images of local weather conditions every four hours. Ellison consulted with navigator Mark Rudiger, an experienced Whitbread race-winning navigator.

"The pictures start coming up," Ellison said. "And I'm sitting next to Mark and my jaw drops. As Mark looks at it his jaw drops, which is not good. We're both looking at this thing dead-silent. And I look at Mark and ask, 'You ever seen anything like this in your life?' and Mark says, 'No.' And I said, 'I have. On the Weather Channel. It was called a hurricane. What the fuck is that thing doing out here?' This horrible low-pressure system is just staring at us. We plot our course and we know why it's calm: We're sitting right smack in the eye of the hurricane. And that which we sailed into we have to sail out of.'"

While Ellison's crew had been repairing *Sayonara's* mainsail, a quarter of a mile away the crew of *Brindabella* was doing the same.

The biggest boat in the fleet, Nokia, took a severe pounding despite her size. Here a crewman is steadied as the boat ascends a swell and is heeled to port by a 75 knot gust. As the storm built on the second day of the race, many boats sustained rig damage when they came out of huge wave troughs that blocked the wind and caught the wind's full force. Going from essentially luffed sails to Force 11 winds in seconds proved too much for even modern rigging, masts and high tech sails. Like Nokia's crew, most boats were on storm watches for at least 24 hours, which means that small deck crews were rotated frequently. Note the safety harnesses and full wet weather gear worn by Nokia's crew. Only a day earlier it was 90 degrees with bright sunshine.

"At dawn we knew that *Sayonara* was to the east of us, because the chopper [from Tasmania] came out to film us, then he went straight on to the east. So we knew *Sayonara* was out there," said trimmer Geoff Cropley. "At noon we spotted her about 1,000 meters from us. They had their mainsail on the deck repairing it. We had our main on the deck repairing it. We hoisted ours and then they hoisted theirs and the drag race started again."

Ellison and the crew of *Sayonara* were in the lead and were the first participants in the nightmare.

"I went back up on deck to do a bit of driving in the nice weather for 15 minutes," Ellison said after seeing the boat's position in the eye of the storm. But it wasn't in the cards.

"It was beautiful," said Ellison, "And then a minute later the wind had gone from 15 to 45 knots on its way back into the 50s. It was astounding how fast it happened. I've been in fronts, but nothing like this as we came out of the eye of the hurricane."

Sayonara went quickly from full sails to a reefed mainsail and a #5 jib as the wind quickly built to a steady 55 knots. Beating into the storm at 16 knots meant that the boat was experiencing greater than 70 knots of apparent wind across her deck. Complicating matters, a huge high-pressure weather system had moved in and was encroaching on the massive low-pressure system that was pounding the Hobart fleet. The pressure gradient between the two systems was so great that it spawned severe and sustained winds. The huge waves in the shallow Tasman Sea and Bass Strait being pushed up by the colliding fronts would take their toll.

The dramatic increase in wind speed cost *Brindabella* back-to-back line honors.

"Toward evening on December 27 the breeze started shifting dramatically to the left and we tacked onto port and *Sayonara* did too," Cropley recalled. "That put us on a heading sort of toward the coast. It was an amazing leg. We had put full mainsail up and one of our big jibs up. And

Sayonara was in sight all the way. Somewhere between 9 and 10 that night the breeze built very quickly again and we got caught with a jib up and the jib split and we had to send Jacko [crewman Jack Young] up the rig and keep him up there and the seas were very big. The jib had gotten wrapped, so we had to sail north to cut the bow lift and keep the rig smooth so [Young] could cut the jib loose. They [*Sayonara*] were sailing south while we were sailing north — and that took about an hour — and that's where they won the race."

Sayonara was sailing into conditions that would make the first night of the race — as bad as it had been — seem like a shakedown cruise, as equipment began to fail and crew injuries mounted.

"The port jib track was lifting right off the deck," Ellison recalled. "This just doesn't happen. This is all titanium, carbon-fiber stuff that is not supposed to break. And certainly it's not supposed to bend and flip around like it was. Equipment is now just falling apart on the boat, right and left.

"What was happening was that not only were the seas bigger, but they were so steep and the wave angle was so bad that as we hit a wall of water it really was like hitting a wall of water. You'd literally be knocked off the (steering) wheel by the wall of water. The guys on deck, God only knows how they survived and did their jobs. We were just getting battered around so bad that we had four guys with broken bones."

The battering from the sea washing over the deck, though, was greatly compounded by the shape of the waves and the punishment they dealt.

As Ellison explained: "The worst part was as you hit the wave, the wave would lift the boat. And normally when you come out of the wave, you angle and surf down the back of the wave. Great fun. That's not what we did. The backs of these waves were so steep the boat would come out of the wave, you'd go weightless and then you'd fall, like down an elevator shaft, and crash into the trough below. It was really unbelievable. Because you just feel the weightlessness and you'd watch the guys on the foredeck leave the boat. They'd be sometimes 5 feet off the deck. You'd see a guy's head nearly hit the first spreader. And I was thinking, 'I want to go home. This is not good.'"

Wishful thinking was not going to solve Ellison's problem. The hour upon hour of brutal punishment continued. At one point a crewman went overboard. A strong and experienced rock climber, though, he was able to get back aboard quickly. Soon the constant dropping off the back of 30- to 35-foot waves began to take its toll on the sailors' nerves and on the boat. Ellison recounted the experience of free-falling in the 25,000-pound *Sayonara* from the waves. "Crash into the wave, get lifted, weightless. Count one-one-thousand, two-one-thousand, three-one-thousand. Boom."

At this point, each time *Sayonara* crashed to a wave trough at the end of a three-second free fall, the crew was checking the hull. "We were hitting so hard, our concern was that literally the bow of the boat would break off," Ellison said.

The gut-wrenching impact of one free fall was so forceful that it exploded a forestay connecting rod made of titanium. Another fall disabled the massive port primary jib winch. And while *Sayonara* is weathering the pounding, her crew is beating her to windward under a storm jib and a tiny trisail. She is bearing about 80 miles off the northeast coast of Tasmania, beyond range of the rescue helicopters that were, at that moment, mobilizing the largest sea rescue operation ever undertaken by Australia. *Sayonara*, some 30 miles ahead of *Brindabella*, was on her own. And it was the first time skipper Ellison gives serious thought to the notion that he may not come out of the race alive.

"As the boat is leaping off these huge waves and going airborne and crashing down, I remember talking with one of the guys about, well, if something happens, how long?" Ellison recalled. "Because we'd heard all the distress calls now. A lot of boats were going down. There's a lot of helicopters in the air. We were convinced that [if anything happened] we wouldn't, couldn't get any help for at least a day. And you don't last a day in those waters."

Ellison and his crew had been through what the Hobart fleet, which was on average 90 miles north, was sailing into Sunday, December 27.

* * *

Aspect Computing's position report at 2 p.m. on December 27 put her 25 miles southeast of Gabo Island (GAY-bow). The island marks "the corner," where the mainland cuts sharply to the southwest and forms the northern entrance to Bass Strait. *Aspect*'s position report was the moment in the 1998 Hobart when conditions would turn from bad to the worst imaginable. But *Aspect*'s skipper, David Pescud, familiar with capricious weather of the Southern Ocean, had a plan to get his boat and his crew, half of which were drawn from his Sailors with DisAbilities program, racing — not sailing for survival.

"We got the weather forecast and had a big look at it and I said to the crew, 'This is what's going to happen. We're going to have a good night tonight [Saturday] and were going to have to go as hard as we can and get as far down [south] as we can,'" said Pescud. "'The further down we are when it hits us the better off we're going to be. There'll be no sleeping tonight. When we hit this front there will be plenty of time to sleep. The storm will last for 24 hours. At the end of 24 hours it'll abate, stay in the west, and move to the south-southeast. Then it's going to move back to the southwest. By that time we should be going up Storm Bay [Tasmania] and out of the weather.' And that's what I said to the crew. And it was pretty well on the money. The pressure was up a bit. And as a result we wound up getting 70 knots of wind instead of the 55 knots forecasted."

With a killer storm in the forecast, radio traffic that indicated boats were in serious trouble and *Aspect Computing's* proximity to shelter in Eden, a case can be made that continuing south was at least imprudent, probably dangerous and showed a lack of care on Pescud's part for the safety of his crew. Such a case can only be made by those who don't know David Pescud. If he is a risk taker, those risks are carefully calculated to help disabled people, as Pescud, a dyslexic, says, "own their disability instead of being owned by it." To that end, the genesis of the Sailors with disAbilities program and its core philosophy is as unique as the program itself.

"I'm a dyslexic and I've got a bit of a thing about disabilities," Pescud said. "There are disabilities that fall through a crack. If you're in a wheelchair you get quite a lot of societal support because people can see that you're in a wheelchair and that you've got one leg or whatever. But when your disabilities aren't apparent, say if you're a woman and you've just had both breasts removed because of cancer, no one knows. Your disability is just as profound and just as invasive in your life as any other disability, but no one knows. You don't get that support. You fall through the cracks of the support networks."

Pescud also saw a seriously flawed approach to the way support programs for the disabled are fashioned and administered in Australia.

"We disabled people allow the able-bodied to put parameters on our lives. We let them say to us, 'You can or can't do this or that.' And we allow that. We have. What we're trying to say is that we'll decide what we will or won't do. We're saying we're going to Hobart. If we die, we die.

"We have administrators doling out money to the handicapped, with the best will in the world — no one's being a bastard. But they're creating programs that will be of benefit to a Martian. And that's the difference. They're not creating a program for humans. They know nothing about being handicapped.

"Sometimes you see someone in a wheelchair and you say, 'Here's $100,000. Fuck off.' You don't want to deal with him. What you've done is gotten rid of the person. We do that so often, just throw money at the disabled. It doesn't fix the problem. What fixes the problem is to be recognized as a person and say 'G'day, I'm David.' It's not easy. But it's a bloody lot cheaper than throwing money at a lot of people. In other words, just give people some dignity and some humanity and you'll be surprised at what happens.

"So I see our job as a facilitator to life between mainstream society and disabled society in a constructive fashion. We can't just go along and say 'You're going about it all wrong.' That'll just get everyone's back up. We've got to say that there's a better way to do this. And 'Have you thought about this in a way that's productive and complementary to what exists?' Rather than tear systems down we need to add to them in ways that are more appropriate, more relevant to the needs of the handicapped. And we think the best focus for that is the younger people. And it is those young children who will be coming along and become able to make constructive change. And if we can get them to own their disability rather than being owned by it then their capacity to contribute becomes much larger, much greater."

The Sailors with disAbilities program got a serendipitous start four years earlier. Pescud's two daughters were grown, he had sold his trucking company and he was enjoying an early-middle-age retirement.

"In 1994 this chap was in a wheelchair and said, 'I'd like to go to Hobart and nobody's going to take me.' He said this on a commercial radio station. I happened to hear him. So I called him and said, 'I've got a boat. How about we get together?' So that's how the program started. I put the program together in a short period of time," Pescud recalled.

"Most of the people who went to Hobart that year [1994] had very limited yachting experience. Two or three had a reasonable amount of experience, but among the 12, most were first-timers, first-timers yachting not just the first time in the Hobart. The idea was to complete the 50th Hobart. Of course, that was an event. And to demonstrate that handicapped people could do this. The idea wasn't to be a gun boat; it was finishing the event, which is what we did.

"We had a sponsor, [Sydney-based] Aspect Computing. They said to us: 'Would you like to do the Hobart under our sponsorship next year?' I hadn't really thought about it, but here we are. We've changed the boat significantly and it's now technically quite a bit faster than the boat we started with."

Since the program's inception hundreds of handicapped have sailed on *Aspect Computing* in Sydney to Hobarts and many other races. But Pescud pointed to members of *Aspect Computing's* 1998 Hobart crew to illustrate the benefits of the Sailors with disAbilities program. Among the crew was the youngest sailor in the race, 14-year-old Travis Mudgee, a dyslexic.

"Young Travis came to me and said, 'You aren't really dyslexic, are you?' I said, 'Yes, I am, mate.' He didn't believe me, so I told him, 'I am, Travis. I can't even write my own address.' Then he asked, 'Well, then who owns the boat? I said, 'I do.' He said, 'How did you get the money to buy a boat like this?' I told him that I owned a trucking company and that I sold it and used part of the money to buy the boat. He didn't believe me and he asked one of the crew who confirmed my story. I think that was the first time Travis ever considered the idea that there might be more potential to his life than he thought. As I did at his age, he thought there was this box that was his life and he would have to be a road digger, a laborer or a farm hand. And that was where he was going to be. He'd worked that out because he couldn't do anything academically. That's a crystallized example of what happens on the boat. And it happens all the time. All the time.'"

While in 1994 Pescud was trying to make a point by finishing the Hobart, the 1998 Hobart was a race for which Pescud, his crew and his boat were well prepared. He wanted to win.

"We no longer sail to demonstrate the ability of the crew," said Pescud. "These people out here know that *Aspect* is going to kick their bum, same as any other boat. So we are now accepted. And I think that's our success story. The people who sail on this boat are considered to be sailors. Whatever their disability is, who cares? Now I walk down the dock [at Sydney's Cruising Yacht Club of Australia], and everybody will kick the piss out of me or one of my crew about something regarding a past or future race. And that's exactly what they should do. That's what human beings should do. If one of my guys or gals walked down the dock five years ago people would have reacted to them like they were weird. What it means is that were now accepted as people — sailors — and that we've leveled the playing field."

Getting to that point was not easy. Each increment toward acceptance had to be earned by superior performance. Early on, at least, if Pescud and his crew were not shunned by members of the yacht club, they were the subjects of well-meaning but misguided pity.

"Another problem with disabled people is the tin-cup brigade, those who rattle their tin cup and say 'help me,'" Pescud said. "Such individuals, which are common on the streets of Sydney, color the perception of able-bodied people about all disabled people," he said.

"We've taken the position: Don't come and help us. We're going to help ourselves," said Pescud. "And that's harder for us to do. It is. If you're the bowman and you don't have any legs, you're going to spend most of your time under water. It's hard. It's harder than for a guy with legs. But when you beat the guy with legs, you know that you're seriously better than your competition. Try sitting on your bum and trimming sails in the bow. It's hard. So at the end of the day, this boat is a very, very competitive racer."

Indeed.

Aspect Computing was 25 miles southeast of Gabo Island on December 27, 1998, heading into the epicenter of the storm that would mark the darkest moment in Australian yacht-racing history. Gray skies hovered seemingly at the top of the Hobart fleet's mast tops. Wind rocketing out of the southwest at speeds few had ever experienced was driving rain so hard that one crewman described it as feeling like being stabbed in the face by a fork. Waves of the size that break the spines of cargo ships were coming at the sail boats in clusters, knotting stomachs already emptied by seasickness. Conditions the previous night that knocked six extremely capable boats and crews out of the race prepared no one for the feral intensity of Sunday's conditions.

Aspect Computing's skipper was in his element.

"I've not raced anywhere else in the world so I don't know how other people race or what conditions they get in," said Pescud. "But as far as the Hobart, it was just another day at the office. That's what were there for. That's the way I look at it. I came up on deck in the middle of a blow on Sunday. I remember looking at one of the girls — it was her first Hobart — and this wave had just broken and it just washed her from one side to the other. I pulled my goggles down and said, 'Don't you love these blows? Isn't this just great fun?'"

Sandy Collins and Sharon Bond, two of *Aspect's* Hobart crew, were less enamored of Sunday's conditions.

"It was terrifying. I think it put us off for a day," said Collins. "But in the end I was grateful for the test. You learn a lot about yourself."

"If you thought about it before you left you might have second thoughts about going," Bond added. "But it was fascinating and overall it was supreme race training."

One of the biggest challenges facing *Aspect* as the storm built in earnest Sunday afternoon was climbing the huge waves, taking them on starboard at a 45-degree angle, and then renegotiating the boat's angle down the back of the waves, "especially the big ones," said Pescud. Twice while driving, Pescud said, he was thrown violently against *Aspect's* starboard safety rail by tons of green water washing over the deck. It was

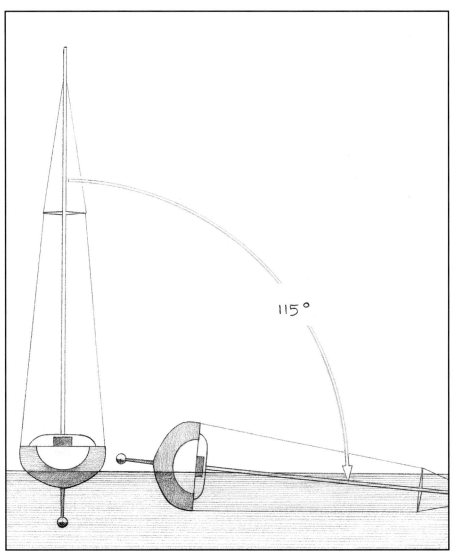

115°

To qualify for a Category 1 race such as the Sydney to Hobart, a yacht must be able to right itself from a 115 degree knockdown. Sail boats are able to self right because of counterbalancing lead weights in the keel.

immediate punishment for miscalculating the angle up or down a big wave. *Aspect's* stern spray rail still bore the evidence three months later.

How big were the waves battering *Aspect?*

"Big. Fucking big," Pescud said. "I don't want to estimate wave size. But when you've got 2 feet of green water over the deck you know you're in big seas. And that was happening a lot."

Aspect came close to a knockdown, heeling over at 50 degrees before recovering. And a spinnaker pole was broken. But, like Ellison and the crew of *Sayonara,* Pescud said the worst part of the storm was launching off steep waves and free-falling to the sea surface.

"The boat was full of bloody water from green water coming over the deck," Pescud said. "We were bailing every hour. I think the scariest thing was a three-second free fall. When she goes airborne we count onnnnne, twoooo, threeee, *BANG!* I thought the mast was going through the bottom of the boat. That was the worst thing. And then after the storm abated a little, that's when we did the damage. We hit the accelerator really hard. The wind was going at about 45 knots and we were jumping off these waves at 9, 10 and 11 knots, just *BOOM BANG, BOOM BANG* for 10 hours or so. I think that's when we really hurt her. But she's glued back together now."

Both legally and morally responsible for the safety of his boat and crew under such conditions, Pescud said his confidence in the crew never flagged — even for a moment.

"The crew was just brilliant," he said. "We were running under a storm staysail. And it takes a fair bit of rigging up, which the crew did under very difficult circumstances. I don't want to single one or two out because they were all brilliant."

A self-described Captain Bligh, Pescud said he nonetheless trains diligently with crew members to devise ways to accomplish sailing tasks that at first seem impossible for certain handicaps. And, he added, better anticipation of required tasks and the additional time it takes for a handicapped sailor to do those tasks is built into *Aspect Computing's* racing tactics.

"I get the shits from the crew," he said. "They'll tell you that I'm a bastard and I ask a lot of them. If someone tells me they have a disability, I tell them to pack it up and go tell someone who cares. But because of their disabilities we can't do things as fast as other crews and we make allowances for that. We anticipate what we need to do and give ourselves a bit more time to get it done. But in terms of someone saying I can't, we say 'Tell us why you can't and we'll develop a system so you can.'"

A man who has overcome great odds in his own life, Pescud sidestepped his own seamanship and leadership skills to praise his crew for their accomplishment in the Hobart.

"I left Sydney thinking that I had six good sailors that I could rely on, and when the storm hit everybody kept working, they just kept going," he said.

Their efforts would put them across the finish line in a position that would surprise everyone.

* * *

AFR Midnight Rambler, skipper Ed Psaltis' untested 35-footer, was five miles west of *Aspect Computing* on the same latitude. Psaltis and his crew of seven, which included his brother Edmund, sailed into the northern edge of the storm at 3 a.m. on Sunday. *Midnight Rambler*, like the rest of the Hobart racing fleet, endured a six-hour battering before the winds dropped briefly on the westerly or "inside" route. But unlike the rest of the fleet, the crew aboard *Midnight Rambler* was still logging its first hours aboard the new boat. In addition to his brother and the boat's co-owner Bob Thomas, Psaltis' crew included Chris Rockell, Gordon Livingstone, John Whitfield and Michael Bencsik. Like Psaltis, the crew members were widely considered among Australia's best amateur offshore small-boat sailors. Among them they had 57 Sydney to Hobart races, and they had years of experience sailing together as a team. In 1997, the last Hobart race for the former *Midnight Rambler*, Psaltis finished a respectable 15th across the finish line, which was good for a third place in the small-boat division.

"We knew in 1998 that the boat was quite capable of winning the race," Psaltis said. "It's a hard race to win but we had an idea that we would do very well in our division. *Midnight Rambler* was built specifically for the Hobart. It's a tough boat, a lot tougher than some of those new boats, and it's substantially built. And we're marginally heavier than some of the very light boats, so it's a good solid boat. It's got a strong mast, but not to the extent that it's not a competitive boat. It's always been a competitive racing machine. It was built specifically for the Hobart so it's not a throw-away boat in the way that some boats are built to race the Hobart four or five times."

In terms of sail boat design, modern ocean-racers are a target of criticism among some heavy-water sailors. The extreme light weight of the boats coupled with the enormous amount of sail they carry make them capable of great speed in "fine" sailing conditions but problematic in rough seas. Their flaw, according to detractors, is that the light, fast boats cannot be slowed sufficiently in high winds and steep seas, which creates handling problems and excessive stress on the boat and its rig.

Even a racing boat overbuilt specifically to endure the unique rigors of the Hobart like *Midnight Rambler* is not immune to the punishment the Hobart can dish out, as it did in 1998, 1993 and 1977. "There was no hull damage," Psaltis said. "Just a bit of cracking in the fiberglass coating from her slamming off the waves. Nothing substantial."

Nor was the storm anything substantial for Psaltis and his crew as they sailed in a 15-knot breeze at midmorning on Sunday, at the top of their game. Psaltis later would say that he was unaware that the storm was anything other than "another gale" until late in the race. It was noon when *Midnight Rambler* faced a hard chance.

"The first change came through at 3 a.m. on the 27th," Psaltis recalled. "That was about 40 knots, and it died at about 9 o'clock in the morning. It was light wind then for about three or four hours and then it came in very hard at about noon, very hard and very fast. It just kept blowing, blowing, blowing. We had lost our wind instruments so we didn't know how hard the wind was blowing. But I'm told it was 70 knots plus. It was very bad, the worst I've seen in the Hobart."

One of the biggest differences between the maxis and the smaller boats is that the smaller boats feel every nuance of the sea as they move through it. It can be described as the difference between driving a family sedan over a bumpy road and driving that same road in a go-cart. The road must be driven far more slowly and with much more attention to the road surface at the wheel of the go-cart than at the wheel of the sedan. In the violent storm that struck the Hobart fleet, a maxi has a slender margin for error. A 35-footer's margin is slim to none.

Such was *Midnight Rambler's* margin of error and the critical necessity for the crew to do everything exactly right, every time as the storm escalated Sunday afternoon.

"I was washed off the helm twice," Psaltis recalled. "We were knocked down in the waves and green water came over the boat. I tried to hang on but I was washed off. The green water pushed me against a spray rail and luckily that didn't break and my ribs didn't break and it kept me from going over the side. And going into another wave I was pushed against the rail and hung on to the wheel. The rig didn't break, my ribs didn't break and my safety harness didn't break. We had one man washed overboard in the bow but he was able to get back aboard quickly and without incident."

A few bruised ribs and a close call or two was the tally aboard *Midnight Rambler* by 1 p.m. So far they were lucky, even considering the vast amount of seamanship that went into manning the boat. As Psaltis noted, he had lost his anemometer, the spinning device at the top of the mast that measures wind speed, the night before. *Midnight Rambler* was sailing in a Force 11 gale, conditions in which few people ever sail a small boat and fewer still live to tell about it.

While there is a correlation between wind speed and wave height, it is not linear. It is exponential. Watching the sea with *terra firma* under foot, the difference between a 55-knot wind and a 70-knot wind can appear to be a relatively fine distinction. But for sailors in the 1998 Sydney to Hobart the difference between Force 10 and a Force 11 was the difference between being at the gates of Hell and passing beneath its solemn greeting: Abandon all hope ye who enter here.

The Beaufort Wind Scale was designed in 1805 by Sir Francis Beaufort, a rear admiral in the British navy, to describe the wind's effect on sailing ships. Based on a scale of Force 0-17, the Beaufort Wind Scale is used worldwide. A Force 3, for example, is a gentle breeze of 8-12 knots. A Force 5 is a fresh breeze of 19-24 knots, the kind of wind perfect for weekend regattas. A Force 8 sea, according to the Beaufort Scale, is a fresh gale of 39-46 knots with "moderately high waves of greater length [than Force 7 conditions]; edges of crests begin to break into spindrift. The foam is blown in well-marked streaks along the direction of the wind."

The Beaufort Scale calls Force 10 a "whole gale." Winds range from 55-63 knots and waves build to 40 feet. The Beaufort Scale description of a Force 10 is: "Very high waves with long overhanging crests. The resulting foam in great patches is blown in dense white streaks along the direction of the wind. On the whole the surface of the sea takes a white appearance. The tumbling of the sea becomes heavy and shock-like; visibility affected."

Force 11 is, on the Beaufort Scale, a "violent storm" packing winds of 64-73 knots. The few sailors who have been on the receiving end of a Force 11 marine weather warning and not made port might agree with the

Beaufort description: "Exceptionally high waves (small and medium-size ships might be for a time lost to view behind the waves). The sea is completely covered with long white patches of foam lying along the direction of the wind; everywhere the edges of the wave crests are blown into froth; visibility affected."

Midnight Rambler faced its first crisis less than an hour after the storm built rapidly from a Beaufort Force 4 to a Force 11.

"Chris Rockell, one of our crew who was down below when the boat lurched and jumped off a wave, was thrown through the air," Psaltis said. "He hit his head on some bolts that hold the mast and he cut his head, quite a deep, long cut. Any head wound bleeds a lot, so there was blood everywhere. And he was concussed. None of us were doctors but we didn't think he was badly concussed. We wrapped him up and put him in a bunk."

If they were thinking about turning *Midnight Rambler* about and running for the shelter of Eden, now was the time.

"I'm sure we all thought about it," Psaltis recalled. "And we talked about it briefly when Chris got hurt. We actually discussed it and decided that continuing was far less of a risk than trying to make it to Eden. The guys making the decisions — myself, Bob Thomas the co-owner, and my brother — we knew that Eden was only about 40 miles while the shelter of Hobart was a couple hundred miles. But it was pretty risky the way the wind was blowing from the southeast to try to make it to the coast of New South Wales. We were all adamant that turning and running with the waves would place us at greater risk of being rolled than going on. And for the next six hours we kept checking on Chris. He kept saying, 'I'm OK. Let me come on up and get on with it.'"

In retrospect, the decision to head for Hobart rather than turn around and run downwind for Eden in the high seas may have been one of the best calls Psaltis, his brother and Bob Thomas ever made. It would be a long two-and-a-half days before they would find out just how right they

Most of the more serious knockdowns in the 1998 race happened in a sequence similar to this.

were. But almost immediately after making the decision to continue, they got verification that it was the right one.

"We saw some bigger boats that had turned around and were going back with just a storm sail up, running back through the waves, and they were just hanging on. They were much bigger boats than us, 45-footers and bigger, and the waves were crashing over them. They were running with the waves, which were, with the wind, coming at their port just aft of the boom. They were running at about 110 degrees of the waves, which were coming southwest to northeast," said Psaltis.

At 4 p.m. *Midnight Rambler* was beating to windward in a Force 11 under a tiny scrap of storm trisail. Overhead there was an ugly gray-black sky reverberating with thunder and spitting rain that hit like bird shot. The enormous waves — any of which could break the back of the strongest oil tanker — taxed the boat and its experienced crew to their absolute limits. There was no respite, no time-out, only the waves and the relentless wind.

"At 70 knots the wind is very loud," Psaltis recalled. "That was one of the scariest things of the whole experience. It was a scream, a constant scream in your ear as it came through the rigging. And it made an odd noise as it came around the mast. The wind was so loud that you could just be heard by someone standing right beside you if you yelled at the top of your voice. The shrieking of the wind was almost as bad as the sea state itself in that it reinforced just how bad it was out there."

Midnight Rambler was in the middle of a maelstrom that bore a striking resemblance to a storm 56 years earlier in the North Atlantic. In late 1942, carrying 15,000 American soldiers bound for England, the *Queen Mary* hit a storm about 700 miles off the coast of Scotland. Without

Overleaf: *The force of tons of green water over the deck is enough to snap safety lines and damage rigging even when the boat remains upright.*

warning amid the violent storm, a single, mountainous wave struck the ocean liner, rolling it on its side and cresting over its upper decks. With the help of a second wave, the ship managed to right itself and continue on its voyage.

A more recent incident happened under conditions eerily similar to those created by the East Coast current off the coast of New South Wales. The Agulhas Current skirts the South African continental shelf. Depending on the prevailing winds, this current often meets a steady wave swell nearly head-on. The collision reduces the spacing between the waves and changes their size and direction. In November 1996, a cargo ship with 29 people aboard sank after being hit by a freak giant wave generated by gale winds countering the Agulhas Current.

If mountainous waves can topple the world's great ocean liners and massive cargo ships, what chance does a 35-foot sail boat have in similar conditions? The answer is that it depends on the skill and courage of the crew, which *Midnight Rambler* had in abundance.

"We've got 57 Hobarts among us and most of those have been done together. So it's a very close crew," said Psaltis. "I think that's one of the big areas that is understated in this race. If you have a crew that knows each other and has spent time together that can really help, especially in a race like the Hobart. Otherwise you have situations where you have one or two big names, professional [sailors] on the boat, very fine individuals, but in a tight situation they don't know the capabilities of the other crew members, which can lead to some dangerous situations. As the saying goes: A crew that is a team will always beat a crew of individuals. That's what we are, I think, a very good team. There are no stars. But we know each other well and we're a very good sailing team."

Sailing across Bass Strait in the late afternoon of December 27, 1998, in the malevolent heart of the storm was the epitome of *Midnight Rambler's* hard chance. But what distinguished Psaltis and his crew from many of the other boats was his knowledge of how to negotiate the huge waves in a small sail boat. There are few books that offer proven tactics for surviving violent storms in a sail boat. One that does was written about the tragic 1979 Fastnet race, a 605-mile yacht race along the English Channel, around Ireland's Fastnet Rock and back to Plymouth, England. Struck by a Force 10 gale on the second day of the race, the Fastnet fleet was decimated. Thirteen sailors died and scores of boats were lost.

"I learned from the Fastnet book that the best way to approach the waves was from about 60 degrees to the wave. That way you go up and over the wave instead of through it and you minimize the chance of getting caught on the crest and rolling over. You can see them coming and you can pick your angle and get up and over the top. I think staying up high [closer to the coast] and hitting the waves at 60 degrees helped us survive," Psaltis said.

Yet *Midnight Rambler's* veteran skipper was not making life-and-death tactical decisions simply by taking another sailor's word for it. In the 1994 Hobart, which was hit by a storm, Psaltis, sailing a 30-footer, the smallest boat allowed in the race, was rolled by a large wave.

"[In the 1998 Hobart] I think if we'd presented the bow at 90 degrees, beam on [directly into the wave] I'm pretty sure we would have been rolled. I was rolled in the '94 hobart in a 30-footer while doing just that and it's something you don't forget or ever want to repeat, believe me," he said.

Describing the process of negotiating the wave, Psaltis said that ideally the boat would approach the wave at a 60 degree angle, ascend the wave, top it and then "pull away." Pulling away means turning the boat at an angle that surfs it down the wave's back side rather than launching it into the air to crash to the trough, sometimes far below. That was the ideal, which the skipper said he and *Midnight Rambler's* other helmsman were able to get right about 80 percent of the time. But it required constant vigilance because each wave required its own angle of ascent and descent.

"Some of the waves were breaking and some weren't," Psaltis recalled. "At the top 10 feet on the breaking waves it was just white breaking water coming at you. So that was the first part, getting up over. The next part was knowing when to pull away. At the top of the wave you've got to pull away hard and just slide down rather than shooting into the air and dropping 20 or 30 feet, which can break up a boat. That can bend and break even Kevlar and carbon.

"That's the two most dangerous things: what angle do you go up the wave and your judgement at the top of the wave, where there's usually breaking water you pull away at just the right time and you slide. Without too much trouble you can get it wrong. And when that happens you can get water crashing down on the deck or worse.

"About 80 percent of the time we got it reasonably right. The other 20 percent of the time, for whatever reason, the helmsman didn't pick it right. We fell at the wrong angle too soon, too late. That's when we'd take green water over the deck. Other times we'd come off the wave and shoot out into the air and fall to the ocean with a huge bang, which the boat would survive. But when you're down below [decks] and experience that, it's just the scariest thing. It's like you're in a big drum and the boat just shudders as if saying, 'Don't do that to me again.'"

Psaltis and crew were in tacit control of this roller-coaster ride on waves as high as 70 feet in wind that gusted to 75 miles an hour while wearing goggles obscured most of the time by the driving rain and the constant lash of sea spray. When you come off the first hill on a roller-coaster there's a certain assurance that it's safe — an amusement. When you come off a 70-foot wave in a sail boat, the bow is pointed nearly straight down and the boat is hanging on only by the thin blades of your racing rudder and keel, the thrill is surviving the moment. Then, immediately, survival depends on whether you've got enough speed to make it over the top of the next monster.

"Going up was dangerous because if you didn't make it to the top the wave would pick you up and roll you," Psaltis said. "Or if you didn't make it over the top you'd slide back down. The key was getting over the top. Then you pick the right angle to go down the wave. If you pull away too hard you'll get rolled, so it's halfway between the two. It's pretty hard to select the right angle each time, but 60 degrees was pretty much right most of the time. But sometimes it was 70 degrees just to hang and stay righted.

"It's hard to estimate the size of the waves. They were certainly huge; the biggest I've seen. I find it hard to estimate the size of the waves because it isn't a big wall; it's a gradual rise. I'm sure the tops of some of the big ones were 60 to 70 feet. We found that we took them in sets and after every two or three waves there was a big and nasty one and then you'd have relative calm. So it was like that. You just survived these sets of big waves. It really wasn't constant big waves, but these sets of them that you had to survive."

Midnight Rambler's crew did everything right, but they still had their share of close calls.

"We got knocked over about 90 degrees," according to Psaltis. "It wasn't enough to wet the sails, but that's when I got washed off the helm and knocked back. I had to hang onto the tiller to get back to the boat, which wasn't much fun. Sometimes we were just lucky. But the boat is really stable. She's got a high stability ratio compared to most of the boats, which means that if she does get knocked down she rights faster. And that really helped us under those conditions. We have a 122-degree righting angle, which is substantially higher than the race requirement of 115 degrees. Some of these new boats right at 115 degrees, which makes them lighter and faster but also perhaps more dangerous in bad sea conditions."

While the crew on deck struggled to keep *Midnight Rambler* afloat, making dozens of critical adjustments every minute, belowdecks, it was as bad — if not worse. The slamming and groaning of the hull under stress whispers disaster. There is no rest, because climbing into a bunk is akin to lying in a coffin going over Niagara Falls. Even something as simple and refreshing as a cup of coffee or soup is impossible because it's too turbulent, and, anyway, the gas stove broke down hours ago. Even if it hadn't, anxiety and seasickness stole your appetite so long ago you can't remember the last time you ate or drank. At best, you sit in a draft-free spot and hang on so that you don't float in zero gravity when the boat free-falls off a wave. You think about loved ones, good times, the last thing you said to them and how you might have treated them better, because it's pretty obvious that surviving the next hour or two is a crap shoot. Above all, though, you keep your game face on for the sake of your fellow crewmen. That's important.

"No one spoke about [dying], which was good because it showed that we were a competent and confident team," Psaltis said. "Nobody said anything negative; it was all positive and upbeat. We discussed it after the race and how lucky we were to have made it and to be back with loved ones. But no one said anything about it while we were in the race. I'm sure we all thought about it, but everyone made positive comments to keep everyone else going, which was key to our survival. It's a credit to all involved that nobody threw their hands in the air and said, 'We're all going to die.' That's what made us a good team."

By now, *Midnight Rambler* was no longer racing in the 1998 Hobart, Psaltis said. The crew was sailing for survival.

"We were just hanging on. It's hard to explain. But we were just trying to survive. So you just try to get the information you need to keep hoping, keep going. The motion of the boat, the storm, the wind, it all has a jarring effect on you and you're hanging on for dear life."

They desperately needed a break. And they got it just before dark on Sunday night.

"About 8 o'clock that night the wind suddenly died out. Which makes me think that we might have been sailing through the eye of the storm. It was blowing so hard and then to suddenly die down to about 15 knots, roughly estimated. I've never seen it 70 knots and then suddenly die out. It happened in about 15 minutes, maybe less. Then two or three hours later the breeze gradually built again to about 45 knots."

Midnight Rambler was still a long way from the finish line. But the worst was over. She and her crew had survived a hard chance. Others were not so fortunate.

* * *

By midmorning Sunday, a half dozen boats, including line-honors favorites *Marchioness* and *Wild Thing*, had sustained disabling damage and were forced out of the race. Many others, confronting the full fury of storm for the first time, were heading for the shelter of Eden's Twofold Bay. At 10 a.m., the Hobart fleet was an average of 25 miles from Eden.

Among the seven boats in the lead Sunday morning was *Team Jaguar*, a 65-foot sloop out of Sydney's Cruising Yacht Club of Australia. Running for the shelter of Eden was not an option. The 1989 Farr design was formerly named *Brindabella* and raced by George Snow to a line-honors victory in the 1991 Sydney to Hobart. The boat's current owner, prominent Sydney lawyer Martin James, had had *Team Jaguar* in a top position in the 1997 Sydney to Hobart only to be thwarted by a broken mast.

James and his crew of 18, most of whom were seasoned offshore racers, left the 1998 starting line with the objective of finishing among the top five, which is as hard to achieve as it is desirable. But James' hope for a top finish was dashed late Sunday when, running well ahead of the pack, *Team Jaguar* was knocked down by a huge wave, which weakened her mast and washed crewman Tony Eggleton overboard. He was recovered an anxious three minutes later.

At the entrance to Bass Strait four hours later, *Team Jaguar's* weakened mast was no match for the strait's storm winds. It snapped, and a line from the downed mast jammed the big sloop's propeller. Adrift and pushed north by the oncoming front, *Team Jaguar* was taking a terrible pounding when her radios failed and her deck began breaking up from the stress of the sea's incessant beating.

Melissa McCabe, a 16-year-old Sydney high school student was among the crew of *Team Jaguar*. She won her berth with a first-place yachting essay in a contest sponsored by skipper James and "Team Jag," as the pocket maxi is known by local yachtsmen.

In the January 2 edition of the *Sydney Morning Herald* Melissa recounted her experience during which *Team Jaguar* was dismasted for the second consecutive year and feared lost.

"Excitement bubbled in my stomach as I left behind the crowded deck at Rushcutters Bay [the location of the Cruising Yacht Club of Australia and *Team Jaguar's* home] destined for my first Sydney to Hobart yacht race. The harbor was filled with a mosaic of sails, spectator boats and white water as we swept past other smaller boats to gain a better starting position.

"The strong northeaster was carrying the boat along like a dream, allowing us to set our spinnaker whilst rounding the Heads and cruise at an average speed of 18 knots. The whole crew was ecstatic. The brilliant conditions heightened our pleasure over our successful start.

"We were making excellent time and had passed Jervis Bay well before nightfall. Although I was still exuberant, we were beginning to see signs of a predicted black southerly change. The swell had been continuously rising, and by dusk dark clouds began to seep into the horizon, soon forming two thunderstorms that enveloped the boat from the east and the west. We removed the spinnaker.

"I had wrapped myself in my wet-weather gear and strapped on a safety harness. Waves were beginning to wash over the bow of the boat. From my position on the boat's rails spray washed over me.

"We started our watch system at this stage — two hours on deck, two hours on the rails to be called in if needed, two hours sleep. At 10 p.m. I clambered below deck and arose again at midnight to find the conditions worse.

"In the dark, the boat made a harsh slapping sound as it slammed down the front of the swell.

"During this watch we tacked unexpectedly. The two crew members on either side of me managed to clamber into the cockpit. I wasn't so lucky. Panic-stricken, I managed to grab hold of the rail as water rushed over the deck and began to rise around my waist. I shouted for help and my crew members grabbed me and hauled me into the cockpit.

"We then had to make it to the rails on the opposite side. Frantically I had to unattach my safety harness in order to reattach it to the other side of the boat. My fingers were too numb to function. Using two hands I managed to unclip my harness. I hated the terror I felt, knowing that for a time I was totally unprotected.

"At 4 a.m. my watch was up. Exhausted, I struggled below deck only to find seasick crew members bailing and pumping because the bilges had flooded some sections of the boat.

"At 6:30 a.m. my watch was greeted with daylight. The sun seemed to soak up the night's miseries. The wind had relented slightly, and Eden was in sight to our east. I felt so glad to be aboard the boat that morning, knowing that we had all those miles behind us.

"At 11:30 a.m. I was lying below deck when I heard the cry of 'All hands on deck.' The mast was beginning to break. It was too dangerous for me on deck so I could only peep out of the hatch and gasp at the mainsail lying limp in the water and the boom sagging. Hacksaws, hammers, screwdrivers were used to pry off rigging to save the boat.

"At the moment that the mast slipped into the sea, I looked around at crew faces full of fear and intensity and knew that my hopes of getting to Hobart had also been gobbled up by the sea. The race was now for safety.

"With the mast gone nothing was left but to motor the 50 nautical miles back to Eden. A huge bang sounded as a mass of water cracked the deck frame above me. I jumped up, knee-deep in water, wanting to escape. I kept having flashes of disaster voyages. It was almost surreal. I was told to get up on deck, and did so swiftly.

"As soon as we got on deck I saw two crew being pulled back on board after being washed off.

"It was worse on deck than below. For our own safety, another two females and I were ordered below.

"Below deck I heard that ropes had been swept overboard and had jammed the propeller. The skipper tried the radio and realized we could make no transmission. This was the moment that I was the most scared. I knew that no one knew that we were in trouble.

"When communication was finally established using our emergency aerial we were informed that a trawler called *Moira Elizabeth* was coming to tow us to Eden. The worst part about waiting was listening to the radio and hearing real peoples' horror stories and frantic Maydays, knowing you couldn't possibly help them, or even yourself.

"Finally, at 4 a.m., we were found. At 12:30 p.m. we pulled into Eden wharf. I had never felt so thankful for seeing so many caring faces. When you suffer a piece of hell everything in life shines brighter."

While it is crushing to watch a hard-won and favorable position evaporate two years in a row, the blows James suffered were primarily to his pride and pocketbook. Other boats in *Team Jaguar's* vicinity were taking a similar pounding. And while some of their crews were getting beaten up, all were getting spooked.

Twenty miles east on a course nearly parallel to *Team Jaguar*, Stan Zemanek, the skipper of *Foxtel Titan Ford*, was giving serious consideration to the concept of death.

"We were just bare-poling [no sails up] and the boat was still leaning over on a big angle," he said. "The boat just hit a wave and flew straight up in the air and I went with it, nothing to hang on to. I hit my head and ribs on the galley, breaking two. I thought I was a goner."

A consummately skilled sailor with a 20-year maritime career and 21 Hobart finishes to his credit, Roger Hickman, the skipper of *Atara*, described Sunday morning's waves: "We were in a 43-foot boat. You'd go up the wave and look to the bottom. And I reckon that they were somewhere between 60 and 65 feet from the bottom to the top."

John Stanley, a crewman on the ill-fated cutter *Winston Churchill*, said he had been warned 16 years earlier that tempting fate and Bass Strait was playing with fire.

"I remember a speech back in 1982 when it was said that sometime in the next 100 years we would get some horrific conditions in Bass Strait. And it looked like we were in those conditions," he said.

It would only be a matter of a few hours before the storm — at its greatest intensity — would start tearing into the Hobart fleet with no holds barred.

VC Offshore Stand Aside was its first victim.

* * *

Skipper Jim Hallion and co-owner Laurie Hallion, both of Adelaide, South Australia, thought they had a good chance of finishing the Sydney to Hobart ahead of the other boats in *Stand Aside's* division. Jim Hallion had skippered the 40-footer to a divisional first and several divisional placings in Cruising Yacht Club of South Australia inshore and offshore events. He was a veteran of two Sydney to Hobarts, but 1998 was *Stand*

Aside's first. The boat had proved particularly fast when running and reaching, sailing with the wind from her stern, the kind of winds initially forecast for the race. So Jim Hallion and his experienced crew of 11 had reason to be optimistic about a good finish.

And even though the storm shifted the winds 180 degrees on Saturday from north to south, *Stand Aside*, at her best when running, had beaten more than 200 miles to windward in 24 hours. Averaging 16 knots overnight in rough seas, *Stand Aside* was running hard at the entrance to Bass Strait by 1 p.m. on Sunday. With steady winds of 50 knots, her crew had gradually reduced sail until *Stand Aside* was running only a small storm jib. With the wind, the seas had built, so most of the crew stood watch on the pitching deck, on alert for rogue waves. Within an hour the winds had escalated to 60 knots, with gusts as high as 80 knots. With such wind it didn't take long for a rogue wave to find *Stand Aside*.

Crewman Simon Clark, a 28-year-old who had sailed since he was a boy, wasn't worried. He had seen only one "green wave," as he called the huge walls of water that were knocking down so many yachts in Bass Strait.

Suddenly, though, a rogue wave Clark described as a tennis court standing on end loomed astern *Stand Aside*, dwarfing the yacht.

"Bear away!" he yelled above the roar of the wind.

"All of a sudden the call came that there was a huge wave behind the boat," said Laurie Hallion, an experienced yachtsman. "The skipper tried to bear away but the wave came down on top of the port side of the boat, crashed the boom down on to the deck and rolled the yacht over."

Eight members of the crew, most tethered to the boat by harnesses, went with it.

"Underneath the boat it was just a mass of bodies struggling to get free of the ropes and the harnesses," Jim Hallion recalled. He remembers being under the water for one to two minutes, feeling other bodies struggling around him. It felt like longer.

VC Offshore Stand Aside *lying dismasted in heavy seas after it was rolled through 360 degrees by a huge wave*

"We must have been hit by an 80- to 90-foot wave," said crew member Charles Alsop, another experienced yachtsman. "It broke over the boat and we took a 360-degree turn."

Alsop, who was thrown overboard when *Stand Aside* was struck, said he nearly drowned as a result.

"As soon as you're underneath the water, ropes all over you, all tangled up, your first thought is: 'I've just got to get to the surface. I'm losing air.'"

Crew member John Culley, a sailor with three years experience taking part in his first Sydney to Hobart, was wearing neither a harness nor life jacket when the yacht keeled over. "I was sitting on the rail, I think I was the furthest forward, and I just heard somebody say 'wave' and then somebody said 'Oh, shit!'

"I had this sensation of a slow-motion roll into the sea. I opened my eyes and I could see the deck underneath the water and a few bodies floating around. When I surfaced, the boat seemed like it was a mile away but in fact it was probably only about 40 meters away. I had my waterproof boots on which were filling up with water.

"I thought, 'I'm not going to make it,'" Culley said.

But the waves and the wind pushed him back toward the boat and he was hauled back on board by strong hands.

By this time, the yacht's mast was gone and its cabin destroyed. The engine was under water, as were the batteries. The main communications system was gone, leaving only a small hand-held radio to send the Mayday call.

The boat was filling with water through a 7-foot gash in its cabin.

All the crew could do was bail water as they sent out a distress call and waited for help.

As the magnitude of the disaster unfolded, increasingly larger government agencies would take control of coordinating rescue services and dispatching increasing numbers of ships, planes and helicopters to the stricken yachts. But for the moment radio operator Lew Carter, a longtime race volunteer, was coordinating rescue efforts from his crowded space aboard *Young Endeavour,* the Australian Navy's bringantine that harked back to the days when sailing ships ruled the seas.

Gary Ticehurst, the pilot of an Australian Broadcasting Network helicopter, found himself in the dual role of on-site rescue coordinator and ABC pilot.

"We went straight for the position that was given us for the yacht *Stand Aside,*" said Ticehurst. "What greeted us was just unbelievable. Unbelievable circumstances. Help was on its way, but it was an hour away. We had just refueled so we were able to stay on station. We were aware of a smaller yacht. *Siena* passed within a couple hundred meters of us and *Stand Aside* but because of the big seas did not see either of us."

Siena, an older 38-foot sloop skippered by Iain Muray of Sydney, was heading for Eden under a storm sail with a crewman who had suffered broken ribs. She passed *Stand Aside* while both were in troughs on opposite sides of the same huge wave. Neither yacht saw the other. But *Siena,* whose crew included Dr. Stephen Grenville, the deputy governor of the Reserve Bank of Australia, responded immediately to a hail from the ABC helicopter. Apprised that *Stand Aside* was dismasted and off her port, *Siena* and her crew of seven came about to offer assistance.

Watching the slow and dangerous maneuver from several hundred feet above, Ticehurst said, "That took a lot of guts. That really took a lot of courage for them in that small boat to turn around in those conditions and assist *Stand Aside.*

With *Siena* tending and Ticehurst hovering the ABC helicopter overhead, the crew of *Stand Aside,* several of whom were badly injured, waited. Below decks the boat was awash in a nauseating cocktail of sea water, spilled food, toilet chemicals and engine fuel. On deck it was just as unpleasant as the boat pitched over each new wave and dropped to the trough far below, all the while bucking wildly at the mercy of the gale winds. Three hours later a civilian Helimed rescue helicopter equipped with a winch arrived, hovered 100 feet above the yachts and made radio contact with *Stand Aside*.

"*Stand Aside*, this is Helimed One. Do you have a motor?"

"No, the motor is not working."

"Can you let the life raft out a bit further [astern]?"

"Yes, we can."

Ticehurst, who had remained on the scene in the ABC helicopter, said: "The worst injured on *Stand Aside* were put in a life raft. The first rescue attempt was made with the rescue swimmer lowered out of the helicopter into the water. But the waves were huge and breaking. We could see the air crewman in the water disappear in a trough as the wave broke. Due to conditions it took some time for the first rescue to be completed, as the pilot was warming to his task. But after that it didn't take very long to rescue the rest of the crew."

Shortly after the Helimed helicopter arrived, a second rescue helicopter reached the scene to replace a Victorian police helicopter that had been diverted en route to another stricken Hobart yacht.

Helimed paramedic Peter Davidson returned to the water eight times until he was exhausted. The Helimed helicopter from which he had been working was running low on fuel. So the pilot wheeled it about and headed for the mainland with eight of *Stand Aside's* crew of 12 aboard. The lives of the four remaining crewmen were in the hands of the crew of the second helicopter on the scene, SouthCare, a civilian air-ambulance service from Canberra, Australia's capital city. On board was Kristy McAlister, a 30-year-old fit and youthful paramedic. Although an experienced paramedic, she had only been working on helicopters for two months, and this was her first ocean rescue. As the helicopter's paramedic, McAlister was the designated "down the wire guy," as air crews refer to the position.

As McAlister hooked the winch cable to her harness and looked below, one of the victims was drifting quickly away from the life raft tethered to *Stand Aside,* which held three other victims. Hesitating momentarily, she inventoried her nightmarish surroundings from the lurching helicopter that was struggling to hold position in the buffeting winds. In the space of a few seconds two monster waves rolled beneath the helicopter, reaching up 60 feet to lick its underbelly. Glancing at the instrument panel, McAlister saw the altimeter gyrate wildly in response to the upreaching waves and their deep troughs. The wind screamed demented notes through the vents of her safety helmet as she gave the "ready" signal, leaned out the starboard door and jumped, rescue strop in hand.

Immediately after a hard landing in the roiling sea she was clutched by a huge breaking wave and driven deep beneath the surface. Her lungs burning for air, McAlister clawed for the surface and came up almost beside the victim. With some hurried instructions, she got the oval-shaped strop over the man's head and gave the thumb's up, the signal to winch them aboard. A second massive wave that McAlister had not seen dragged them both under for several long seconds. When they surfaced, the wire tightened and hoisted them to safety.

After a perfunctory check of her first victim's condition, McAlister was back in the churning ocean, landing near the life raft and its three hypothermic occupants. With the last man rescued and the ruined and abandoned *Stand Aside* passing beneath the helicopter as it headed for the mainland, McAlister could hold out no longer. She began vomiting sea water in a series of violent spasms that would last for 10 minutes.

It was a difficult rescue for McAlister and the rest of the helicopter crew. As one of the pilots remarked: "One minute we had 80 feet under the aircraft and the next minute 10 feet. It took all our training and effort to get these people out."

One of the major points of confusion in all of the 1998 Hobart helicopter rescues was communicating with victims. Many of the stricken boats had lost their radios, so pilots could not explain to those below the high risk of tangling the rescue cable in the boat's rigging or slamming the rescuer against the boat when attempting to pluck a victim from the deck of a yacht. Even novice sailors are trained to "stay with the boat" as long as possible. So leaping into the sea, especially a wild sea, is not a comfortable proposition for sailors. But it is almost always the safest position for the helicopter crew from which to rescue a person, rescue pilots agree unanimously.

The four crewmen of *Stand Aside* with the worst injuries — Mike Marshmon suffering a severed finger, Clark with tendon damage to one of his knees, one with broken ribs, and another with head injuries — were flown to Traralgon District Hospital.

Jim and Laurie Hallion, Andy Marriette, Bevan Thompson, Bob Briggs, Charles Alsop, Hayden Jones, John Culley, Mike Marshmon, Rod Hunter, Simon Clark and Trevor Conyers had survived a hard chance.

* * *

Like *Stand Aside*, *Solo Globe Challenger* was entering Bass Strait Sunday evening and was handling the mountainous seas well, according to her skipper Tony Mowbray. "Cliffs of water," as Mowbray called them, were hammering down on *Solo Globe Challenger* with the force of thunderclaps, one after another. When the big ones struck, all the topside crew could do was hang on and turn away as tons of water pummeled the boat, and she shuddered in response.

At 43, Mowbray, a laborer from the middle-class coal-mining seaport town of Newcastle, 70 miles north of Sydney, thought of the 1998 Sydney to Hobart as a shakedown cruise. He had mortgaged his house and drained his savings to buy and outfit 44-foot *Solo Globe Challenger*. The veteran sailor with 32 years experience planned to sail solo, non-stop and unassisted around the world to raise money for an Australian children's hospital. Mowbray entered the 1998 Sydney to Hobart, his 14th, to spotlight his charity venture and to spend time with his sailing buddies, including his mentor and veteran of 22 Hobarts, Bob Snape, before circumnavigating the globe 10 months later.

In addition to Mowbray and Snape, *Solo Globe Challenger's* crew included David Cook, David Marshall, Glen Picasso, Keir Enderby, Keith Molloy and Tony Purkiss. Mowbray knew each of the crewmen, but with few exceptions the crewmen had not met each other before the race.

The yacht and crew withstood Sunday's battering until a 65-foot monster wave crashed on *Solo Globe Challenger's* stern at about 4 p.m. The yacht yawed sharply to port and rolled on its side at 145 degrees with its mast and rigging in the water. Like a body surfer, the knocked-down boat was pushed before the wave for nearly 30 seconds before it slowed and righted itself. Water gushed into the cabin through a broken skylight.

"I hadn't been to bed since the start of the race," Mowbray recalled. "And so on Sunday afternoon I went down below to get some rest. Not long after, the first monster hit us and laid us over. Before I had a chance to recover, the second one threw us over further and put the mast in the water. It just snapped off like a twig. The huge volume of water that came through the cockpit area smashed out the windows and blew out all our navigational and radio gear. We had no communication at all."

Crewman David Cook, from Lake Macquarie, in New South Wales, was below decks with David Marshall when the giant wave struck. "The next thing I know, a great wall of water came through the hatch and I ended up on top of Dave [Marshall]," Cook said.

Cook, an experienced ocean racer sailing his first Sydney to Hobart, remembers finding his way up out of the hatch after the yacht had righted itself again and finding sail trimmer Tony Purkiss sitting there, stunned, on deck with a huge gash on his head and blood everywhere.

Purkiss, taking part in his fifth Sydney to Hobart, had been hit on the head when the mast came down. And deck hatches had come down on his legs, fracturing his left leg below the knee.

"Glen Picasso was hanging over the side, dragged by his safety harness. [Tony Purkiss] had his leg pinned by the mast and was in a lot of agony and screaming out," said Mowbray

Picasso managed to drag himself back aboard. Purkiss was so entangled in the fallen rigging that he had to be cut free. Both men suffered head injuries and broken ribs.

After the initial shock, Mowbray quickly realized that the mast, still connected to *Solo Globe Challenger* by the rigging, threatened the boat as much as the next wave did.

"The biggest danger was the mast puncturing the side of the yacht, which would sink us. We had to cut the mast away and get rid of it. So we sent 35,000 bucks worth of gear to the bottom of the sea," the skipper said.

The yacht was now completely disabled and adrift.

"We had no mast, no engine, no communications, no rig," Cook recalled.

After bailing out the cabin and activating two EPIRBs (emergency position indicating radio beacons), all the skipper could do was stay at the wheel and use what little steerage he had to avoid another rogue wave. Nearby, the racing yacht *Pippin*, which was en route to Eden with seriously injured crewmen, some of whom had seen the knockdown, made a hazardous turn to come to *Solo Globe Challenger's* aid. Mowbray waved the yacht off, believing the sea was too dangerous for any rescue attempt by another boat. Also, *Pippin* had its own problems. *Pippin* continued on its course, but not before alerting the fleet's radio-relay ship that Mowbray and his crew were in trouble.

Two hours after the knockdown, two aircraft circled the stricken yacht within 30 minutes of each other. Shortly after that, a container ship slowed some 300 yards from *Solo Globe Challenger,* then resumed its course. Mowbray and his crew, unsure if they had been identified by the planes or the ship, fired a parachute flare, but the ship continued.

* * *

With two activated EPIRBs but no radios, *Solo Globe Challenger* headed into the maelstrom with the last of the gray sky turning to black.

The storm that was taking a terrible toll on the Sydney to Hobart fleet was to test the entrants to the absolute limits of their physical and mental endurance. In the process, it would also produce a number of heroes and heroines. One of them was 19-year-old Australian Elizabeth Wardley.

An experienced sailor at 19, Wardley had fallen in love with sailing big boats five years earlier. Disenchanted with school, she sailed on a big boat with an experienced skipper for the first time when she was 15. The skipper, she said, told her she should follow her love of sailing. Wardley took the advice and worked her way up to racing big yachts. After finishing high school, she began delivering yachts all over Australia. By the 1998 Sydney to Hobart race, Wardley had sailed the event once, she was ranked number two in the world in 16-foot catamaran racing and she had recently passed a difficult national test to become a charter-boat skipper.

At the Sydney to Hobart starting gun, Wardley was the skipper of the 40-foot sloop *Dixie Chicken*, which she and her father had bought a year earlier. She commanded a crew of seven men.

At the 2 p.m. radio sked, *Dixie Chicken* was 25 miles off Gabo Island, struggling to negotiate the huge seas and winds that were recorded two hours earlier at Wilson's Promontory in Bass Strait at a steady 80 knots. During one 10-minute interval the wind speed was a steady 92 knots — greater than 100 miles an hour.

It was in such conditions that skipper Alan Quick and the 10 crew of the Victorian yacht *Outlaw* was knocked down by an enormous wave and seriously damaged. It was Wardley's *Dixie Chicken,* five treacherous miles away, who came to Quick's aid.

After five hours of tending the 44-foot *Outlaw* as it struggled to Eden, Wardley pulled *Dixie Chicken* out of the race, believing she had lost too much time. One of Wardley's crew, Carl Sriber of Sydney, called his skipper's actions courageous. Even coming about in Sunday's conditions to go to *Outlaw's* aid was a dangerous 30-minute maneuver, he said.

Wardley's self-sacrifice, courage and heroism would not be the last in the 1998 Sydney to Hobart.

After a day of "screaming down the coast," as her skipper described it, *Sword of Orion* was among the Hobart fleet's lead boats Sunday afternoon. She was running a close race with Roger Hickman's *Atara,* which was a half mile off *Sword of Orion's* port bow and in the same Division B size class. *Yendy's,* a smaller Division C yacht skippered by Cruising Yacht Club of Australia Director Geoff Ross, was beating to windward off *Sword of Orion's* port just a large wave or two distant.

A Sydney-based boat with a new owner, *Sword of Orion* was on a major winning streak. Owner Rob Kothe had campaigned the 47-footer to a surprise victory in the prestigious Hamilton Island Race Week a short time earlier. Formerly the *Brighton Star,* which finished well in the difficult conditions of the 1997 Sydney to Hobart, *Sword of Orion* had been race tuned, including being refitted with a lighter, faster carbon keel. Signalling his intent to continue the winning streak, Kothe recruited several crew members with world-class racing talent. Among them were Admiral's Cup yachtsmen Steve Kulmur and Andrew Parkes, bowman Darren Senogles and helmsman Glyn Charles of Great Britain, who represented his country at the 1996 Olympics regatta in Savannah, Georgia.

The Cruising Yacht Club of Australia listed *Sword of Orion* as "extremely competitive" and "a definite chance" in her class.

Kothe, like many skippers in the 1998 Hobart fleet, knew about the low-pressure system in Bass Strait. And like many skippers, the 52-year-old Sydney to Hobart veteran considered the forecast — a Force 9 gale — literally par for the course. But the conditions at the time of the 2 p.m. "sked," the radio roll call that fixed each boat's position, were far worse than anything Kothe had expected. Wind gusts greater than 90 miles an hour were piling up series of sharp waves that were crashing down on *Sword* from heights of 50 feet. Those on deck watch were getting thrashed about like rag dolls each time one of the monsters struck. All were wearing standard nylon-web safety harnesses clipped to lines secured to the deck. But the force of tons of green water moving at enormous speed was straining the safety lines to their limit.

Drenched and shaken by the repeated dousings, Kothe made his way gingerly down the companionway to the navigation station and the boat's high-frequency (HF) radio. The 2 p.m. skeds were about to begin. Right on schedule, radioman Lew Carter aboard the race escort ship *Young Endeavour* began taking the roll alphabetically. When hailed, each boat responded, gave its position and signed off, which is standard race protocol. Offering or requesting additional information is typically reserved for emergency situations, under which the boat is no longer racing. More commonly, racing boats offer less information than more. For example, although the practice is frowned upon by race officials, skippers sometimes feign radio difficulties during skeds to mask their positions from other boats. Kothe listened to this litany until it came to boats whose names began with the letter S. When *Sayonara* reported, there were nine more boats — 45 seconds — before *Sword*. Kothe made a tough decision. Breaking with protocol and giving away what is considered top-secret tactical information, Kothe gave a weather report for the benefit of the many boats far astern.

"*Young Endeavor,* this is *Sword of Orion.* The forecast is for 40 to 55 knots. We are experiencing between 65 and 82. The weather is much stronger than forecast."

Radioman Carter, equally surprised by the wind speeds and Kothe's unusual disclosure, repeated the message to the Hobart fleet. Almost immediately, 20 percent of the fleet, some two dozen boats, headed for the shelter of Eden to weather the storm in retirement from the race or to continue racing after the storm abated. Among the boats that heeded Kothe's weather warning were Queensland yacht *Midnight Special* and *Polaris,* a New South Wales yacht whose owner and skipper John Quinn was washed overboard during the 1993 Sydney to Hobart then miraculously plucked from the ocean.

Kothe's call probably saved lives, but it spawned its own controversy. Because the storm was moving northeast toward the fleet in *Sword of Orion's* wake and nearing its greatest intensity, scudding or close reaching to Eden was one of the most dangerous routes in the 1998 Hobart, as *Midnight Special* learned. *Polaris* laid over in Eden for 12 hours and then proceeded to Hobart, where she crossed the finish line in 30th place overall and in seventh place in her division. *Midnight Special* was in for a nightmare.

But Kothe's weather warning to the fleet, as unusual a procedure as it was, was not the first. Ninety minutes earlier, Gary Elliot, the skipper of *Doctel Rager,* had issued a similar report from his position at the head of the pack. Elliot, a lifelong sailor, had won the Plympton Cup in 1998, South Australia's oldest sailing trophy, and he had taken line honors in the race. In 1997, he had competed in the Sydney to Hobart with his son, who was 14 years old. When he issued his weather warning at 12:35 p.m., *Doctel Rager* was 15 miles west of *Sword of Orion* and closer to the building storm. Also, Elliot had his son and his 16-year-old daughter aboard. Elliot reported severe weather ahead with winds of 50 to 60 knots and gusts of 70-plus.

Fifteen minutes later, the yachts *Secret Mens Business, Wild One* and *She's Apples II* issued severe weather advisories over the single radio frequency used by the entire fleet. The three yachts were strung out for 45 miles behind *Doctel Rager.*

Within the hour, all three would head for Eden and shelter, along with the yachts *Sea Jay, Henry Kendall Akubra* and *Indian Pacific.*

After his radio report, Kothe went back on deck where the winds had suddenly dropped to 50 knots, conditions Kothe and fellow Hobart veterans consider a walk in the park. But it was a brief one. At 3:35 p.m., by Kothe's watch, a wall of wind he estimated at 80 miles an hour slammed into *Sword* without let-up. He ordered everyone below except young and nimble bowman Darren Senogles and Olympian Glyn Charles, who was at the helm. Next Kothe scrambled below and radioed *Young Endeavour* that *Sword of Orion* was withdrawing from the race and heading north, to the shelter of Eden's Twofold Bay.

Turning north for Eden was not an easy way out. It meant that *Sword* was sailing on a Force 11 following wind and the mountainous seas it was generating. Fifteen minutes after *Sword* changed course, Kothe, who was on the radio, felt the boat rising sharply up a huge wave. Without enough speed to top the monster, the 47-foot sloop was thrown backward. For two long seconds *Sword* was upside down and airborne before it slammed to the ocean with a horrible concussion. The boat somehow righted itself after several more seconds, and Kothe found himself facedown on the cabin deck covered in broken equipment. It was while staggering to his feet that Kothe heard Senogles' frantic wind-torn words from top side that all skippers dread: "Man overboard! Man overboard! Man overboard."

Almost as one, Kothe and the seven crewmen below deck scrambled up the companionway and onto the ruined deck, which had separated from the hull during the knockdown. Charles, 30 yards away, was encouraged with yells of "Swim! Swim!" Senogles, a close friend of Charles, tied himself to a rope and prepared to dive in. Charles, upwind and clearly dazed, raised an arm. A life ring was immediately tossed, but the wind blew it back on to the deck. Simultaneously, a second huge wave struck, knocking the crew down and tumbling them like bowling pins. When they recovered, Charles was doomed, 150 yards away.

"When the wave hit us we just rolled over with a great crashing roar as we fell down the face of the wave," Kothe recalled. "When the boat came back up Glyn Charles was in the water. There was a lot of yelling, a lot of anguish. One of the young guys was about to dive in the water and was restrained. It didn't make any sense. We didn't have a line that would go back 150 feet. We were all in danger of drowning. The boat was at enormous risk."

The struggling Englishman stayed in view for five minutes before he was lost from sight, forever.

Kothe went through a futile two hours of broadcasting urgent may-days. *Sword's* mast had snapped in five pieces when she plummeted off the monster wave. Atop the mast had been the boat's broadcast antenna.

Dangerously damaged and without radio communications, *Sword of Orion* was now adrift in huge seas with a shocked and disheartened crew, some of whom were injured, one with a broken leg. Less than an hour later they thought that their luck had changed.

Sword of Orion crewman Steve Kulmar and another crew member were on deck at about 4 p.m. when they spotted the *Margaret Rintoul II* sailing straight at them, about 500 yards away. One of the oldest yachts in the Hobart fleet, *Margaret Rintoul* shares the record with *Mark Twain* for the most Sydney to Hobarts. She and *Sword of Orion* both sail from the Cruising Yacht Club of Australia.

"We let off four or five flares and waved them," Kulmar said. "By the time we came up she was 150 to 200 metres dead to windward with a storm jib up only. We were somewhat amazed they didn't see us."

The *Sword of Orion, abandoned after it came demasted, rocks in the mountainous seas.*

Richard Purcell, the skipper of *Margaret Rintoul,* did see them. "We had sailed past him (*Sword of Orion*) when we sighted him," Purcell said. "We saw one flare, for five seconds. I saw the flare, no one else saw it. I decided what we could and couldn't do for them.

"The total responsibility number one I have got is to my crew. All of them are married, except for two. All of them have children. I had to take responsibility."

Cruising Yacht Club of Australia Commodore Hugo van Kretschmar said, "There is an obligation on all the yachts to render all the assistance they can safely provide to a yacht in distress." The CYCA commodore, who competed in the 1998 Hobart and retired to the shelter of Eden, called failure to offer assistance gross misconduct. "It is not dissimilar to not stopping after a car accident," he said.

Sword of Orion's skipper Rob Kothe neither reported nor pursued the incident, hoping "it would just go away." But *Sword* crewman Steve Kulmar was angered by the snubbing.

"We were in a life-threatening position," he said. "We had no rig, no means of power. The boat had cracked open. We had a metre of water in the boat. Surely he had a duty just to stand by. He could have heaved to, dropped his sail and attempted to make some form of communication. We could have told him Glyn was overboard. He could have started the search. He could have contacted the radio relay vessel for us. There's a lot of things he could have done without physically endangering his boat or our boat."

Purcell insisted that by the time he spotted *Sword of Orion* and seen its flare, Charles had been overboard for several hours. "The English professional skipper was already dead. They saw him go under. He wasn't wearing a life jacket," he said.

When the two crews met in Hobart after the race, what is usually a jocular recounting of the race on New Year's Eve turned into a bar melee.

As this book was going to press, the Cruising Yacht Club of Australia was continuing its investigation of Purcell's actions during the race. He could be banned from ocean racing for life. Too, a coroner's inquiry into the death of Charles and others that was not concluded by press time could recommend its own sanctions.

The fact remained that *Sword of Orion* and her crew were left adrift in a Force 11 storm in a boat that was literally coming apart at the seams. At 7:30 p.m., halfway across Bass Strait, their distress beacon's signal was finally distinguished by rescue authorities, whose computer screens were lighting up like Christmas trees from 11 distress beacons all broadcasting on the same 121.5 megahertz frequency.

Thirty minutes earlier, faced with multiple knockdowns, retirements and Maydays, the Cruising Yacht Club of Australia let the fleet know that it was not going to call off the race. A message broadcast by *Young Endeavour* reminded skippers that the responsibility for and the decision to continue racing rested solely with them. Five minutes later, the Australian Maritime Safety Authority (AMSA) declared a Mayday for the entire Sydney to Hobart race course.

As soon as *Sword of Orion's* EPIRB signal was distinguished from others, a search by a Navy Sea King helicopter with infrared night-vision equipment began. But it was nearly 12 hours later when *Sword of Orion* was spotted and her crew winched to safety aboard a rescue helicopter.

* * *

At the Canberra headquarters of the Australian Maritime Safety Authority, Sunday's series of emergencies began with a false alarm. At 3 p.m. as the Hobart fleet headed into the worst storm in the race's 54-year history, a computer in AMSA's third-floor "ops" center, which houses Australian Search and Rescue (AuSAR), received a signal from a satellite that had picked up an emergency distress beacon broadcasting on 406 megahertz in Bass Strait.

Minutes later, another message came in by telephone: The distress signal was not from a Hobart yacht but from an EPIRB accidentally dropped overboard from the Thai-registered freighter *Thor Sky.*

With the freighter's beacon eliminated, a second EPIRB signal was picked up by AMSA. It was broadcasting on 121.5 megahertz, a frequency used by pleasure craft and fishing vessels worldwide. Knowing that the Hobart fleet was sailing into a violent storm, AMSA dispatched a small airplane from Mallacoota, 30 miles south of Eden, to reconnoiter the EPIRB's location. Thirty minutes later the pilot confirmed the worst: the first yacht of many, *VC Offshore Stand Aside,* was in serious trouble.

For the staff of seven maritime and aviation rescue officers, thus began the greatest crisis AMSA and AuSAR had ever confronted. The computers began to receive distress signals in rapid succession as yachts got into trouble.

Every hour, one of seven satellites in polar orbit passed over Bass Strait — three Russian, four American — giving the yachts a 15-minute window in which to transmit an EPIRB signal to a satellite that in turn relayed it to ground stations at Albany in Western Australia, Bundaberg in Queensland and Wellington in New Zealand. They were relayed to AMSA instantaneously, with a detailed location of the transmitter. Mayday calls were also coming in, voice transmissions on VHF yacht radios. These dramatic calls for help were relayed by three coastal receiver stations and telexed to AuSAR.

Fortunately for those sending the distress calls, the AuSAR officers into whose hands these signals were delivered understood their plight. All of them were veterans of the sea and air, many recruited after leaving naval or merchant marine commands, others from careers as pilots and air safety control officers.

The Australia Maritime Safety Authority and its rescue activity, AuSAR, are unique to Australia. Like the United States Coast Guard, AMSA is

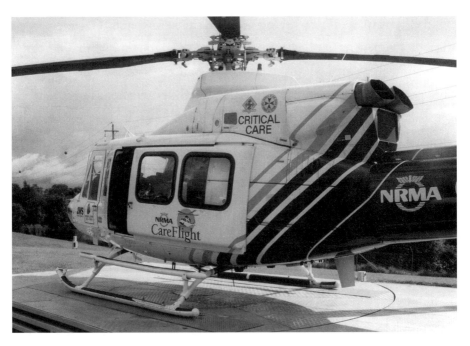

The twin engine four blade helicopter, a variation on the famous Vietnam era "Huey," that pilot Dan Tyler flew during the rescue of the Business Post Naiad *crew*

responsible for sea rescue. Unlike the U.S. Coast Guard, AMSA operates on a smaller budget and relies on a network of volunteers, as well as designated civilian and military vessels and aircraft it can call on in emergencies.

Until recently AMSA's responsibility was restricted to maritime rescue. A second agency, Airservices Australia, was responsible for the search and rescue of civilian aircraft. AMSA and ASA had separate search-and-rescue operations that fulfilled obligations under separate international agreements.

The earlier of the two agreements, the Civil Aviation Treaty of 1944, gave rise to Airservices Australia. With the advent of World War II and the huge role aircraft were playing in the war, civil aviation officials worldwide saw the handwriting on the wall. The 1944 convention in Chicago, Illinois, saw the development of sweeping standards affecting pilots, crewmen, safety, radio frequencies and legal standards for international flights. The 1944 accord, signed by virtually every developed nation, granted reciprocal rights to fly over other countries and paved the way for international civil aviation as it is known today. An outgrowth of the Civil Aviation Treaty — that all participants provide search and rescue for downed civil aircraft within their borders — gave rise to Airservices Australia.

The 1974 International Safety of Life at Sea Convention and the International Search and Rescue Convention of 1979 mirrored the earlier aviation accord. The maritime accords gave Australia responsibility for search and rescue over a vast 30 million square miles of the Indian, Pacific and Southern oceans. The international pacts also created the need for a national maritime safety organization, and the Australian Maritime Safety Authority, AMSA, was born.

Because both rescue agencies were routinely participating in aircraft and maritime rescues, AMSA and ASA merged their search-and-rescue activities in mid-1997 and created Australian Search and Rescue, AuSAR. Pilot Dan Tyler, president of the Helicopter Association of Australia, who would emerge a hero of the 1998 Hobart race, explained what the merger means to pilots and their crews.

"AuSAR is only a coordinating authority," Tyler said. "They're not given the budget to actually own their own aircraft and train their own crews like the U.S. Coast Guard and Civil Air Patrol, neither of which Australia has. AuSAR has to rely on the aircraft they find in the civil fleet, and they have the authority to requisition those aircraft.

"Also, AuSAR doesn't have a budget to fund a standing rescue force. They use the defense forces to the extent that they can and the civil resources to the extent that they can. They do have semi-dedicated civil air-rescue providers or civil SAR units. It's a program where they provide some training and some funding for specialized [rescue] equipment that participants agree to store on their premises without charging them rent. Participants agree to that in exchange for being the first cab off the rank in the event of a search and rescue operation and getting to charge full charter rates. Every year, in our case [Careflight One], AuSAR pays for us to go out and practice precision liferaft placement.

"Search and rescue in Australia is a combination of civil and military aircraft which are loosely retained by AuSAR. There's enough of us around that they can quite easily muster a fleet of aircraft if they need to."

In the 12 months preceding the 1998 Hobart, AMSA had directed 338 rescues, nearly 90 percent of them at sea, mostly coastal yachts and fishing boats. Within the next 40 hours it was to direct 35 planes and helicopters on more than 250 search-and-rescue sorties and to bring seven ships, including the missile frigate *HMAS Newcastle*, into Bass Strait. It was also receiving messages from two media aircraft overflying the fleet. One reported: "It's just chaos down there. There's yachts in trouble all over."

* * *

By 6 p.m. Sunday AuSAR had nine distressed yachts listed on its control board. "It got frenetic," said senior aviation rescue officer Garry Callow, an ex-Royal Navy lieutenant commander. "It just punched in. I've never known anything like it."

One of the distress beacons that blinked on the screen at AMSA's Canberra headquarters was from the Tasmanian yacht *Business Post Naiad*.

Naiad's skipper Bruce Guy typified the sport of sailing. A 51-year-old family man and business owner in Launceston, near Tasmania's north coast, he was a lifelong sailor who taught local youngsters the sport he loved. Guy's entry of his 40-foot ketch in the 1998 Sydney to Hobart race was a dream come true. Guy was one of Tasmania's leading yachtsmen with two Sydney to Hobart, six Melbourne to Hobart and six Melbourne to Devonport races to his credit. But 1998 was his first time entering the Sydney to Hobart in a boat he owned.

Guy had a reputation in the Australian yachting community as a careful and prudent sailor who was a stickler for safety. Yet he also had a lion's heart and the racing blood it takes to quarterback a winning boat. Earlier in the year Guy had sailed *Business Post Naiad*, a former New Zealand Admirals Cup yacht designed by famed American yacht designer Bruce Farr to victory in the Three Peaks race, one of Tasmania's premier sailing events. Guy, who bought the yacht in 1994, had also skippered *Business Post Naiad* to good finishes in several Melbourne to Hobart races, a shorter version of the Sydney to Hobart.

When Guy was laying plans to enter the Sydney to Hobart it was only natural that his neighbor, Phil Skeggs, be part of the crew. Guy and Skeggs were not only neighbors (their families separated only by a back fence), they were friends. Guy had introduced Skeggs to the sport about five years earlier. Thirty-four-year-old Skeggs had crewed on *Business Post Naiad* when she won the 1998 Three Peaks. A locksmith by trade, Skeggs was a family man with two young children, an ardent SCUBA diver and yacht racer. He seized the opportunity to crew on *Business Post Naiad*, even though it meant he would miss Christmas with his family.

When skipper Bruce Guy and his crew of eight (Skeggs, Jim Rogers, Matt Sherriff, Peter Keats, Rob Matthews, Shane Hansen, Steve Walker, and nephew Tony Guy) lined up in Sydney Harbor for the start of the race, they were one of the few who had just sailed the 630-mile race course in the opposite direction. And they and *Business Post Naiad* were in the hunt.

Off the starting line and throughout Saturday's downwind conditions, *Business Post Naiad* steadily made its way through the pack. Its crew considered the waters of Bass Strait "home waters." They considered the strait's steep, sharp waves and its winds of 60 miles an hour normal, when it wasn't flat calm — as it often was. In fact, when the forecast was upgraded to a storm Saturday afternoon, skipper Bruce Guy and crewman Rob Matthews, a housing inspector, saw it as a tactical advantage. "The guys who haven't been in Bass Strait before, they're going to get a bit of a dustup," Matthews predicted.

By Sunday afternoon, *Business Post Naiad* was ahead of the main Hobart fleet and about 20 miles astern of *Sword of Orion*. *Naiad's* crew had heard Rob Kothe's weather warning from *Sword* during the 2 p.m. position report and decided to continue the race. Almost everyone aboard *Business Post Naiad* had been in a southerly "buster" in Bass Strait and had been down to bare poles in 70-knot winds. So such a prospect did not dim the crew's high spirits. Too, they were looking forward to partying with friends from the Melbourne to Hobart race. A much shorter sailing race than the Sydney to Hobart, the Melbourne to Hobart is timed so that the yachts in both races reach Hobart in time for the annual New Year's fiesta.

As the winds and seas built in the hours after Kothe's weather warning, the crew of *Naiad* was unaware that race officials had postponed the start of the Melbourne to Hobart yacht race. Weather experts applauded the decision, saying that it saved lives. Terry Ryan, the Melbourne Bureau of Meteorology's senior forecaster, said: "They would have killed people going through the [Melbourne] heads into that wind." Phil Jackman of the Derwent Sailing Squadron, which sponsors the Melbourne to Hobart race, said it was the first time the event had ever been postponed.

A second race that was already under way, the Around Alone, the marathon of sail boat racing, was rerouted to avoid the storm in Bass Strait. Leg 2 of the solo ocean classic would have taken the boats through the storm but in the opposite direction of the Hobart fleet. The Around Alone "singlehanders" had sailed this south-to-north route through Bass Strait and up the coast of New South Wales to Sydney

since 1982. In 1998 the Around Alone was diverted to Aukland, New
Zealand. On Sunday night, when the Hobart fleet was getting steam-
rolled by the storm in Bass Strait, Around Alone leader Giovanni
Soldini, some 150 miles east of Hobart, reported "traveling in a light
breeze and averaging a less-than-thrilling 4.8 knots."

Throughout Sunday afternoon the crew of *Business Post Naiad* continued to reduce sails as the winds built. By 5 p.m. it was under "bare
poles," meaning that the wind was howling through the rigging at such
speed that its force on the mast alone was enough to keep *Naiad* moving
forward — the key to keeping control of a sail boat. Without forward
motion a sail boat can not respond to its rudder and change course, and
its ability to stay upright in wind and high seas is severely diminished.

On Sunday evening winds of 60 knots and gusts of 80 knots were
recorded in Bass Strait. But the wind-speed indicators on *Business Post
Naiad* had been destroyed and only the eerie moans and piercing shrieks
of the wind through the rigging belied its speed and power. With the mast
bent like a scimitar and straining at its cable anchors, Rob Matthews, who
was driving, steered *Naiad* up the steep face of a 50-foot wave, one of
many the boat had ascended in the last two hours. To the shock and surprise of Matthews and the other four crewmen on deck watch, *Naiad*
stalled just as the wave crested. The boat was thrown to the left and down.
Three seconds passed before the boat slammed into the wave trough
upside-down. The deck crew was hurled off the starboard side and into
the ocean, but each crewman's safety harness and tether held. Below decks,
bulkheads and doors cracked at the impact, and the four men below were
pinned against the underside of the inverted deck by heavy sail bags,
soaked mattresses and dislodged and broken equipment.

Almost as quickly as she was knocked down, *Naiad* righted itself,
again slamming those below against the now righted galley deck, angular
bulkheads, tables and fittings. Awash in knee-deep water below decks,

skipper Guy had struggled halfway up the companionway when someone yelled, "Fuck, the mast is over the side."

Broken at the second spreader, the mast pitched at a wild angle to starboard, its top submerged. "That wasn't in the bloody brochure," joked easygoing Phil Skeggs, who, like the others, had anted up $500 to help with costs and ready *Naiad* for the Hobart. Guy had pooled the money with a $4,000 sponsorship from Australia's postal service to race tune *Naiad*.

It took all nine of *Naiad's* crew to retrieve the broken mast and lash it to the deck. Once done, Guy radioed *Young Endeavour* that he was out of the race and heading for Eden, nearly 50 miles northwest, under power. Heading back into the biggest seas and the strongest winds at 2 knots — all the speed the motor would allow — the crew settled in for a long night. Below decks the refrigerator's contents mixed with calf-deep sea water, broken plates and cups and waterlogged nautical charts. The bilge pumps had evacuated some of the brew but had broken down when they became clogged with detritus. The heavy steel stove had been ripped from its mounts and rumbled around like a drunk with the impact of every sharp wave. With no other option, skipper Guy had activated *Naiad's* EPIRB and, with a jury-rigged antenna, radioed a request for helicopter evacuation.

Compared to the knockdown, the next five hours under power were uneventful. Around 10 p.m. principal helmsman Steve Walker was spelled by Matthews. Skeggs assisted Matthews by shouting compass readings into the black night so Matthews could stay on a course for Eden. Both men, lashed by spindrift and 70-knot wind, struggled to keep their balance when *Naiad* was overtaken by huge following waves that loomed suddenly from the dark. A few moments of moonlight showed both crewmen what they were up against.

At 11 p.m. another wave rolled the boat. This time, unlike the first time, the boat did not right itself. *Business Post Naiad* stayed upside down for five minutes, said Matthews.

"I was trapped over the back of the boat in underneath the cockpit behind the aft lifelines," Matthews said. "When the boat initially rolled I thought it would do like it did the first time and just pop back up again. So for the first 10 to 15 seconds I made no attempt to unhook my harness because I didn't want to leave the boat."

"Then when it stayed inverted I started to try to get my harness undone, which I found really difficult even though I had the hooks on my chest, because I was being pulled every which way and I was right at the end of the harness and I was using all my strength.

"I had nearly run out of breath when the boat was lifted by another wave and I just sucked enough air to keep me going for another 10 or 15 seconds, I don't know how long, and I forced the harness off.

"Then the back of the boat was only 2 feet behind me and I popped to the surface and hung on to the ropes at the stern.

"I am the luckiest man alive."

Skeggs was still trapped beneath the overturned boat.

Below decks, Steve Walker, Bruce Guy, Jim Rogers, Matt Sherriff, Peter Keats, Shane Hansen and Tony Guy were also trapped. Believing the boat was sinking, Bruce Guy and Walker hurriedly cleared the companionway of debris as an escape route to the sea below and the surface. With the pressure inside the cabin now stopping more water from gushing in, Guy tried to force one of *Naiad's* life rafts out the inverted companionway. Walker stopped him, guessing that the next wave would right the boat. On deck, meanwhile, Matthews was trying to locate Skeggs.

"We heard Rob [Matthews] calling for Phil [Skeggs]," Walker said. "We didn't hear Phil answer and couldn't do anything.

"Then another huge wave righted the boat," said Walker. The righting movement funneled a cataract of sea water through the companionway, threatening to sink the boat. As one, seven crewmen waded through 3 feet of water to get to the companionway and up on deck to avoid being trapped in the hull of a sinking boat. "Bruce [Guy] was beside the main hatchway. As he tried to get up [the companionway] he had a seizure and died in my arms and I tried to keep him above the water," said Walker, who dragged his friend's body to a bunk before making his own escape.

In the five minutes before the boat righted itself, Matthews had managed to cling to the slippery hull of *Business Post Naiad* by standing on the piece of broken mast lashed to the submerged deck. But without a safety line, the wind and waves threatened to cast him adrift. With nearly the last of his strength, Matthews was able to pull himself upward and get a firm grip on *Naiad's* keel. Needing additional support, he had just placed a foot on the submerged mast when the boat began righting itself. In the roll, the mast catapulted Matthews into the air. He landed with a painful thud in the cockpit just as the boat finished righting itself. To his horror, Matthews had landed inches from the lifeless body of Phil Skeggs, who had been unable to escape the serpentine tangle of broken rigging in which the sea had enmeshed him. Beyond exhaustion, Matthews could only watch as crewmen boiled out of the companionway and administered CPR. But it was too late.

Shocked and exhausted by their ordeal, the crew sent an additional Mayday to say that *Business Post Naiad* was taking on water. Then they began bailing and waiting for rescue, hoping it came before the next rogue wave tore the boat apart.

* * *

With the death toll rising, what may arguably rank as the longest and most terrifying ordeal suffered by a crew in the 1998 Sydney to Hobart began with these words:

"Mayday! Mayday! This is *Winston Churchill. Winston Churchill.* We are taking water rapidly."

That was the chilling radio distress call issued at 5:30 p.m. Sunday, December 27, by the oldest yacht in the fleet, the *Winston Churchill.*

The 50-footer's hull had been laid in Hobart, Tasmania, in 1942, and the boat was used to service Tasmanian lighthouses during World War II. British wartime Prime Minister Winston Churchill had personally approved the cutter's name. She competed in the first Sydney to Hobart in 1945 as a line-honors favorite, but came in third. *Winston Churchill* had raced in the event 16 times since, with at least one close call eerily similar to her fate in 1998. In the 1958 Sydney to Hobart, *Winston Churchill* narrowly avoided sinking after she fell off a huge wave in Bass Strait, which punched her wooden mast through the bottom of the boat. With sails wrapped around her hull to cover the gaping hole in her hull, *Winston Churchill* was listing sharply and nearly awash when she was dragged onto a Victorian beach. A decade later she was chartered for an around-the-world expedition, and was later used to train Australian Navy midshipmen.

A crewman who sailed on *Winston Churchill* in the 1963 Sydney to Hobart said the boat should not have been entered in the 1998 event. "She was never designed for racing," said Raymond Brooks of Sydney. "She was designed for long-distance, comfortable cruising. I'd go any-where in the world on her. But not in the Sydney-Hobart."

In 1996, *Winston Churchill's* new owner/skipper Richard Winning had undertaken a $500,000 restoration of the ketch-rigged boat in prepa-ration for the 1997 and 1998 Sydney to Hobart races. Most of Winning's crew of nine were lifelong friends who had sailed with him many times, with the exception of 19-year-old Michael Rynan, an experienced sailor in his first Sydney to Hobart. Indeed, although she was the oldest boat in the fleet, *Winston Churchill's* crew was also the most experienced, with some 50 Sydney to Hobarts among them.

"The crew on *Winston Churchill* were mainly old yachties who sailed for the camaraderie and the yachtsmanship rather than sailing to win," said John Winning, Richard Winning's cousin. "They were out for six days' good hard fun sailing; they never expected what they got."

Crewman Paul Lumtin agreed. "We were sailing in what you would call the veterans' division. It could be simply described as gentleman's ocean racing. It's not out there to win; it's not out there to make the fastest time. It's out there to sail and do the job properly."

The *Winston Churchill* cut quite a figure in Sydney Harbor as she paced the starting line under a perfect sky on Saturday afternoon. She was widely believed to be the safest boat in the fleet. She was certainly the grand entrant. Winning, her skipper, was the archetype of a sea captain, with a weathered, angular face complete with pipe and framed by a trimmed graying beard. Tall and athletic, Winning was the scion of a Sydney family whose household-appliance business had prospered through several generations.

Like the rest of the Hobart fleet, *Winston Churchill* had made a fast run down the coast on Saturday. By the 2 p.m. radio "sked" Sunday she was approximately 25 miles due east of Gabo Island and 40 miles southeast of Eden. That put her square in the middle of the pack and less than an hour from the cyclonic low-pressure system's strongest winds and biggest waves.

At the time of *Winston Churchill's* distress call, 37 yachts had been forced from the race with damage or had opted to take shelter along the New South Wales coast. Rescue helicopters were in the air looking for disabled boats and their crews.

At this point, the sea was what sailors call confused, meaning there was no regular pattern to the waves. *Winston Churchill* was negotiating each as it came. And the waves were enormous, reaching extreme heights of 80 feet and averaging 40 feet. The ketch's anemometer, a rotating device for measuring wind speed, was pegged at 60 knots, the fastest wind it could measure. But experienced heavy-water sailors don't need an anemometer when the wind is extreme. The rigging voices its warning to the trained ear. At 75 knots of apparent wind, *Winston Churchill's* crew members were hearing a high, keening shriek as the wind tore through the rigging. During higher gusts, the noise dropped several octaves to an ominous moan.

Scientists can define how waves develop, but only fairly well. Speed, duration and fetch are the underlying principals that determine the energy of a wave. Speed and duration refer to the wind, the engine that drives the wave. Fetch is the amount of sea room the wave has in which to develop.

Theoretically, the harder and longer the wind blows, the greater the wave's size and strength. Yet while the violence of a wave driven by a 40-knot wind is predictable, it does not increase in a linear proportion with the wind speed. Rather, the wave's power is quadrupled by the speed of the wind.

Thus, with winds of 70 knots, *Winston Churchill* was experiencing devastating waves. And coupled with the peculiar hydrodynamics of Bass Strait, *Winston Churchill* found herself in a witch's brew. Even boats that dwarfed her in size found the going hazardous. The 25,000-ton ferry *Spirit of Tasmania* that runs between Melbourne and Tasmania took waves over her bow during the storm and suspended service until the storm blew itself out.

Atara skipper Roger Hickman was shaken when he saw something similar. "We saw a 40,000-ton merchant ship off our bow pitching over waves that exposed her bow and rudder. And that was eye-opening because here we are very small. And maybe we've got more than the waves and the wind to contend with," he said.

Conditions on deck for the crew of *Winston Churchill* were treacherous at best. Sailing under storm sail, the boat's deck pitched crazily as Winning took her up the crests at 70 degrees and sought to bear off at any angle that would not launch the boat into thin air off the wave's steep back.

"You couldn't stand up," crewman Paul Lumtim said, describing the conditions. "You had to crawl around on all fours. If you stood up you would be thrown down."

It was in these chaotic conditions that *Winston Churchill* was dealt a fatal blow, one that would finally end her long and distinguished career.

It came in the form of a huge rogue wave.

"The wave literally picked the boat up so high that the boat fell off the wave," Lumtin said. "So we didn't actually go over the top of the wave. The wave got so high and so steep that the 25,000-pound boat literally fell 20 or 30 feet into the wave below, and that's when it smashed."

Skipper Winning said that although the going was tough, *Winston Churchill* was handling the windward beat well, until the giant wave struck.

"We had pretty hard conditions all day and the sea was getting bigger and bigger," he said. "We were handling it all right until we got to that one sea that was just a little bit bigger that the others. It had a breaking crest on it and it turned the boat over a little bit.

"The breaking crest came down right on the leeward deck and, we think, pushed the mast through the bottom. Next thing we know, we were taking on water faster than we could handle it. So we knew the time had come [to abandon ship]."

John "Steamer" Stanley, a 52-year-old Sydney marina manager, was below decks when the boat fell off the monster wave. "It was like hitting a brick wall," said Stanley. "I was just waking up. The force of the water broke out the galley windows and the water came through and pinned me against the bulkhead."

Winning and crewman John Lawler were hurled into the sea and were pulling themselves toward the overturned yacht by their strained life lines when *Winston Churchill* righted itself.

The gouts of sea water coming through the imploded galley windows were nothing compared to what Stanley saw next. A huge section of the galley was open to the sea, and the boat was shipping water even faster. *Winston Churchill* had ruptured its hull. She was doomed. Stanley scrambled up the companionway to the deck, where Winning was trying to disentangle his safety line from the mass of rigging on the deck to which he had been thrown when the boat righted.

"After Richard untangled himself I told him that we've got to start the motor to get the pumps going," Stanley, Winning's most experienced crewman, said.

Winning quickly agreed and detailed crewmen to bail and others to work on the boat's engine. Within minutes the small engine coughed to life, but only momentarily. It died and would not start again.

"I thought, 'Dear God, it's not looking good.' So we brought the life rafts up on deck," said Stanley.

Meanwhile, Winning had rushed to the navigation station below to get a position fix to send with the Mayday. "GPS was gone. The paper chart was gone. It had become fairly obvious that [*Winston Churchill*] was going to go. So the Mayday was the next go. We couldn't give an accurate position because all of our navigation was gone," Winning said.

With the ocean beginning to lap over the boat's deck, the distress call was issued: "Mayday! Mayday! This is *Winston Churchill. Winston Churchill.* We are taking water rapidly. We are taking to life rafts."

The order to abandon ship resonated particularly strongly for Lumtin, who watched the venerable ketch slip beneath the waves 30 minutes later.

"She'd circumnavigated the globe two or three times," he said. "She's been in 18 Sydney to Hobarts. She's been in numerous races. She's been at sea all of her life. Here I am in the water watching her die. And that is just a horrifying thing. Just horrifying."

Although the boat was sinking quickly, Winning was reluctant to abandon *Winston Churchill* until the last moment.

"I was very mindful of the fact that you step up to a life raft and not down [stay with the boat as long as possible]," Winning said. "So we inflated the life rafts and hopped into them. I took the EPIRB. And off we went."

For the crew of *Winston Churchill* it was the beginning of a 24-hour epic struggle for survival that three of them would lose. When the crew took to life rafts, Winning, Lumtin, Bruce Gould and 19-year-old

Michael Rynan boarded one. Jim Lawler, John Dean, John Gibson, Stanley and Mike Bannister took to the other.

"We started off roping the rafts together, which is usual practice because we only had one position indicator [EPIRB], which was on our raft," said Winning. "The light line holding the two rafts together broke, which was lucky because otherwise it might have damaged the rafts. We didn't get that far away from the other raft. I glanced out regularly to check on them and just before dark they were about 150 meters away and seemed to be riding steady."

That changed quickly. Though both rafts deployed sea anchors, a device that works like a parachute to slow the raft, the anchor line on Winning's raft broke shortly after it was deployed. The anchor line on the other raft held for less than a half hour. As a result, the two groups separated quickly shortly after dark. Shortly after nightfall, Winning's canopy raft was overturned in the high winds and seas, which Winning called "bloody frightening."

"You have got four of us underneath this little canopy and the next thing is you are upside down. So one poor bastard has got to go out and right it while the other three are inside," Winning said.

It was another crew member who reported that it was 61-year-old Winning who righted the raft each time it overturned. "That happened twice and it was twice too many," Winning said.

In the capsizing, most of the raft's safety equipment, including signal flares, was lost, and the raft was filled with water. Winning and his shipmates used a plastic bag and a mariner's boot to bail the small craft. But within minutes the raft was overturned again, and Winning again leaped overboard to right it. And without the sea anchor, the raft had begun to surf at frightening speed off the backs of five-story waves. The raft's terrified occupants believed the events were a countdown to an inevitable death at sea.

"Every time a wave would come, I could just see the terror in everybody's face," Lumtin said. "We knew that it was coming for us. We didn't know whether we were going to get tipped over. We didn't know if this was the wave that was going to take us out."

As bad as the situation was on Winning's raft, Stanley's crew had it worse. The odyssey began inauspiciously, with four of the five crewmen hurrying to get off the sinking *Winston Churchill* and struggling to get through the raft's canopy opening while wearing life vests. Twenty minutes after they were aboard the raft, the line holding their sea anchor broke, leaving the five with no way to control the raft's speed or direction. As the raft's movement became more erratic, the canopy shuddered and boomed in the high winds, striking its occupants on the backs of their heads repeatedly. All the while, an emergency tube meant to collect and deliver rainwater was instead deluging the men with cold sea water, spume and rain.

Shortly after losing the sea anchor, the raft began bucking wildly in the wind and waves. The five men, all except Stanley wearing bulky flotation vests, crowded the small raft, leaving little or no room to move around. It was the crowded conditions that led to the first serious injury. With the raft rocking violently and with his leg pinned beneath the weight of the others, Stanley's ankle fractured and his hip ligaments tore under the tremendous strain. Wearing only shorts and a light rain jacket, Stanley braced himself for a long and painful night.

* * *

ABC pilot Gary Ticehurst was hovering nearby so his camera crew could film the rescue of the 12 crew of *VC Offshore Stand Aside* when he heard *Winston Churchill's* Mayday. It was a frustrated Ticehurst who later said, "If I wasn't with *Stand Aside*, if I'd been combing the area we would have been there instantly. But we can't be everywhere at once. And we had no fuel to go to the assistance of *Winston Churchill* at that stage. The plan was to go back to Mallacoota for fuel and go straight back to Winning's position. But when we got back to Malacoota we got a Mayday call from *Kingurra*, a man overboard. That became a priority."

EPIRB distress signals and Mayday hails were popping like popcorn all over Bass Strait, and *Kingurra's* was only the latest. At AMSA's operation center, which was receiving the EPIRB signals, rescue officials were struggling to get an accurate picture of the scene in Bass Strait. Three problems were complicating their critical and high-pressure task. First, all of the activated distress beacons were transmitting on the same 121.5 MHz frequency. Since an EPIRB's location can be pinpointed to approximately a 12-mile radius, it was difficult to distinguish one distress signal from another. Secondly, yachts were issuing premature Maydays. And responding rescue helicopters were arriving at the scene to find that the distressed yacht had found its way out of danger. Crews of Navy Sea King and Sea Hawk helicopters searching for them found some of the yachts anchored safely in Eden. Thirdly, most of the yachts that needed the most assistance had been dismasted, losing their radio antennas with the mast. Without antennas, the crews had no way to radio their locations or further information that could have expedited their rescues. As darkness fell, it would get worse.

It was just about dark when the Queensland yacht *B-52* took a disabling punch from what meteorologists call a "king" wave.

Wayne Millar, *B-52's* owner and skipper, and his crew, were highly regarded among fellow ocean racers throughout Australia. Typically a racing competitor's skill is grudgingly acknowledged by a collegiate, backhanded compliment. Not so with Millar and his crew. They were admired, as characterized by Sydney to Hobart skipper David Pescud's observations. "They're a great bunch of sailors; a lot of skill there," Pescud, the skipper of *Aspect Computing*, said. Even in Sunday's perilous conditions it surprised Pescud and other Hobart veterans that *B-52* "copped it." "They may just be the unluckiest boat in the race this year," was Pescud's speculation.

Millar, a prudent skipper, didn't need to hear *Sword of Orion's* weather warning to the fleet to know that discretion is the better part of valor. Giving up a substantial lead over the rest of the pack at noon, he ordered navigator Will Oxley to plot a course for Eden. At that point, said Oxley, "We were in survival mode rather than in race mode."

Oxley and the rest of the experienced crew knew that turning for Eden and running in such high wind and waves was potentially more hazardous than staying the course for Hobart. But they figured that they could make it to Eden in a six-hour run. Hobart was at best a punishing 36-hour beat away. "Instead of trying to sail to Hobart we were letting the breeze take us to Eden — the safe and prudent thing to do," the navigator said.

Helmsman Mark Vickers and his friend Russell Kingston, a bowman, weren't far into their watch, but they were on full alert. As their other eight crewmen rested below, Kingston tended the tiny storm sail while Vickers kept *B-52's* keel and rudder knifing laterally across the faces of the huge following waves. Both men kept a wary eye astern of the 41-foot sloop, on guard for any large waves. Even in the gathering dusk the big greenish-black waves stood in sharp contrast to the grayish-purple storm skies astern. For both men, but especially for Vickers, seeing an oncoming wave was helpful because they could brace for its impact and Vickers could steady his footing for the powerful rush of water off the cockpit and back over the stern. What they could not do was avoid it.

Shortly after 6 p.m., Vickers, a 32-year-old ceramic tile mechanic, glimpsed a king wave building just off *B-52's* stern. As it continued to build, Vickers was awestruck by the monster's size, which he said loomed taller than the sloop's 60-foot mast. Kingston, in a tight crouch in the bow, had seen it too. As it began to crest and crash toward the boat, Vickers hollered, "Oh, shit, Russell! This one's going to hurt!"

As the freak wave crashed hundreds of tons of sea water onto *B-52,* the boat pitchpoled, standing on its bow then crashing upside down through a full half-circle roll.

Below decks, the crew was hurled about like so many automobile crash dummies. Many had been sleeping on stowed sails and awoke abruptly to find themselves pinned under water to the ceiling under half-ton sails. "We were standing on the roof with water up to our knees," said Oxley. With the companionway blocked by the incoming sea, the crew was trapped and could not reach the deck crew, both of whom had been thrown overboard.

The tremendous force of the wave had driven Vickers through the metal spokes of the steering wheel, breaking two and bending the massive wheel. Dazed and trapped, Vickers did not know the boat had capsized until he saw a cabin light above him. Running out of air and with his safety line tangled around the wheel, Vickers unhooked his safety harness but still found himself trapped in the snaking tangle of rigging from *B-52's* broken mast. With the last of his breath, the helmsman finally kicked free of the morass of cables and surfaced 10 feet behind the boat. Too shocked and exhausted to call out, Kingston, clinging to a rope, could only watch as his friend drifted away. Despite swimming with all of his waning strength, Vickers was not getting any closer to the boat, which was 100 feet away and upwind.

Miraculously, Vickers was able to reach a rope trailing from *B-52* just as the boat righted itself. The rest of the crew immediately scrambled on deck to help Vickers and Kingston aboard. To their horror, they found the mast shattered and wide cracks in the fiberglass deck. Like so many others that day, the enervated crew began bailing while the boat's EPIRB was activated.

* * *

The second day of the 1998 Sydney to Hobart will long be remembered for its tragedies. But it also had its share of miracles. With its many knockdowns, dismastings, injuries and deaths, it is easy to think of

Sunday's glass as being half empty. But for each of the 1,000 or so crew-men and women who came out of the race unscathed, it is likely that chance or a legion of guardian angels was hard at work. Most of the stories will never be known except to the individuals and perhaps friends and fam-ily members. But it's a safe bet that each experienced a moment, perhaps more, of danger when the outcome could have gone either way. One such crewman is John Campbell, a 32-year-old American sailing aboard Peter Joubert's yacht *Kingurra.*

The last thing Joubert wanted out of his 27th Sydney to Hobart race was attention. The 74-year-old engineering professor at the University of Melbourne told the Cruising Yacht Club of Australia that *Kingurra* and her crew of 10 "prefers a quiet time and are not really interested in attract-ing too much attention." But as a family member of Australia's most famous yacht designers sailing in the nation's most famous race, anonymi-ty is not an option — at least until you cross the starting line.

By 6 p.m. Sunday night the wry Joubert had tired of helming the 47-foot sloop of his own design. Even with goggles on, the wind and sea spray stung like swarming fire ants every time *Kingurra's* bow yawed off a wave and dropped, which was often. It was even worse when green water came over the deck and threatened to knock the skipper's feet out from under him and break his firm grip on the giant steering wheel. Too, the pound-ing the boat was taking was being telegraphed — not pleasantly — through Joubert's knees and shoulders. He had sailed many Hobarts, and a souther-ly buster was not his favorite conditions for the race. Younger men revel in such conditions, so Joubert had yielded the helm and gone below.

Joubert was in a deep sleep in his bunk an hour later when he was awakened abruptly by "a horrific crash." *Kingurra* heeled hard to port, tossing a sleeping crewman across the cabin and into Joubert's side. The stabbing pain the skipper felt was several broken ribs and a ruptured spleen. Stumbling through bolts of pain and several inches of sea water that had poured down the companionway, Joubert made his way aft, to the nav station and turned on the pumps. Once done, he glanced up through the companionway. Three crewmen were hauling 32-year-old American crewman John Campbell back on deck.

On deck, the still-unfolding chain of events went from bad to worse.

"All of a sudden Anthony [Vautin] yelled 'Watch out!'" said crewman Peter Meikle. "We all ducked our heads in anticipation of getting wet. But what happened was worse than getting wet."

"We got hit by a rogue wave," Campbell said. "And in the process of the boat being rolled I hit my chin and was knocked unconscious. So I don't remember a whole lot about the first part of the incident." He was later diagnosed with a fractured jaw from hitting and destroying the compass binnacle.

"When the boat righted itself, my first observation was 'Where was everybody?'" Meikle recalled, "I looked around the boat and I couldn't see Anthony or John. I looked astern and both of the guys were hanging there. John was face-down with his strop around his neck so I lifted him by his harness as high as I could but I wasn't tall enough to lift him over the safety rail."

Campbell, unconscious, had his arms pulled above his head by the rescue attempt and he slipped out of his safety harness.

"When John slipped out of the harness I grabbed his hand and hung on for as long as I could," Meikle said. "But he was torn out of my grip and started disappearing behind the boat. I didn't think it was really happening. But I also knew that if we didn't do things correctly John was going to die. I was very aware, too, that even if we did everything right, John might die."

Campbell had slipped out of not only his safety harness, which was built into his protective clothing. He was also drifting away from *Kingurra* in the gathering darkness wearing nothing except navy blue longjohns.

From below, Joubert heard the cry of "Man overboard!" Grabbing the radio, Joubert shouted: "Mayday! Mayday! Mayday! We have a man overboard!" Unable to start *Kingurra's* motor and with its storm jib in tatters, Joubert and his crew had no means of rescuing Campbell. In desperation and the first stages of shock from his hemorrhaging spleen, the skipper grabbed the radio microphone again. "Mayday! Mayday! We need a helicopter!"

Still stunned from the hard blow to the chin and bleeding badly from the open wound that resulted, Campbell drifted rapidly away from *Kingurra.*

"The first time I saw the boat it was a quarter-mile away," said Campbell. "I was disoriented and didn't know how I got there. I was having this internal debate about whether this was a dream or reality. And it slowly became clear that this was reality and what my predicament was."

According to Meikle, Campbell was in view briefly every few minutes when a wave lofted him into view. But as the anxious minutes stretched on, Meikle said, "we lost sight of him and only estimated where he was."

Twenty minutes after Campbell drifted away from *Kingurra,* the crew of a Melbourne-based Polair police helicopter was refueling its Duaphin SA 365 to go to the aid of *Stand Aside,* the first yacht rolled and dismasted in the storm.

Climbing east over the coastal mountain range at top speed had siphoned fuel the crew might need for a prolonged rescue, so the helicopter touched down briefly in Malacoota where the tanks were topped off. Gary Ticehurst, who was also refueling the ABC helicopter in Malacoota, scrambled to follow.

The Polair helicopter had barely cleared the headlands into the maelstrom of Bass Strait when the call came from AMSA's operation center diverting Polair to *Kingurra.*

"Man overboard is the worst situation a boat and skipper can find themselves in," Ticehurst said. "And the chances of finding Campbell were very, very small. But the Polair helicopter was launched immediately. We launched two minutes later. Because of the 70-knot tailwind, he must have been doing 220 knots." (One hundred eighty knots is fast for even the fastest helicopters.) At those speeds, the Polair helicopter reached *Kingurra's* last reported position in less than 10 minutes. But there was nothing there but a windswept, empty sea. "I think we've overshot them," pilot Daryl Jones said to the two crewmen. "I'm heading back."

But before Jones could turn the helicopter, winchman Barry Barclay spotted a red flare rocketing skyward. Jones dropped altitude quickly and hailed *Kingurra.* A shaken Joubert reported that Campbell was 300 yards downwind. The growing darkness and the size of the waves made sighting anything on the surface nearly impossible.

"It was like finding a needle in a haystack," said Senior Constable David Key. "The water was black, the victim was in dark clothing and his head was face down."

But within moments of the flare sighting, it was Key who yelled, "Got something!"

Bobbing on the surface was a white life preserver, but as the helicopter neared it the rotor's powerful downwash blew the life preserver into the air. It was flotsam.

At almost the same instant Barclay caught movement in his peripheral vision. Someone was waving at them from sea. It was Campbell.

"I've got him!" Barclay exclaimed, almost in disbelief.

Dangling from 100 feet of taut cable that was blown at a constant 45-degree angle, Key was smashed by huge waves three times before he got Campbell into the rescue strop. At the top of the lift, just below the doorway, the cable jammed hopelessly. Barclay grabbed Campbell by his longjohns and hauled him aboard, followed by Key. An exhausted Campbell lay on his back and kept repeating the words "Thank you."

A short time later Campbell recounted the rescue for Channel 10 news, saying: "It was evident that they could see me, but what they actually saw was a nearby life ring. When they realized it wasn't me they bore away but they saw me at the last minute and came back. There was a moment when they were flying away that I thought they had missed me.

"The pilot did a fantastic job of dropping the rescuer near me. As soon as he hit the water I swam toward him. He got me in the harness and took me up right away. I was absolutely grateful. I thanked them again and again."

Aboard *Kingurra,* a rousing cheer and high-fives applauded the rescue. "We couldn't believe how lucky we were when the chopper arrived. I was elated," Meikle said. But it quickly occurred to them that they did not know if Campbell was dead or alive. After a frantic scramble to the radio and a call to the helicopter, *Kingurra* got the good news.

Fellow rescue pilot Dan Tyler, who would see his own skills tested in the rescue of the Hobart fleet, said Campbell's rescue was among the most difficult.

"The Victorian Police rescue of John Campbell scored the most points for the most dramatic and luckiest of the civil rescues," Tyler, a Vietnam combat pilot, said. "They apparently had headwinds of up to 70 knots at the rescue site and at one stage on the way back they hit a 110-knot headwind, which meant they were only moving about 20 knots forward. Had the squall not abated they were going to run out of fuel before they got to shore.

"Spotting Campbell and keeping him in sight and rescuing him in those conditions was really difficult. With a wind like that you absolutely have to be straight into the wind. It was a real challenge to keep him in sight and keep the helicopter in the wind while they were preparing to go down the wire. I think they did a really fine job."

* * *

For rescue coordinators manning computers and telephones in AMSA's Canberra operations center, Campbell's rescue was the high point of a long and frustrating day. Since its creation 24 years earlier, the maritime-rescue agency had never participated in a rescue of this magnitude. As the number of yachts in trouble continued to climb, AMSA officials were dusting off contingency plans devised for theoretical mass-casualty situations. With dozens of yachts in trouble and the expectation that the worst was yet to come, AMSA, its small budget rapidly dwindling, was calling in every available aircraft and boat — military and civilian — it could muster. At dawn AMSA planned to throw everything it had into the rescue attempt.

Meanwhile, AMSA's operations center late Sunday night was a scene of chaos and frustration for its staff of 12. Military helicopters searching 2,000 square miles of the Sydney to Hobart race course were without night-vision equipment, which hampered their efforts significantly. The huge battle helicopters were equipped with powerful spotlights and infrared detection, but both are inefficient when searching a large area. Helicopter spotlights are designed to flood small areas with bright illumination, usually from a hover, once a subject is located. When flying at 150 knots in low-visibility storm conditions, a search light is not a helicopter crew's preferred search tool. Infrared (heat) detectors are almost as limiting. Infrared images are received by an outboard camera and relayed to a cockpit viewing screen. Although not as restricted in scope as a focused search light, infrared cameras can cover only a fraction of the area of the human eye assisted by night vision.

With what equipment they had, the four Australian Navy helicopters searched through the night for Glyn Charles, the British crewman washed overboard on *Sword of Orion,* and stricken yachts. AMSA staffers were left to assemble the search crews' garbled radio transmissions to piece together "the puzzle" as AMSA officials called it, that was Bass Strait and the many yachts in trouble. With so many missing pieces, "the puzzle" would remain unsolved until well into the next day.

By midnight, 37 of the race's 115 yachts had been forced out of the Sydney to Hobart with disabling damage or had withdrawn from the race in Eden. A half dozen other boats had sought temporary shelter in Eden to ride out the storm. Within 12 hours and the arrival of many more boats, picturesque Twofold Bay, sheltering Eden from the savage Tasman Sea, would be nicknamed "the junkyard."

Aboard *Sayonara* by late Sunday, the worm of doubt and fear had begun to turn.

The crew had sailed into a mariner's no-man's-land. The intense low that had spawned the storm was moving east and colliding with a stationary high-pressure system northeast of Tasmania. *Sayonara* was right in the middle of the meteorological battle zone. The occluded front caused an abrupt wind shift, forcing *Sayonara* onto a port tack, southeast, into an endless series of huge spiking waves. As Ellison's boat fell off the back of one wave after another, it was like sliding down a set of stairs while sitting on a cafeteria tray. Men were getting hurt and equipment was breaking. It was when Phil Kiely, a 44-year-old who heads Australia's branch of Ellison's software company, broke his ankle that Ellison's concern turned to worry.

After finishing a watch, Ellison had just sprawled on a bunk when he noticed a crewman forward, in the sail locker, examining *Sayonara's* carbon-fiber hull. Mark Turner told Ellison he was "trying to make sure the boat's OK." Alarmed, Ellison sprang from his bunk and struggled against the boat's wild pitching and yawing to reach Turner. Ellison's alarm turned to near panic. The constant impact of the boat into the wave troughs after falling 30 and 40 feet from their crests was delaminating *Sayonara's* hull, a worst-case scenario. No one knew how much longer the hull could withstand the punishment before it peeled apart like an overripe banana. Ellison wasn't about to find out.

"How much more could our boat take of this going airborne and crashing into the water? That was what worried me the most, that we would lose our rig [sails and mast]," Ellison recalled. When the titanium forestay rod exploded, it was a signal that *Sayonara* was at risk. "I decided that staying out about 80 miles off the coast of Tasmania in this sea state was crazy. I thought, 'What a stupid way to die. At least the pros are getting paid for this. I was paying to be here.' I could either have continued to be afraid of dying or I could go back to the nav station and decide to tack and get into the lee of Tasmania."

To his soft-spoken and placid navigator Mark Rudiger, Ellison yelled, "This is wacko! I'm not sure how much more of this the boat can take."

Rudiger and principal helmsman Chris Dickson resisted Ellison's suggestion that they turn west for the relative shelter of the Tasmanian coast. Such a move, they argued, would give *Brindabella* a chance to take the lead.

Ellison was now more concerned about surviving the Hobart than winning it.

"If there had been a magic button, I think we would have all pushed the button and gone home. But there's no magic button," Ellison said. So over his helmsman's and his navigator's objections, Ellison issued a peremptory order: "Tack the fucking boat!"

"Man, it's just chaos. We've got 11 distress beacons going and 15 mayday calls. We've already rescued one guy by helicopter and there's other crews we're trying to rescue. It's all happening down here."

—policeman Scott Constable
(as told to Dan Tyler, pilot of Careflight)

Day Three: *Armageddon*

In the pre-dawn chill of December 28, a Royal Australian Air Force flight crew went through a detailed checklist of its big antisubmarine warplane, a P3 Orion. Once completed, they started each of the four powerful turboprop engines, ran them up to flight speed with the brakes on and gave the ground crew the signal to pull the wheel chocks. Lifting off from South Australia's Edinburgh Air Base, the Orion, its distinctive "stinger" extending from the rear of the fuselage, banked northeast for Bass Strait.

While the Orion's crew was pre-flighting the aircraft, nearly three dozen other aircraft — military and civilian, helicopters and planes — were being readied for the same mission. It was the beginning of the most massive search-and-rescue operation ever mounted by Australia. Within a few hours it would also include an Australian warship, another P-3 Orion sub hunter, a military C-130 Hercules troop-transport plane, helicopters of all types, commercial fishing boats and dozens of volunteers manning radios and watch stations strung along the coast for hundreds of miles.

The rescue fleet had been coordinated overnight by the Australian Maritime Safety Authority. AMSA chose Merimbula Airport, about 25 miles north of Eden, where many of the yachts were taking refuge, as the base for air operations, because of its proximity and the stocks of aviation fuel it maintained for civil airlines. Four additional tankerloads of fuel were ordered. In addition, AMSA staffers had spent the night and early Monday tracking Sunday's distress beacons and Mayday calls as well as the additional Maydays and EPIRBs from stricken yachts during the night. At its Canberra headquarters, AMSA officers mapped the locations of the boats, calculated their drifts, prepared search grids and faxed them to Merimbula for the search crews.

The EPIRB signals kept coming in on the hour, giving the latest positions of the distressed yachts. The AuSAR officers mapped the locations of the boats, calculated their drifts and prepared search grids which they faxed to Merimbula.

The top priority was given to the crew of *Winston Churchill*, whose nine men were adrift in life rafts, and to British yachtsman Glyn Charles, washed overboard 12 hours earlier from *Sword of Orion*. AMSA knew there was little chance that Charles could have survived the night in the violent wind and waves, yet, interestingly, his rescue — or the recovery of his body — was a must. The yachts *Wild Thing, Sword of Orion, Business Post Naiad, Winston Churchill, B-52* and *Kingurra* topped the rescue fleet's list at first light. But the list would grow quickly as the storm continued to wreak havoc on the Sydney to Hobart racers.

Merimbula, a small, quiet beach town, was unaccustomed to the tumult. For the past 24 hours, emergency services, support personnel and equipment had been staging at its small municipal airport. The rudimentary airfield was usually the domain of summer visitors in their Piper Cubs and tourists booking hourly air tours of the area's magnificent beaches. On the morning of December 28, it looked like the set for an updated World War II John Wayne movie.

It could not have surprised Merimbula's residents and summer visitors when they were awakened as the first 17 search aircraft took off into a red

Crewmen of a C-130 Hercules *search Bass Strait for stricken yachts. The big C-130 troop transports and sub hunting P-3 Orions swept thousands of square miles of ocean during what became Australia's largest sea rescue operation. At the height of the operation, three dozen aircraft, navy ships and fishing vessels were called in to assist the 115 boat racing fleet and pluck more than 50 sailors from certain death. For many sailors, the sight of one of the huge aircraft overhead meant the difference between life and death.*

dawn at 4:30 a.m. Each was assigned one or more yachts to look for, its last known location and the grid pattern to fly in search of each yacht. Further north, in Canberra, other aircraft joined the search.

At first light, flying and search conditions were far from optimal. Officially they were reported as a low ceiling of 3,000 feet and winds of 40 knots. Below, on Bass Strait, the conditions had not improved. Westpac medevac helicopter pilot John Klopper, flying 30 miles off the coast, reported 30-foot swells and mountainous, white-capped seas. "The boats that we have seen in the more rough area have all been demasted. One we saw being towed in, another one was just adrift and we discovered the *B-52* boat, and it had lost its mast," Klopper reported.

The big P-3 Orion, loaded with an array of sensitive detection equipment, was airborne less than 90 minutes when its crew spotted the first yacht, *Midnight Special*. Even from the air the 40-foot sloop looked almost funereal. Adrift and wallowing with its mast broken and sea water sluicing across its deck, the boat was at the mercy of the huge swells and breaking waves. Even to the untrained eye, *Midnight Special* looked like she had been through a ferocious battle. She had. The Orion pilot blinked his strobe light and tipped the plane's wings to a lone sailor in the cockpit and radioed the boat's position to AMSA.

Sail number 9000 out of the Mooloolaba Yacht Club, near Brisbane, identified *Midnight Special*, co-owned and skippered by Peter Baynes and crewed by a group of friends and veteran sailors. Like the crew of the *Winston Churchill*, Baynes and his crew were sailing in the "gentlemen's ocean-racing division." It was their first Sydney to Hobart race in the 3-year-old boat and the crew, mostly men in their 50s, were out for some fun. "Their only goal is to avoid having a midlife crisis in the middle of Bass Strait. A boat-full of regular blokes out to have some fun," is the way they were described in pre-race reports from the Cruising Yacht Club of Australia. Perhaps such a description was intended by the crew to sand-bag the competition. They were winding up a full season of competitive ocean racing during which they had campaigned *Midnight Special* to several outstanding finishes that could not have been achieved by casual sailing.

But on Sunday it still came as a pleasant surprise when they learned that they were the 18th boat to reach Bass Strait. At 2 p.m. *Midnight Special* was in a virtual dead heat with the race leaders in her division, *Midnight Rambler*, which was a mile off her port bow, and *Chutzpah*, 60 miles east. Baynes and his crew had heard Rob Kothe's warning during Sunday's 2 p.m. radio sked, but they sailed on, believing from the weather report that the worst of the storm was well south of their position. Sails were shortened progressively from full mainsail and a #3 headsail, to a reefed mainsail and a storm jib, to a storm jib alone. Crewman Roger Barnett later speculated that had *Midnight Special* not been in such a favorable position Sunday, her veteran crew would have opted for the shelter of Eden right after the 2 p.m. position report and Kothe's warning.

Nevertheless, *Midnight Special* kept racing south and into the worst of the storm. After an hour of the fearful pounding she and the crew were taking, Baynes and the boat's other owners gathered below decks to discuss their options. During the debate, Neil Dickson recalled, a freak wave struck the boat, throwing Ian Griffiths, a lawyer, across the cabin. He hit the cabin floor with a broken leg and a serious back injury, which erased any doubt about the advisability of heading for shelter.

Shortly after Griffiths was injured, the motors were started and *Midnight Special* began a perilous 40-mile run to Eden. As conditions worsened toward late afternoon, the boat was knocked down twice by huge following waves. Both knockdowns tossed crewmen below decks about the cabin, breaking ribs and dislodging dishes and equipment that struck the men with the force of bricks.

Shortly after midnight the storm was at its peak and *Midnight Special* was motoring along its northern edge. Then, disaster struck in the form of a huge rogue wave that crewman Barnett described as sounding like a freight train before it hit the boat.

"It was absolutely terrifying and very dark," Barnett, a 48-year-old Queensland life raft technician on his first Sydney-to-Hobart, told reporters for the *Sydney Morning Herald*.

The huge wave pitchpoled the 40-foot boat through a full 360-degree underwater roll. The somersault tore off the boat's mast and left its rigging in tangles across the deck and over the port side. Below decks, the cabin fractured and all of its windows imploded, allowing in a river of sea water. Neil Dickson, 49, a veteran sailor, was knocked cold when he was driven into the ceiling during the pitchpoling. Crewman Peter Carter was slammed into a forward bulkhead and suffered a crushed vertebrae in his back. The others got off with a variety of head wounds, cracked ribs and deep contusions.

Midnight Special was able to send a radio distress call to Sydney immediately, and her EPIRB was activated. Remarkably, the crew was able to restart the engine and continue moving north. Their most immediate problem was patching the large cracks that had begun to open in the deck. Sleeping bags were used, but the wind and waves over the deck soon tore them loose. Next, the boat's spinnakers were jammed into the widening cracks, which worked. But the trimming lines from the sails soon caught in the propeller and stalled the engine for good. *Midnight Special* was now dead in the churning sea and her radios had given out. One of the boat's red distress flares was sent aloft to join others arcing skyward all around them. With that done, there was nothing to do but bail and hope for another dawn. Those who could did.

When the P-3 Orion's sighting of *Midnight Special* was learned at AMSA's Canberra operations center, a SouthCare medevac helicopter already launched was alerted. Within 15 minutes, paramedic David Dutton and the crew of the SouthCare chopper were hovering 50 feet above the stricken yacht. Wasting no time, Dutton motioned for a crew member below to jump into the sea. Dutton immediately went down the wire and brought up Dr. David Leslie, a dermatologist. He was sent first because, the waiting crewmen figured, he could brief the helicopter crew about the numerous injuries. Six crew members below decks crowded the companionway to see Leslie winched aboard the helicopter. On deck, nurseryman Bill Butler and Trevor McDonough, 60, a brick mason, looked skyward and waited their turn. Thus distracted, the wave took them all completely by surprise.

A towering wave turned the boat over, leaving it upside down. Of the eight crew still on board, six, including Roger Barnett, were trapped in the cabin. Water pressure had jammed the cabin doors closed and the cabin was rapidly flooding. Dickson waded waist-deep across the flooded ceiling and dived through a small opening in the companionway doors. He made it halfway to freedom before his life vest was snagged. Dickson kicked with all his strength and was running out of breath when Barnett began to cut him loose.

"We were just working frantically to get up on deck," Barnett said.

McDonough and Butler, who had been on deck, were under the submerged deck and hopelessly tangled in the spent rigging. The two, as well as Dickson, were teetering on the brink of panic and consciousness when the boat righted itself. Dickson and the others scrambled on deck to find McDonough laying in the cockpit gasping for air and coughing sea water. Butler was standing nearby, dumbfounded, streaming sea water and the rigging that had nearly killed him.

The three had no time to celebrate their survival. Overhead, the helicopter, low on fuel, wheeled around and headed for the mainland. The crew, not knowing why their means of rescue had deserted them, moved forward as *Midnight Special* sank slowly by the stern. It would be a half hour and several threatening waves before a second helicopter plucked them from the sea.

About the time the second helicopter was clearing the headlands with the rest of *Midnight Special's* crew, the second wave of rescue vessels and aircraft had been launched. *HMAS Newcastle* sailed from Sydney with only 70 crew, a third of its normal complement. The missile frigate is fast and highly maneuverable for her size. (Its American prototype, built at Maine's Bath Iron Works, has a speedometer on the bridge that goes to 90 knots. During sea trials of the Oliver Hazard Perry, FFG7, the first model, it was said that someone standing on the bridge rail could dip their hand in the sea during a tight turn.) With its extended stern, *HMAS Newcastle* could also launch and recover search helicopters, such as the Navy's sub-hunting Sea King and Sea Hawks.

The second Orion P-3 had arrived from Edinburgh Air Base in Adelaide. Able to stay airborne for hours in all kinds of weather, the C-130 Hercules from Richmond Air Base in New South Wales had joined the rescue operation.

By 3 a.m. Monday, *Sayonara* was off the northeastern tip of Tasmania, leading the race and her closest rival, *Brindabella,* by 33 miles. It was Larry Ellison's biggest lead over the Hobart defending champion since the start of the race. Perhaps more importantly, Ellison, with his crew of hired professionals, had managed to outpace his business nemesis' 1996 race record so far. *Sayonara* had enjoyed a 120-mile lead over Hasso Plattner's race record set by the German software magnate sailing his maxi, *Morning Glory,* two years earlier. But the violent storm in Bass Strait, especially late Sunday night, had taken its toll. Now, at 3 a.m., Ellison's lead was a mere 30 miles, and he had to cross the finish line in 24 hours and seven minutes to beat Plattner's record. At the time, it looked like a sure thing.

Sayonara had fallen off the pace shortly after Ellison ordered the westward tack some hours earlier to escape the storm's brutal beating. Time was lost because the wind would not allow the most direct course southwest to Hobart. Instead, *Sayonara* had to sail due west to reach the shelter of the Tasmanian coast. Then she could turn south for Storm Bay, the Derwent River and Hobart. But as *Sayonara* tacked west, out of the worst of the storm, the winds shifted in Ellison's favor, and the boat was put on a direct southwest course for Storm Bay. With favorable 25-knot winds, media predictions put *Sayonara* across the finish line at 9 p.m., well ahead of the race record.

While Ellison remained within striking distance of the race record, he expressed concern that *Brindabella* might be in trouble in the huge seas in *Sayonara's* wake. Ellison later said he was aware that *Brindabella* was 30 miles astern, sprinting to catch up after she had been forced to sail north for an hour Sunday night so that a crewman could cut a fouled sail from the top of her mast. His concern stemmed from the fact that *Brindabella* failed to report on any of the radio skeds since Saturday.

Under better racing conditions, *Brindabella* might be masking her position from *Sayonara* for tactical reasons. But in the conditions that existed, Ellison thought *Brindabella* might be in trouble. And he insisted that he would have gone to the aid of the rival maxi had she reported being in trouble. The veteran ocean-racing skipper said his motivation for doing so stemmed from the Fastnet ocean race 19 years earlier in which 15 sailors died. Ellison said the extraordinary danger to *Sayonara* and crew of returning to assist *Brindabella*, if necessary, was outweighed by the deadly results of not doing so, as happened in the 1979 Fastnet.

"One of the most difficult things for people who'd been in the Fastnet was almost no one came to the assistance of anybody else. And we talked about that," Ellison said.

One of the primary rules of the Sydney to Hobart yacht race is the requirement that skippers render all possible aid to a yacht that is in difficulty. It is a rule of ocean racing worldwide and adopted by the Cruising Yacht Club of Australia for the Sydney to Hobart and other races it sponsors.

Yet under long-standing maritime law, a skipper's primary responsibility is to his boat and crew. According to the spirit of the law, if in rendering aid to a stricken boat a skipper must put his boat and crew in grave danger, the skipper is held faultless if he or she withholds assistance to avoid imperiling boat and crew. The facts of each case and the letter of the law, by which they are measured, decide the outcome.

Ellison's willingness to help notwithstanding, *Brindabella* was struggling with the same conditions as *Sayonara*. But she was not in trouble.

Brindabella had not reported her position on the radio sked, because her radio had been disabled by sea water when the storm began Saturday night, according to sail trimmer Geoff Cropley. New holes drilled in the stern — above the navigation/radio station — to secure the boat's new permanent backstays (cables supporting the mast) had allowed water in and destroyed the radio. Also, during Saturday's fast spinnaker run, the boat had struck a basking sunfish, which often tip the scales at 800 pounds or more. The mishap damaged the rudder stalk and allowed water aboard near the navigation station. Sail trimmer Cropley was quick to point out that since *Brindabella* had been equipped with a special tracking transmitter, her course and status were known to race safety officials.

"We knew that they knew where we were because we had Satcom-C," said Cropley. "They had provided 20 of the boats with Satcom-C and *Brindabella* was one of them. Satcom-C provides real-time tracking of the yachts. One of the officials had a laptop computer that was receiving 20 Satcom-C signals. They could see that we were sailing south on our course and that we did not have a problem."

Too, shortly after incoming sea water disabled all of *Brindabella's* communications late Saturday except VHF radio (HF radio was used for fleet communications), she tried contacting *Sayonara* without success. And about the time Ellison was considering going back to look for the rival maxi, *Brindabella* had again contacted *Sayonara* on VHF radio but got no answer, crewmen told investigators after the race.

At Monday's 2 p.m. radio sked, for the first time, *Sayonara* had fallen behind the race record. Ellison had gotten his boat and crew out of danger by tacking west to Tasmania. But in doing so, he had sailed into much lighter winds. With his substantial lead now evaporated and with *Sayonara's* mainsail and some of her rigging damaged, Ellison no longer had a margin for error. The outcome now rested largely with the capricious winds of the Tasmanian coast. By late Monday, radio and television reports continued their optimistic projections of *Sayonara's* winning finish time.

Sayonara and her crew would continue to race. But the calmer conditions of the Tasmanian coast offered the crew's first respite from the epic storm. Most had been suffering from seasickness and had not eaten or had anything to drink for 24 hours. And with the death and destruction the storm had dealt the Hobart fleet, it was enough to finish the 1998 Hobart. Breaking the record and winning line honors loomed less large than it did at the starting line, as evidenced by Ellison's defense of his decision to run for the coast.

"It was the right decision for the safety of the crew," he said. "It was the right decision for keeping the boat together. And as it turned out, although this was not the reason [I] did it, it was a brilliant racing decision on my part."

As night fell Monday, *Sayonara* was slowly gaining the time it had lost on the race record.

By Monday's 3 a.m. radio sked, *Aspect Computing* was 150 miles astern of *Sayonara* and tracking for its best Hobart finish. While *Aspect* was still in huge seas and lashing winds, her skipper and crew, half of whom were handicapped, sensed that the worst was over and that a personal best was within their grasp.

"We were patching ourselves and the boat up and continuing to race," said *Aspect's* skipper David Pescud. "We had hurt her a bit during the night, but we hit the gas because we knew that we were in a good position [for a high finish]."

Aspect, designed as an around-the-world ocean racer, was closer to the low front when the storm intensified than the faster maxis, which raced south of the storm. Despite "taking it on the chin," as Pescud said, the crew suffered "bumps and bruises," but no serious injuries. Through Sunday night and Monday the crew was on duty in short deck watches fueled by 14-year-old Travis Mudgees' sandwiches and a second wind springing from the chance at a high-place finish. Winchman Paul Borg, a burly and powerful blind man, said of getting through the storm and to a shot at a good finish: "There was no free ride for anyone on board. We're grateful for that because it got us through that terrible storm."

After midnight and early Monday, Ed Psaltis and his crew aboard 35-foot *Midnight Rambler* were still "hanging on by their toenails," as Psaltis said. Opting to forge on instead of taking shelter in Eden, *Midnight Rambler* sailed ahead of *Aspect Computing* on a similar course and had taken a similar beating from the storm.

In the past 24 hours, the boat had been through two knockdowns, extensive adjustments to the sails and a serious crew injury. And, as was true for many Hobart crews, the crew of *Midnight Rambler,* while well provisioned, had no appetite for food or water. By dawn the crew was tired, but not exhausted. Physical conditioning was one of the top priorities among the crew. In the months before the race, Psaltis and his six crewmen, who averaged 40 years old, held group workouts specifically to make sure they could handle anything the Hobart race could throw at them.

So far it had paid off, and *Midnight Rambler* had dueled with 36-foot *Chutzpah* as vigorously as the maxis *Sayonara* and *Brindabella* had fought for line honors. Like Psaltis, *Chutzpah* skipper Bruce Taylor was a legend for his skill with small boats in big races. In fact, the head-to-head competition between Psaltis and Taylor in the 1998 Hobart had been going on for more than a decade. Taylor had overshadowed Psaltis and dominated the Sydney to Hobart in his division for 10 years. But he had never managed to cross the finish line in a top-three spot overall (on handicap).

And like Psaltis, Taylor had a new boat and a veteran crew with whom he had sailed for years. Taylor's fourth *Chutzpah* in 13 years — all 34- to 36-footers — was delivered weeks before the start of the 1998 Sydney to Hobart. It represented the latest in design and technology. Taylor, readying for his 18th Sydney to Hobart, had pulled out all the stops. *Midnight Rambler,* trucked from Melbourne to Sydney just weeks before the race, was Taylor's old *Chutzpah* and Psaltis' new *Midnight Rambler.*

By Sunday afternoon, ABC News reported that, so far, Taylor's dream was on track: "On handicap, the little Melbourne yacht *Chutzpah* leads in the IMS overall standings from Roger Hickman's *Atara* and Stewart Niemann's *Terra Firma,* Geoff Boettcher's *Secret Men's Business* from Adelaide and Syd Fischer's *Ragamuffin* from Sydney."

All of the boats in the news report were larger than *Chutzpah* and in a different racing division. *Midnight Rambler,* sailing even with rival *Chutzpah* on a more conservative course 55 miles west, got no mention.

At the 2 p.m. radio position report on Monday, Bruce Taylor reported that *Chutzpah* was retiring from the race and heading for the shelter of Eden. But Taylor's decision had not been made solely on the basis of prudent seamanship. Taylor had heard *Kingurra's* man-overboard Mayday call late Sunday and had immediately gone to the boat's aid. Sailing under a tiny storm jib and with the boom lashed to the deck, Taylor sailed the perilous westward course toward Eden and *Kingurra* at the height of the storm. It was the same course that had been the ruin of many boats in the hours before and after *Chutzpah* took it on. Arriving at the beleaguered *Kingurra,* Taylor spotted the same white life ring that the crew of the

Victorian police helicopter minutes later thought held John Campbell, the *Kingurra* crewman washed overboard. Taylor sailed to the life ring only to find that it was empty. It had simply washed overboard from *Kingurra.*

Minutes later, the police helicopter arrived and made for *Chutzpah,* believing it was the yacht in trouble. A red flare from *Kingurra* caught the chopper's attention and cleared up the misunderstanding. After standing by the badly damaged *Kingurra* stricken yacht for nearly four hours in the wild seas, Taylor contacted the radio-relay vessel *Young Endeavour* and announced *Chutzpah's* retirement from the race. Taylor's burning desire to win the Hobart in his division would have to wait. Like many who find courage and heroism under extreme duress, Taylor did not think of his assistance to *Kingurra* in such terms. He never mentioned the incident officially or publicly. *Chutzpah's* pulling out of the 1998 Hobart was officially recorded as "prudent seamanship."

The news about *Chutzpah* was not greeted with elation by Psaltis and his crew, who knew that his longtime rival faced a long and perilous run to Eden. But the twist of fate put *Midnight Rambler* in a position that would surprise even her skipper.

Meanwhile, Tony Mowbray and the crew of the dismasted and damaged *Solo Globe Challenger* had just survived a night of terror in waves reaching heights of 60 feet and winds roaring at up to 80 knots. *Solo Globe Challenger* had been at the mercy of the sea for a 16-hour eternity.

"We were out of control," Mowbray said. "It was just a whiteout."

But his luck was about to change.

With dozens of rescue aircraft flying search grids over Bass Strait Monday morning, *Solo Globe Challenger* was spotted shortly after a P-3 Orion tipped its wings at the first to be rescued, *Midnight Special's* crew. Shortly after dawn a rescue helicopter appeared overhead and airlifted three of the most seriously injured of *Solo Globe Challenger's* crew to safety. But to do so, the crewmen had to jump into the sea because the yacht was pitching wildly. Helimed One paramedic Cam Robertson went down the wire three times to fish the men from Bass Strait.

Determined not to lose his boat, Mowbray and his remaining crew jury-rigged a mast from two spinnaker poles and continued to limp *Solo Globe Challenger* west under sail toward shelter many miles and a turbulent sea away.

Since dawn, a twin-engine Cessna 404 from the New South Wales Volunteer Rescue Association had been circling the stricken *Business Post Naiad*. The Cessna pilot had reported the boat's position to rescue authorities who asked him to stay put until a rescue helicopter could reach the boat and crew. Medevac pilot John Klopper flew over *Naiad* en route to the aid of another yacht. The scene, Klopper said, was one of the saddest moments of his nearly round-the-clock participation in the Sydney to Hobart rescue.

"It told a tragic story. All the rigging lay over the deck and you could see the body of the deceased quite clearly," he said. "They are images which will stay with me for quite some time."

As the surviving crew of *Business Post Naiad* shivered in two feet of cold water below decks, a helicopter sent to back up another rescue was diverted to their assistance. The pilot was American Dan Tyler, 49. He has been a search and rescue pilot since 1979, but this was only Tyler's second winch at sea; the first was in the 1997 Sydney to Hobart. In the right seat was flight coordinator and winchman Graeme Fromberg, 35, who had been in helicopter rescue since 1985. This was his sixth ocean rescue. Thirty-four-year-old paramedic Murray Traynor rounded out the crew. With a dozen years experience and three years on helicopter rescue, Traynor had four water rescues under his belt.

Tyler's arrival at the rescue site as the pilot of the twin-turbine CareFlight helicopter began 28 years earlier. A Nebraska farm boy and a veteran of more than 1,000 sorties as a Huey helicopter pilot with the 1st Air Cavalry in Vietnam, Tyler met his bride while on leave in Sydney in

1970. After his military service, Tyler flew helicopters in Australia and the Persian Gulf. He took a foray into the legal world after studying law in Sydney, but he quickly returned to what he loved best — flying helicopters. "I wasn't having any fun," he says of his time as a lawyer. All the while Tyler was witness to and a participant in Australia's adoption of the helicopter as an emergency rescue vehicle, the roots of which lie with the country's surf lifesaving clubs.

Because mainland Australia has an arid interior, much of it true desert, 90 percent of Australians live on or near its vast coastline. Much of the coast is tropical or semi-tropical, especially the populated east coast, the location of Sydney and Melbourne, Australia's largest cities. With temperatures in the 90s and humidity to match during the summer (which is winter north of the equator), Australia's beaches have long been well used. Surf lifesaving clubs evolved early in the 20th century to promote life-saving skills and to protect Australian beachgoers, and are now synonymous with the country. So important are they that virtually all Australian beach communities have a lifesaving club that is supported with local tax dollars. Surf lifesaving clubs are to Australia what the 4-H Club or the Boy Scouts are to the United States. The Australian clubs recruit youths and teach them the skills of life saving, a progressive process that includes local, state and national "surf carnivals" at which lifesaving clubs compete and showcase their rescue skills. That competition is how the helicopter was introduced to Australia's surf-rescue efforts.

Sports reporter Ian Badham, a surf lifesaving club member since boyhood, had been covering surf carnivals for years for Sydney newspapers. In 1971, he covered a demonstration in New Zealand that would change his life and transform Australia's rescue services, according to Tyler.

"They were using a tiny helicopter, a Bell 47, with a rope hanging off the cargo hook," Tyler, who now works for Badham, recalled. "Lifeguards would leap into the surf to be rescued and the pilot would fly with the aid of a mirror to see beneath him. The rescuees were lifted just above the water and to the beach, so that if they fell off the rope they'd just fall back into the water again and wouldn't hurt anything."

The helicopter's potential in surf rescue so impressed Badham that he persuaded the management of Australia's oldest bank to explore the idea.

"Initially there was just the Wales rescue helicopter," said Tyler. "Wales because it was the Bank Of New South Wales, which dates back to 1817 and is Australia's largest financial institution, that provided funding. It was purely as an advertising gimmick or a public relations exercise. But they provided the entire funding to the Surf Lifesaving Association of Australia to mount this helicopter operation. Initially they chartered a helicopter but later bought their own."

With Badham's continued support and the helicopter's own impressive performance, Australia's lone civilian rescue helicopter quickly gained legitimacy. But not among Australia's established rescue services. Australia's municipal emergency services — police, fire and ambulance — are provided, administered and funded by its five states. And the tradition-bound New South Wales Ambulance Service and its bureaucracy initially rejected the helicopter service as "renegades." But the helicopter's continuing high-profile performance could not be ignored.

"The Ambulance Service was eventually brought into the fold," said Tyler. "They had to work under the statutory monopoly that exists in New South Wales."

Tired of practicing law, Tyler, who looks just as natural in a flight suit and ball cap as in pinstripes, signed on with the New South Wales Surf Lifesaving Club in 1979 as its chief pilot.

Five years later, in 1986, Australia's helicopter rescue service, which was now using modern Bell Jet Ranger helicopters outfitted with winches, stretchers, medical equipment, medics and rescue crews, underwent its second major evolution.

Two factions of the New South Wales Surf Lifesaving Club split over the philosophy of the helicopter's future in lifesaving and emergency rescue. One side saw the future of the helicopter as a medically-oriented rescue activity. Opponents of that view, Tyler said, "just wanted to focus on the rescues and not get too deep into the medical side of it." Reporter Ian Badham, now a senior member of the club, "saw that the future of air medicine lay in having a greater capability in terms of crew and equipment to be able to carry patients in comfort and safety," Tyler recalled.

Fifteen of the 18 people associated with the Sydney club's helicopter rescue operation walked out as a result of the rift and formed CareFlight, headed by Badham and a medical board of directors. It was Australia's first independent non-profit civilian medevac organization. The pioneering emergency service, located in the west Sydney suburb of Paramatta, staffed all flights with medical doctors specially trained for trauma care, thereby setting the standard for the many helicopter emergency services that would soon follow. Even the New South Wales Lifesaving Club, from which CareFlight split, came around.

"They continued to focus on rescue and eventually realized that was not where the future lay," said Tyler. "We were going ahead by leaps and bounds here at Careflight and they were going backwards. So they changed course and adopted the same crewing and tasking. Basically the entire operational methodology that we embrace, they embrace."

CareFlight now has a $4 million annual budget and transports 1,000 critically ill or accident victims (to whom the service is free) 365 days a year, around the clock. CareFlight is now called out primarily by the New South Wales Ambulance Service, the helicopter's early nemesis. But it, like other civilian air medevacs, can be called upon by New South Wales police, fire brigades, hospitals and Australian Search and Rescue.

On Sunday, December 27, it was Australian Search and Rescue who made the call.

"As the Hobart rescue happened, CareFlight left on December 27 to go way the hell [inland] on the western fringe of our range to bring a patient to a hospital." Tyler said. "It's such a long flight that they didn't get back until about 9 p.m. While they were out AuSAR rang up and asked if our helicopter was available, which it wasn't. Then the news started to break that there was something extremely big happening down there."

CareFlight next got a call to transport a patient to a Canberra hospital, a job usually taken by its sister service, SouthCare, in Sydney. But the SouthCare helicopter was already on its way to the Hobart racing fleet.

"So I thought I should at least let AuSAR know that we were going to be in the area in case they wanted us down there, instead of coming all the way back and going all the way down again and costing everyone a lot of money flying around doing nothing," Tyler said.

At 9 p.m., just before CareFlight headed south for Canberra with a patient, Tyler called AuSAR to inquire if CareFlight was still needed.

"On the radio, policeman Scott Constable told me 'Man, it's just chaos. We've got 11 distress beacons going and 15 mayday calls. We've already rescued one guy by helicopter and there's other crews we're trying to rescue. It's all happening down here.'"

"I told Scott we were headed for Canberra and asked if AuSAR would need us in the morning. 'Almost certainly,' he said."

Tyler and his crew stripped the CareFlight chopper down to the essentials they would need for the Canberra patient transport and to make room for their own ocean-rescue gear — wetsuits, flares, a crew life raft and other equipment.

At first light Monday, Tyler and his crew, working on less than two hours of sleep, were on the flight line in Merimbula.

"There were already two helicopters out in the fray, with three helicopters standing by when we got there," Tyler recalled. "One of them had already winched several people off *Midnight Special* but it didn't have enough fuel to get them all. So this police helicopter was diverted to winch some more people off *Midnight Special* but they said they didn't know if they had enough fuel to get everybody or not. We were sent to back up the police helicopter and winch off anyone it couldn't get."

CareFlight launched and was 15 minutes over Bass Strait monitoring a cacophony of traffic on two radios when its mission began to change.

"When we were 40 miles out I thought I heard a conversation between a Cessna and AuSAR. The Cessna said that they had just come across a boat that had fired a red flare when they flew over the top of it," Tyler said. "They had homed in on a radio beacon and when they flew over the boat the boat fired a red flare but they were having a hard time seeing the name of the boat. But it was dismasted, there were several people on board and there were two life rafts near the stern that were being blown away rapidly. They couldn't tell if there were people in the life rafts or not. Then they flew lower and could read the partial name, *Business Post.*

"Meanwhile I'm listening to another conversation between AuSAR and a police helicopter that was saying they just took the last of the survivors off *Midnight Special* and were headed for Malacoota with them. Dispatch was still in the process of briefing my rescue crewman about how we were going to do the *Midnight Special* rescue. And I said, 'Listen to this radio!' Finally I got [dispatch] to listen, and I said, 'That job's off and there's another one developing close by here.'"

Tyler said confusion reigned for a few more moments as AuSAR attempted to understand that *Midnight Special* was a completed mission and that *Business Post Naiad* should be the next rescue. During the urgent exchanges among the Cessna, CareFlight and AuSAR, the Cessna pilot radioed that *Naiad* had activated a distress beacon. That was enough for Tyler. He homed CareFlight on the stricken yacht's distress signal, dropped the aircraft's nose and sped into the oncoming gale.

"We got our GPS set just as we flew over the top of the boat. I was looking at the GPS and not at the boat when I suddenly realized that we'd gone over the top of the station," Tyler said. "I didn't even notice this boat there among the whitecaps. We missed seeing it. I flew over it at 500 feet and I never saw it. That's how bad the whitecaps were. I didn't even notice a 40-foot boat down there. So we turned around and came back."

Naiad's life rafts were no longer attached to the boat and were quickly blowing away. Not knowing if there was anyone in the two rafts, Tyler asked the Cessna pilot to check.

"Meanwhile," said Tyler, "we came to a hover and noticed seven people sitting in the cockpit of the boat and there was one guy laying on the deck. We didn't know if he was resting, injured or dead. In fact, dead wasn't one of the things we were even thinking about. Injured was what we were thinking about."

Well-practiced in the logistics and contingencies of helicopter rescue, Tyler focused immediately on the man lying on deck. If he could be moved, the man could be thrown overboard to a waiting rescue swimmer. If he had a back injury, that would complicate matters. The man would have to be taken off *Naiad* on a stretcher. If that were necessary, Tyler would need the manpower on *Naiad* to load the injured man onto the stretcher. Lowering a rescue swimmer onto the deck was something Tyler did not want to do unless he had to.

"The chance of a cable snag with the mast hanging over the side with sharp bits poking out everywhere and cables everywhere and with the boat pitching back and forth was too great," Tyler said. "Plus, the heave of the bloody seas was between 25 and 40 feet, sometimes as high as 60 feet. So winching anybody off was going to be a real bag of shit, a real bag of shit. We didn't want to do it. We hadn't ruled it out completely. But we didn't want to do it unless it was absolutely necessary.

"We discussed this and several other scenarios in the space of two to three minutes as we were circling and thinking it through. We decided that what we would do, since we didn't have radio contact — their radio antenna went over the side with the mast — was with hand signals try to convince one of them to jump into the water. We'd winch him up and we could learn what the hell was happening — find out how many people were injured, were they injured so badly that they couldn't be winched aboard, was anybody in the life rafts? Did they have a beacon in the rafts?"

All this time, Tyler was flying blind, directed by winchman Fromberg, who was hanging out of the starboard hatch, maintaining an incessant patter on their headset intercoms: "Survivor 2 o'clock. Forward 15, right 10. Stand by. Steady. Steady!" Hand-signalling, Fromberg and paramedic Traynor conveyed what they wanted to the survivors. They wanted one to put on a safety harness, leap into the huge seas and swim clear of the boat, an act they knew required considerable courage. With relief, Traynor reported: "One's going to go in."

Traynor was going down the wire. He would drop into the sea and pluck the swimmer to safety. To their knowledge, no paramedic anywhere had ever gone into the sea to make seven rescues, even in calm conditions. But this didn't worry them. After all, they had winched nine schoolchildren to safety in a dry-land rescue two years earlier.

Tyler was worried only about the time it would take. He had three hours of fuel. Traynor was so relieved he didn't have to winch onto the boat that he wasn't worrying about anything. "I was a lot happier going into the water," he said.

On board *Business Post Naiad*, a brave man leapt into the sea. "Those guys were great," Tyler said. "They were brave. As soon as the hand signal was given one of them stood up, put the harness on and went straight over the back of the boat and started swimming away from the boat. Those guys were really excellent victims. There was no bullshitting around. They knew their shit was flaky and they did exactly what they were told to do."

Traynor went down the wire. The moment he left the helicopter, the gale tore at him, spinning him around. Using his swimming flippers as airfoils, "paddling on the wire," the paramedic steadied himself to face the crippled boat and its desperate crew. In 30 seconds Fromberg, the winchman, had dropped him into a wave trough 20 feet from the survivor swimming in the sea.

Traynor was wearing thermal underwear, a full body wet suit, lightweight helmet, thermal boots and gloves, life vest, snorkel and face mask. Attached to him was a rescue harness, a round collar stuffed with buoyant and lightweight bean bag beans. He had his own emergency locating transmitter.

The noise of the sea and wind was overwhelming. Spume choked them. As he reached the survivor, a wave drove them under. On the helicopter, Fromberg frantically played out more cable, and then, as Traynor emerged out the other side of the wave, winched it in again.

Traynor had to support his own body weight plus the drag of more than 100 feet of the steel cable streaming in the wind. Three times he was dragged under the water, going down deep, trusting in the cable to pull him out again.

The biggest threat from the lifeline was entanglement. Driven by the wind and sea, a sudden jerk of the cable can tear off a limb or a head. Twice the cable got beneath Traynor's legs and he had to go under to clear it.

Signalling, Traynor got the survivor to hold his arms in the air. Supported by a life vest, he was able to do it, and Traynor slipped the rescue harness over his neck and beneath his arms. He spun the survivor around and once more went under, this time to fasten the harness. The wire got tangled around the survivor. Once more, Traynor went down.

Above them, the helicopter danced in the air, the rotors blasting out five tons of downdraft. Using a hand-held console, Fromberg winched frantically in, out, in, out, controlling the wire, sending instructions to Tyler: "Up 10, left 20. Steady!"

As another wave drove them under, Traynor thought: "I've had enough of this. Let's get out of here." He gave the signal Fromberg was waiting for: right arm extended, thumb up.

They were coming out.

With Fromberg calling the directions, Tyler blindly maneuvered the helicopter until it was directly overhead. Now the waves were an even worse threat. If the sea caught Traynor and his human cargo while they were suspended in the air, the water, moving at frightening speed, would slam them under with tremendous force.

Fromberg waited until a big wave had swept over them and spat them out the other side. He wanted the maximum time before the next wave hit. The winch lifts at a rate of 150 feet a minute. Fromberg hit the button and pulled them out at top speed, lifting them clear as another wave tore beneath.

On board, Traynor was clearly exhausted. But he did not detach from the cable as he quickly checked the survivor, then they asked him for a status report.

"We put a headset on him and asked, 'What's the story? How many are on board and how many are injured and how bad are their injuries.? He said, 'We've got seven people with minor injuries or no injuries and two dead.'

"Shit, you've got two dead down there! That wasn't one of the things I was expecting to hear," Tyler said, recalling his reaction. "That was the first anyone other than *Naiad* crew knew of any death aboard. That was the first confirmed dead in the whole race. They suspected that Glyn Charles [from *Sword of Orion*] was dead. But so far there was no confirmation. They were still searching for him."

Helicopter rescue pilots and crews do a job that calls for split-second decisions and emotional detachment while maintaining their primary focus on those they are sent to rescue. And when there is more than one victim and a cascade of changes from minute to minute, the rescuers are trained to make fast and final decisions about the fate of victims. The realm in which helicopter rescue crews perform is exacting and far removed from the mainstream of human experience. As such, a glimpse into their world provides a picture of an alien, hard-edged landscape.

"That they were dead was great relief," said Tyler, "because that made the rescue a lot easier. And it didn't put the rescue swimmer at risk, as well as the rest of the helicopter crew and boat crew. We could leave the dead there. I didn't have to worry about putting a stretcher down there in the middle of all those bloody cables with the boat pitching around wildly. And the chance of smacking the crewman into the boat pretty hard and hurting him was pretty good. Also the chances of getting the cable tangled and having to cut it would mean not only failing to rescue the survivors but actually adding one survivor to the list of people needing rescue.

"The object of any rescue is to make things better, not make things worse. And in a rescue situation you always have to stop and think for a moment about what seems like a good idea and evaluate if it's going to make things better or if it's going to make things worse. And you have to do the things that have a reasonable assurance to make things better, because there are plenty of factors that can make things worse in a hurry. So if we put Murray [Traynor] down there and he became tangled or injured, we'd just made things a whole lot worse."

The rescue crew had just learned that the man on deck was dead and the skipper was also dead in his bunk. With barely enough time to catch his breath, Traynor went down the wire again.

Traynor and his SCAT colleagues, the Special Casualty Access Teams, are a distinctive breed of men and women. SCAT paramedics, are the medical SWAT teams of the New South Wales Ambulance Service. And as their name implies, SCAT paramedics do whatever is necessary to get to a patient. As New South Wales SCAT paramedic Roger Bowen, who was on temporary duty with CareFlight shortly after the Hobart rescue, explained. "Our main role is to assist a patient, and to do that we need to have the ability to get to the patient, whether they go down in an airplane in a remote area or are bitten by a snake. And we use whatever vehicle it takes to get to the patient, be it four-wheel-drive, helicopter or motorcycle," he said. (New South Wales paramedics routinely respond to accidents in Sydney, because they can get through the city's traffic quicker than a traditional ambulance. It is one of the few places in the world that has such a service.)

Chosen from the ranks of the Ambulance Service after a minimum of four years of duty, SCAT candidates undergo a rigorous eight weeks of basic training, "a weeding-out process," Bowen explained. During the course, candidates focus on physical fitness and the fundamental mountaineering skill of rappelling, though from helicopters. Those who don't wash out move on to cave access, then to bush training, which involves rappelling down cliffs and waterfalls in remote areas. Graduates of the training are then assigned to a Special Casualty Access Team, where training focuses even tighter on the types of rescues most common in the area. It may be mine rescue, bush aircraft rescue, sea rescue or working with firefighters on a hazard-material team. To develop the greatest range of skills, SCAT paramedics are transferred every two years to new areas that require different skills. Throughout their career, SCAT paramedics must pass a physical fitness test every 10 weeks. Its standards are a 2-mile run in 12 minutes, 45 sit-ups and 12 chin-ups followed by a 250-yard swim in 10 minutes or less.

"They make sure we can do our jobs," said wiry and middle-aged Bowen.

Hovering above *Business Post Naiad,* Tyler fought the controls of the bucking CareFlight helicopter as Traynor went down the wire and into the sea again. Seven times he went into the killer seas and lifted men to safety. Each time, he was driven or dragged beneath the waves several times. It took 35 minutes.

If there was any up side to the horrendous conditions faced by CareFlight it was that the winds, while strong, were steady and blew the powerful rotor downwash away from rescuer, victims and the rescue cable.

"In fact, the winds were so strong that the rotor wash was going behind us, so the guys going up and down the wire were in relatively undisturbed air," Tyler said. He added that when the cable is in the rotor wash more cable must be payed out to compensate for the slack caused by the downwash. Such slack exists even with the weight of rescuer and victim at the end of the cable, which can be deadly.

"When the cable is in the rotor wash and is getting blown around and you start to pick someone up who has an extra turn of cable around their neck, it will pop their head right off," Tyler explained.

But what advantage the howling wind was offering, the sea and its huge swells were more than negating.

"We try to keep just the right amount of cable out, but when you've got seas that size, you go from 20 to 30 feet of clearance from the sea to about 100 feet. That's a lot of cable to have out. And when someone attached to the cable is riding up on a swell there's a tremendous amount of slack created. And it sinks. So it's tremendously difficult to lift a person without giving them a bit of a jerk."

When Traynor brought the seventh sailor to safety, Tyler relayed a message to the exhausted survivors: "I'm sorry, but we're not going to get the bodies. Our job is to look after the living."

It may have been over for the crew of *Business Post Naiad,* but not for Tyler, Traynor and Fromberg.

"Once we had them all aboard we asked them if they were sure the people were dead. Usually a person isn't dead until a doctor says they're dead,"

Tyler said. He had left CareFlight's doctor behind to make more room for rescued yachtsmen.

Tyler's and his crew's concern arose from the brutal pragmatism of their training and experience.

"I'd hate to have the vessel recovered four days later with a message scrawled on the wall: 'Why did you leave me?'" Tyler said. "We needed to be absolutely sure that someone we're about to abandon is really dead. The thought of them not being dead and being left behind is truly horrifying."

The rescued yachtsmen assured Tyler that there was no doubt that their shipmates below were dead. Shortly after the CareFlight crew learned of the two deaths from the first yachtsman rescued, winchman Fromberg had hand-signaled instructions to the waiting crew below to secure the bodies in place. The ropes and cables ensnaring Phil Skeggs to the deck were immediately tightened and the door to the cabin where skipper Bruce Guy lay dead was closed and latched. To make sure that the boat and the bodies would be found, Traynor had left a special distress beacon on *Naiad* that broadcast on a frequency of 119.4 Megahertz rather than the 121.5 of the racing yachts' EPIRBs. Tyler radioed the information about the special data buoy and its location on *Naiad* to Australian Search and Rescue.

When Tyler apologized to the seven huddled, cold and exhausted survivors that their dead shipmates were to be left behind, he knew what was at stake.

"I felt bad that we had to leave the bodies behind. I've heard people say that you should never take risks to recover a body. That's bullshit. You do take risks. You obviously don't take as great a risk as for a survivor. But you do take risks because it's very important for people to bring closure to their loss by having a body to bury," Tyler said.

CareFlight one and its crew had done everything possible as it wheeled from its hover and headed to the mainland, giving Tyler a chance to flex fingers that had gripped the controls hard for the last hour. As the aban-

Police inspect the disabled yacht, Business Post Naiad, *after it was towed into Eden harbour with two deceased crewmen aboard.*

doned yacht passed beneath, Tyler's last thought was that the bodies would be lost if *Naiad* was rolled again in the giant waves.

During the flight to the mainland the rescued crew of *Business Post Naiad* did little more than exchange glances among themselves through salt-reddened eyes. It was familiar to Tyler, and it brought back a flood of memories for the Vietnam combat pilot.

"I only had a bit of a chance to glance over my shoulder at them while the rescue was under way," he said. "My impression was this. When I went to Vietnam I thought that everybody would be somber on the way over and cheering on the way back. We were all sort of goofing around and carrying on on the way to Vietnam. And when we left to come home, everyone was somber all during the flight. There was a small cheer when we landed at Travis Air Base [California], and that was it. Otherwise it was just somber. They just sat there. One guy sort of gave me a thumbs up. But everybody else just sat there. I mean they were feeling really bad.

"One of the big things about it was survivor guilt: I survived and other people died. And no matter if you're in Littleton, Colorado, Vietnam or the Sydney-Hobart yacht race, survivor guilt is one of the strongest emotions that sets in. When the plane lifts off at Bien Hoa or you get rescued off the *Business Post Naiad*, suddenly survivor guilt starts to get you. You've got two of your buddies down there on the boat, dead. And I think that's why it was a pretty quiet ride back."

In the port town of Eden, the scene was far different than what the yachtsmen of the Sydney to Hobart had come to expect. The halfway point of the race, Eden is usually a gathering place for those who sail the race strictly for fun. The stop in Eden is a chance to renew acquaintances, grab a shower, a good meal and have a drink with friends and crew. Among its regulars in the Sydney to Hobart race, the fishing port and the race itself have become known as the Sydney to Eden. But on Monday, the port's usual leisurely camaraderie had been replaced by shocked silence.

Nearly half of the racing fleet's 115 boats crowded the small harbor. Less than two days earlier, most of the boats were in their slips, gleaming under the summer sun at Sydney's Cruising Yacht Club of Australia. Now, under a leaden sky, many were damaged almost beyond recognition. Once vaulting masts lay at odd angles across decks, some with their tops in the water. Carefully crafted sails now draped cracked decks and drooped over gunwales like flags draping coffins. Here and there, bent and broken rudders hung precariously from battered sterns, conjuring up the image of a bar brawl's aftermath or teeth that needed pulling.

On the wharf, race yachtsmen who knew each other well passed without speaking or, at most, with bewildered head shakes. Most had monitored the increasing radio traffic through the night and through Monday morning. Also, the yachting disaster was beginning to take center stage on commercial radio and television stations, and it was front-page news in the press.

"There were a lot of boats looking a bit shabby, torn up," said *Wild Thing's* sailing master Scott Gilbert. "The mood was very, very somber. We sat on the boat and had a few drinks and then went up to the fishermen's club and saw a lot more than one guy walking around with tears in his eyes, that's for sure."

For 27 hours, Gilbert and the crew of *Wild Thing* had limped the storm-crippled maxi to Eden. The boat was at anchor when a vivid tableau in the form of the yacht *Kingurra* ghosted alongside.

"They were just exhausted and had a couple injuries on board," Gilbert said. "And seeing them, it really struck me just how bad it had been for some of the smaller boats."

Shortly after midnight, *Team Jaguar,* dismasted, her propellers fouled by downed rigging and her radios dead, was drifting north, ahead of the storm. Her crew had jury-rigged an antenna and had managed to get a radio message to the fleet radio ship *Young Endeavour* about their plight.

The crew of Quest of Hobart begin the job of clearing up their yacht after surviving one of the worst storms on record.

Tom Bibbey, skipper of the 85-foot fishing trawler *Moira Elizabeth,* who was heading south near *Team Jaguar,* agreed to Telstra Control's request that he go to *Team Jaguar's* aid.

Using a hand-held GPS unit, the crew of *Team Jaguar* fixed their position and relayed the coordinates to the fishing trawler. But according to Bibbey, the GPS aboard *Team Jaguar* was malfunctioning. For four treacherous hours the yacht and the fishing boat were unwilling partici-pants in a game of hide-and-seek in the towering seas. Finally, at 4 a.m. the *Moira Elizabeth* found *Team Jaguar* and took the stricken sloop under a slow and careful tow. They reached Eden at noon, 30 minutes before the yacht *B-52,* also rolled and dismasted Sunday, limped into Twofold Bay under its own power.

Brian Northcote was the navigator aboard *Sharpe Hawke V,* which was damaged by a freak wave Sunday and forced to seek shelter in Eden. He called the scene in Eden a tragedy.

"There are a lot of upset people down here because you go sailing for the enjoyment and really when you experience these conditions you don't really expect them to take the toll that they have," he said.

The only bright spot in Eden Monday morning were the many tele-phone calls to family and friends on shore who had heard the news and were waiting anxiously. Monday was still the height of the Christmas hol-iday, and many who had friends or family in the race knew that the fleet was facing a storm. Some, like the girlfriend of *Sayonara's* Larry Ellison, had begged the yachtsmen not to go.

The 1993 Sydney to Hobart race was still remembered, but its more sanguine details were fading in memory. The 1993 event saw a strong storm smash into the racing fleet almost from the starting line and howl at full force for three days. Of 104 boats that began the race, only 38 finished. Having finished the race in 1993 is a badge of rank among vet-erans of the Sydney to Hobart. True esteem comes to those who finished both the 1993 race and the 1977 Hobart, which was ambushed by a devastating storm. Ultimate status would arise from finishing the triple crown, the 1977, 1993 and the 1998 Hobart. But it was the 1993 race that was pivotal for the Sydney to Hobart.

Taking lessons from the disastrous 1979 English Fastnet race in which 15 people died and the 1993 Sydney to Hobart, the Cruising Yacht Club of Australia (CYCA) made a number of compulsory changes to the race and its administration. Chief among them were:

• The introduction of entry applications for each boat. The move gave the CYCA the ability to assess the quality of boats and crews in the race and to reject those deemed not up to the challenge.

• Transfer of race control to Hobart from Sydney after the first day of the race. Transferring control to Hobart stemmed largely from the increasing difficulty of maintaining radio contact with the fleet as it sailed south.

• Requiring a radio certificate from each yacht, insuring that the boat's radios were installed and maintained properly and that they were in good working order.

• The inclusion of the Australian Maritime Safety Authority as advisors to the CYCA's race management team.

The 1993 race review gave rise to eight other proposed changes to the Sydney to Hobart yacht race, primarily crew education and changes in safety equipment and radio procedure. But they were not officially adopted by the CYCA.

Underscoring the need for any change was the weather and the batterings it had meted out to the Sydney to Hobart fleet over the years. Hewing to the seagoing tradition that it is a skipper's decision to race and continue racing, the CYCA was silent on all matters of weather forecasting in its 1993 review. In the 1998 Sydney to Hobart, weather forecasting took center stage.

Virtually all of the race's 1,135 crewmen were aware that the perfect conditions that prevailed during the afternoon of the first day of the Sydney to Hobart would not last. They knew that a gale was forecast for Bass Strait. What few knew was just how bad the conditions would get.

Australian Bureau of Meteorology forecasters in Sydney and Melbourne had been tracking a number of weather systems in the seas around Australia just before Christmas. On December 24, a ridge of high pressure was sitting over the Tasman Sea, off the coast of New South Wales. A strong low front had sprung up in the Southern Ocean, approximately 1,000 miles south of the continent, and was headed for Australia. A major cold front was bearing onto southwestern Australia. And a broad band of low pressure hovered just off the country's north coast. Such a mixture of weather components could mean trouble or it could mean nothing. By Christmas Eve, when government forecasters were scheduled to give their initial briefing to the Sydney to Hobart racing crews, it was, for Meteorology Bureau forecasters, too early to tell.

Wearing a festive red cap, Kenn Batt, a forecaster from the Meteorology Bureau's Sydney office, arrived at the Cruising Yacht Club of Australia's unobtrusive brick waterfront headquarters in Rushcutter's Bay right on time. Two hundred and fifty yachtsmen who would be competing in the Sydney to Hobart two days later were in attendance. The meteorologist was in a difficult spot. Batt's computers, his primary forecasting tools, were giving him information that was varied and inconclusive. There was no consensus and some conflict among the eight Meteorology Bureau weather-modeling programs used to project results of the weather systems off Australia's coast. For nearly a half hour, Batt stuck with what he knew — the positions and bearings of the various weather systems. In the final minutes of the briefing, he advised the group to keep an eye on a low front forming southeast of Gabo Island. Too, he said, the low could cause steep breaking seas.

Competitors would have to wait until the morning of the race for a more definitive forecast, Batt informed them.

To further illustrate Batt's plight, on December 24, two of the Meteorology Bureau's main computer weather-modeling programs were predicting entirely different outcomes from the same weather data. The ECMWF (European Center for Medium-Range Weather Forecasts) model was predicting a low near Tasmania and winds of 30 knots near Gabo Island Sunday night. The Australian GASP (Global Assimilation and Spectral Prognosis) model was predicting a high-pressure system near Gabo Island Sunday night, with light and variable winds.

In the next 48 hours, the weather bureau's meteorologists in both bureaus would remain unsure of the forecast for the race. By late Friday, the day before the start of the Sydney to Hobart, the storm began to swim into focus for forecasters. The Meteorology Bureau's GASP model and UKMO (United Kingdom Meteorology Bureau) models were both predicting stronger southerly or southwesterly winds of up to 35 knots for Sunday night. Forecasts for a storm of the magnitude that struck the fleet never came. But hours before the starting gun on Saturday, the Bureau of Meteorology's computers all saw the storm nearly for what it was.

The weather bureau's models — European, Australian, Japanese, United Kingdom and United States — all predicted a deep low-pressure system developing approximately 200 miles southeast of Gabo Island by Sunday night. Gale winds of 45 knots were forecast. By this time, most of the Sydney to Hobart fleet was on the water preparing for the start. Getting the updated forecast was left largely to individual boats. Even so, such a forecast was standard fare for the Sydney to Hobart sailors. And they would be 200 miles from the low, on its edges at most.

Almost as the starting gun fired and 115 boats sped across the line, a Meteorology Bureau modeling computer used for looking at small areas of land or sea kicked out a startling forecast. It predicted an intense low-pressure system 80 miles off Gabo Island — in the middle of Bass Strait — for Sunday afternoon with westerly winds of 55 knots, gusting to 70 knots, or 80 miles an hour. Waves were expected to reach heights of 25 feet.

The various weather systems that lurked off the coast of Australia in the days leading up to the race had conspired and fooled most forecasters and their machines. The modeling image that came up on forecasters screens at 1 p.m. was an enormous and malevolent wraith that spread out south over thousands of miles of the Southern Ocean and focused in a tight, clockwise twist over Bass Strait. It was no longer a "southerly buster." It was a violent storm, one whose fury would exceed the government's predictions.

With dozens of friends in the race that was already under way, Kenn Batt sped from his downtown office, through the bohemian neighborhood of King's Cross to Rushcutters Bay and the Cruising Yacht Club of Australia to deliver the storm warning. It was 2 p.m. After a sendoff from 300,000 holiday revelers, the fleet was just rounding the sea buoy at the Sydney Heads for the spinnaker run south.

"Those poor people are heading into a massacre," a distraught Batt told a friend after realizing the full implications.

The warning was also sent to the Australian Maritime Safety Authority and the Eden Coastal Patrol. The report upgrading the forecast from a gale to a storm in eastern Bass Strait was passed from AMSA to the CYCA's radio-relay vessel *Young Endeavour* and broadcast on coastal radio. Even though most of the yachts got the updated forecast in whole or in part, it was widely misunderstood.

"At the first [radio] sked we got a weather update. Nothing in the weather forecast indicated that we were going to get anything more than 55 knots," said Peter Meikle, a crewman aboard *Kingurra*.

Meikle's comment about forecasted wind strengths on the 8 p.m. radio sked were typical of many in the fleet who interpreted the report to

mean that winds would reach 55 knots. Fifty-five knots in the Sydney to
Hobart is not a cakewalk, but most of its competitors had sailed the race
or others like it under similar conditions or worse. What they weren't
expecting were higher winds and the huge waves they generate. One competitor would later describe the unexpected conditions to race investigators as looking "like the gates of Hell and building the greatest bitch of a
sea you could ever design."

Most didn't expect such conditions. But some did.

Dr. Roger Badham of Sydney is a private weather consultant to racing
yachtsmen and others worldwide, a job he has done for 20 years. Twenty
skippers in the 1998 Sydney to Hobart used his services. The quiet, reserved
meteorologist is known as "Clouds" among yachtsmen, a moniker earned for
his effectiveness at predicting weather for yacht races. Like the Meteorology
Bureau, Badham had been watching the various fronts converge on Australia
for a week before the race. And like the state forecasters, he had used the same
computer tools to come to his conclusions or forecasts. The critical difference
between Meteorology Bureau forecasts and Badham's was timeliness and the
fact that they were understood by competitors.

When he's not performing his role as sailing master aboard the racing
yacht *Wild Thing*, Scott Gilbert delivers yachts to destinations around the
world. He has come to depend on Badham's forecasts. Gilbert and *Wild
Thing's* skipper Grant Wharington were among the Sydney to Hobart
crew who consulted Badham before the race.

"We had a long talk with Roger before the race and he certainly predicted that the breeze could get up quite strong, to 70 knots plus," Gilbert
said. "So we had a pretty good idea what we were getting into.

"I think the difference between Roger's forecast and the weather
bureau's is that Roger had absolutely up-to-the-minute information, especially within the last two hours preceding the race. When something
forms as quickly as the low did in the Hobart race, hours literally make all

the difference. The night before, Roger was saying that there wasn't going to be any bruising weather of the type he was predicting an hour before the race. An hour after the race started he rang up a few of the people that he knows quite well, which is probably not the right thing to do [by a strict reading of the race's rules] and said you've got two options: Either head due east or come home. Don't go into it."

Badham said that in the days and hours leading up to the race, he knew that a powerful low would develop somewhere near Tasmania. He thought it would be east of the island state, away from the Sydney to Hobart racecourse. But at the same time state meteorologist Ken Batt saw the projections of the severe low in Bass Strait, so did Badham.

"Oh, shit," Badham recalled thinking, "This is Armageddon. It was at least going to be as bad as 1993."

On *Aspect Computing,* skipper David Pescud and his crew of able-bodied and disabled sailors knew what to expect.

"We knew the front was coming. We had Roger Badham's package and he said, 'Look, it's gonna get you,'" Pescud said.

The dueling maxis *Sayonara* and *Brindabella* both had consulted Badham before the race. *Brindabella's* Geoff Cropley said Badham's accurate forecast helped the crew avoid the worst of the storm.

Said Cropley, "Roger came to us that morning and he had three computer models: the American model, the European model and the Australian model of what the computers were indicating would happen with that storm. And he said he favored the American model. The American model was showing an intense low developing. He briefed us that when we entered Bass Strait we would get 55 knots of wind from the west. As he calculated, we would be slightly to the west when the storm moved in. And he said to prepare for a lot of wind because it's going to be beam on as we were heading south. And he was spot on. The breeze was exactly west and at the levels he predicted."

Sayonara had Badham's forecast, but skipper Larry Ellison and his key crewmen did not appear to pay particular attention to its details until late Sunday, when Ellison saw the severe low on the boat's weather computer and reacted in shock. "What the fuck is that thing doing out here?" he exclaimed rhetorically to his navigator, Mark Rudiger, who had consulted Badham about the storm often in the days before the race, and who had no answer.

Ed Psaltis and his crew on the diminutive *Midnight Rambler* did not consult directly with Badham, but they did get his fax weather updates. Psaltis said that while Badham's forecast did not anticipate the full extent of the storm's power, it did prepare *Midnight Rambler* for "a very nasty front."

"If I had known that the winds were going to blow 70 to 80 knots, well, I can't say," said Psaltis. "But you always expect the worst. The forecast only gives you average wind. It doesn't give you the puffs, which were extremely strong. But ocean racing is a sport of skill and experience. You take the forecast and factor that in to your race strategy, assuming that the weather is going to be worse than forecasted. And if it happens, that's the chance you take."

Just before the race, Badham let *Atara* skipper Roger Hickman know what he was in for. "Roger came to me and put his arm over my shoulder and said, 'Hickman, you are in for a *big* wind.' I said, 'Gotcha.'"

Two hours after the starting gun, Badham told longtime race commentator Rob Mundle, "If I were on half these boats I'd be lowering my spinnaker now and coming home because this is going to be worse than 1993."

Weather forecasting would continue to be a heated issue long after the 1998 Sydney to Hobart race. The Cruising Yacht Club of Australia would launch an investigation that would describe the Meteorology Bureau's forecasts as inept, delayed and confusing. The weather bureau would launch its own pre-emptive strike, an exhaustive report in which it would absolve itself of any nonfeasance, insisting that its race weather forecasts were accurate and timely, though misunderstood by race competitors.

Four months after the race, months before either of the two reports were published, Scott Gilbert of *Wild Thing* said that assigning blame to the Australian Bureau of Meteorology was misguided. He added that any assignment of blame is a useless exercise akin to armchair quarterbacking.

"I think it's important to say that it looks like a lot of people are on a witch hunt trying to blame the Weather Bureau for not giving out the correct information," he said. "From my experience and what I know about it, it was the fact that the Weather Bureau simply couldn't get the information out in time.

"As far as allocation of blame, maybe individual skippers may have made the wrong decision as to whether to keep going or to turn around. But there's no point in identifying who that is. It's a bloody yacht race. Whoever second-guesses the actions of the boats and skippers is wrong, because they weren't there and weren't experiencing the situation as the decisions were being made."

It is one thing to willingly participate in an ocean race as a sport, a pastime or a passion. It is voluntary. None of the 1,135 participants was on board because he or she was required to be. Certainly, crews, such as half of Ellison's on *Sayonara,* were being paid as professional sailors to participate in the race. But their participation was not compulsory. It is surely a different matter for those who were called upon to risk their lives rescuing Sydney to Hobart sailors.

Dan Tyler was working the day he piloted a CareFlight helicopter to the rescue of *Business Post Naiad.*

"I don't consider myself legally bound to go out there and rescue them," said Tyler. "But I'm enough of a civil libertarian to think that the Sydney-Hobart yachties have a right to go out there and race. I'm not happy with people who go out and do foolish things, because there is some moral obligation to go out and try to rescue them. So when people foolishly put themselves in a position like that I'm critical of them.

"But the Sydney-Hobart people had a weather forecast that, had it been accurate, would have presented them with conditions that they could have handled. They were not totally unprepared. They were prepared for an ocean yacht race. And they weren't told how bad the weather was. There were a few who were, who consulted a private meteorologist who forecasted the storm pretty closely. But the Weather Bureau forecast called it too late. The boats were already out there.

"So I don't think anybody can point any fingers at all and I certainly wouldn't. Ocean racing is a pretty legitimate sport. It's got pretty good safety regulations. Occasionally acts of God occur and you're taken by surprise. I don't consider this a guarantee that I or somebody like me will go out and rescue them, but they have a right to do what they do."

The crew of *Winston Churchill* had spent a cold and dangerous night in two separate life rafts waiting, hoping and praying for someone like Tyler to rescue them.

Twelve hours into Richard Winning and his crew's ordeal Monday morning, 17 aircraft were looking for the *Winston Churchill*, whose EPIRB signal had not been detected among the many activated. All rescue authorities had to go on was Winning's Mayday position. With all of *Winston Churchill's* navigational equipment destroyed in the knockdown, Winning was only able to estimate his position for authorities, an estimation that was now many hours old and counting. Through the day, Winning and his shipmates huddled in the liferaft, battling the winds and waves as much as they could to stay upright. At one point hopes were raised and dashed when a plane passed in the distance but failed to see the tiny craft among the waves, troughs and spindrift.

"By daybreak the seas had abated, so we were a lot more sanguine about our chances," Winning recalled. "Emotions rose and fell during the afternoon. Around 4 p.m. I thought I could hear an aircraft. But all of us had been hearing aircraft and seeing ships and submarines all day. It's

This is the pilot's view from the flight deck of a C-130 aircraft searching Bass Strait for stricken Sydney to Hobart racing yachts. With limited visibility and storm tossed seas, the yachts were difficult to spot. Air crewmen said they could pass near a yacht that was hidden by a wave trough and never see it. And when they were able to locate a yacht in trouble, its radio was usually inoperable, making identification difficult. New rules proposed by the race's sponsoring yacht club are expected to prevent most of the communications and identification problems that hampered the 1998 rescue effort.

incredible the way you engage in wishful thinking with your eyes. But more than one of us agreed that we heard this aircraft. And sure enough after a little while we saw it coming, a fixed-wing.

"When we saw him coming on our track we broke out our next-to-last parachute flare and let him have that. But when he got to the end of his search leg he turned off and disappeared. We couldn't hear his engines and we were pretty disappointed. But he soon came back on another leg of his search, which brought him even closer to us. So we let him have the last flare. He saw it." Said grateful Paul Lumtin, "When we heard that helicopter coming, we all had tears in our eyes and were ecstatic and we knew we were going home to see our families."

One by one the shipwrecked crew was plucked from the raft by a rescue swimmer and winched aboard a hovering helicopter. From there, Winning, Lumtin, Bruce Gould and 19-year-old Michael Rynan were taken to a hospital in Mallacoota to recover from hypothermia.

Winning said he was thankful to have been spotted in the failing light. "I wouldn't want to have spent another night out there."

Winning said that a short time after his rescue he was informed that *Winston Churchill's* second raft had been sighted and that signals had been exchanged between the aircraft and raft's occupants.

"So I went to bed confident that they would be rescued," Winning said.

Meanwhile, Jim Lawler, John Dean, John Gibson, John "Steamer" Stanley and Mike Bannister were on the point of a fateful decision. Shortly after dark Sunday night, their raft had been overturned by a monster wave. The rectangular raft was heavier than the one Winning had twice risked his life to right in the storm. And during a brief debate among the five trapped beneath the overturned raft, it was decided that anyone trying to right the raft would be in grave danger of being swept away. Moreover, no one knew how to right the raft. And, with the submerged canopy enveloping them from the water pressure, it would have been impossible to get through the canopy hatch while wearing a life vest. The only one not wearing one was Stanley, who was incapacitated with a broken ankle and other injuries. Instead, they decided to cut a hole in the floor, which was now the roof. The men had been trapped beneath the raft for several hours and had found that it was more stable while inverted and that it offered them better protection from the storm. What it did not offer was air. They were beginning to suffocate. "You could just feel the air starting to get a bit tighter," is how Stanley described it.

Shortly after a 10-inch cut was made along a floor seam, the raft was righted by a wave. Its canopy was in tatters from the men standing on it while submerged, and the craft's safety kit was gone. Immediately, the weight of the five men strained the cut floor seam, which parted from gunwale to gunwale. Almost as quickly, the entire bottom shredded. The five were left clinging to an oversized life ring.

Despite their desperate situation, Stanley said, "The spirits were great. The guys were just fabulous blokes. We were all helping each other and carrying on."

Then disaster struck.

"We got hit with this almighty wave," Stanley recalled. "And normally we could hear them coming, the breaking surf, and you'd hang on. This particular one, there was no warning. All of a sudden we were just crashing off the top of this huge rogue wave. So I hung on to the roof rope and was able to hang on pretty well. I just took a breath and away we went. And when it stopped I was on the outside of the raft. And when I finally came up for air I gasped and yelled 'Who's here?' And the only reply was Gibbo (John Gibson). I looked back and there was white water for about 300 meters and I could see two people.

Horrified, John Gibson, who had survived what he described as "going over Niagara Falls in an inner tube," wanted to go back to the men cast adrift by the rogue wave.

"We can't do anything for those boys," Stanley insisted, "because the wind is blowing us so fast away from them."

The two survivors could do nothing more than lift their faces to the black sky and say a prayer for their friends.

Throughout the night Stanley and Gibson clung to each other and the raft. Although the raft was overturned repeatedly in the storm conditions, the pair managed to hang on. Gibson was attached to the raft by his safety harness, and Stanley, without one, held onto Gibson during the worst capsizings.

The unlikely pair of longtime friends — Gibson, a gregarious lawyer; Stanley, a quiet working man — made it through the ordeal with each other's help and in their own separate ways. Gibson wanted to talk. Stanley kept his fear and the pain from his injuries at bay by containing it, by remaining silent. After futile attempts to draw Stanley out, the exasperated 64-year-old Sydney lawyer said, "John, you're not much good at conversation, are you?"

Toward evening Monday, after a long, cold day in the storm-tossed seas, Stanley and Gibson saw an aircraft only 300 yards away. Stanley waved Gibson's yellow life jacket, and both men thought they saw the plane flash its wing lights in acknowledgement. But they were not seen.

Two hours later, the pair was nearing emotional and physical exhaustion when a second plane appeared.

"It was a Navy Orion," Stanley recalled. "And it was coming in really low."

Again, Stanley waved the yellow life vest at the plane. This time they were spotted. The P-3 Orion pilot blinked the plane's strobe lights and dipped its wings to let the men below know they had been seen.

"We are spotted!" an elated Stanley yelled at Gibson, who had lost his contact lenses and could not see the plane's signal lights or wing dip. Almost simultaneously, a helicopter passed overhead, which Stanley guessed correctly was going to the aid of Winning and the crew in the other life raft.

Winston Churchill *skipper Richard Winning shortly after he and three other crew were rescued from a life raft 24 hours after the cutter was smashed and sunk by a huge wave. Three crewmen in a second raft were not so lucky.*

Overhead, the Orion alerted the Navy frigate *Newcastle*, which dispatched a Sea Hawk helicopter, the last remaining aircraft with night-vision capability.

As the Sea Hawk helicopter sped to the scene, darkness closed in on what would be one of the most difficult and dangerous rescues of the 1998 Sydney to Hobart. It was also the last.

Commanded by Lieutenant Commander Rich Neville, 41, the Sea Hawk is a large and powerful helicopter configured for various operations at sea. It was piloted by Lieutenant Nick Trimmer, 29, and the crew included sensor operator Lieutenant Aaron Abbott, also 29, and winch-man Petty Officer Shane Pashley, 33.

In the short time it took Trimmer to lift off from the *Newcastle* and reach the raft, night had completely closed in. The interior of the aircraft, lit in combat red to preserve night vision, stood in sharp contrast to the pitch blackness, roiling seas and 70-knot winds just beyond its thin aluminum skin. Once in the area where the Orion had spotted the life raft, Trimmer dropped to 200 feet and flew over the raft at 80 miles an hour the first time. With a position fix on Stanley and Gibson, Trimmer made his next approach with the help of the Sea Hawk's auto-hover system. He put the big machine in a hover 65 feet above the huge waves and downwind of the stricken raft.

Now control of the aircraft was passed to Abbott, who flew the helicopter from a wall-control unit near the lifesaving winch. Set to maintain its altitude automatically and sensitive to within 2 feet, the aircraft bucked repeatedly to avoid the waves welling up beneath it.

Now it was Pashley's show. Three years earlier he had gone down the helicopter's wire and into the ocean to rescue French solo yachtswoman Isabelle Autissier from her stricken sail boat. But that was in daylight. And the sea did not look like the inside of a washing machine. Compared to what Pashley faced now, the Autissier rescue was a piece of cake.

Attached to the wire and standing at the door, Pashley glimpsed the entrance to hell. A cone of light from the helicopter played down to the violent surface of the sea, alternately illuminating and losing the terrified men in the raft as they bobbed over the huge waves. The helicopter did its own macabre dance in the night sky as it dodged the waves and fought to maintain its position in the battering winds.

Blown at a sharp angle as he descended to the sea, Pashley hit the water near the raft, swam to it and clambered aboard, only to disappear beneath the surface. Pashely did not know the raft had no bottom. After recovering, he made a quick decision that Gibson was in need of the most immediate attention. He put the harness over Gibson and gave Abbott the thumbs-up signal to hoist him and Gibson to safety. The rescue went smoothly for about 10 feet. But then two things happened that imperiled the entire crew. The autopilot system that maintains altitude failed and a huge gust blew the helicopter sideways and down, plunging the two men on the wire into the ocean. In the seconds it took to regain control of the helicopter, Pashley and Gibson were dragged through and across the giant waves. "A pretty horrific feeling," Pashley called it. Then they were brought aboard.

The Navy had never done a helicopter rescue in such high winds, and Neville knew he was pushing the envelope, especially with the overburdened auto-hover. He was unwilling to endanger 33-year-old Pashley by sending him into the sea a second time to rescue Stanley.

Instead, Pashley dangled a rescue strop over the remnants of the raft. Stanley, broken ankle and other injuries notwithstanding, managed to drag himself into the strop. But it wasn't going to work.

"When I put the strop on I must have put a rope from the raft into the harness," Stanley said. "Because when he started lifting, the raft was following. I was up about 25 feet when I realized what was happening. So I just put my hands in the air and bailed out and went straight back into the water."

After fighting his way back to the surface, Stanley again managed to get into the rescue strop. This time he was hoisted to safety.

The 28 hours in the ocean without food or water had taken a toll on both men. Gibson's tongue was so swollen with thirst that he could barely speak. Stanley was on the edge of hypothermia.

"I'm pretty sure those two men would not have been able to take it much longer down there," Pashley recalled. "Their skin was like prunes from the salt water and they were as thirsty as hell. We just kept giving them water and talking to them all the way back."

On the way back, Stanley and Gibson learned the good news that Richard Winning and the men in the other raft had been rescued. They told the crew of the Sea Hawk the bad news: three of their crewmates had been swept away.

An Australian Air Force spokesman expressed confidence that the missing men would be found alive the next day because they were wearing special suits to survive long periods in cold water. Winning appeared on an early morning television interview the next day. The host's first question was: "How do you feel about the loss of three *Winston Churchill* crewmen from John Stanley's raft?"

It was the first time Winning learned that Jim Lawler, John Dean and Mike Bannister had perished. Bannister and Dean had been his lifelong friends.

Shortly before the aborted television interview, the bodies of Bannister and Lawler were pulled from the sea 50 miles off Eden. When John Dean remained missing after a daylong search, rescue authorities gave him up for dead. His body was never found.

Glyn Charles, the British crewman washed overboard from *Sword of Orion,* was also given up for dead late Monday by the Australian Maritime Safety Authority. The body of the 33-year-old Olympic medalist in sailing events was never found.

"Right now I'm not anxious to go back again, not if I live to be 1,000. It was by far the toughest race I've ever done in my life. It was horrible."

—Larry Ellison, skipper *Sayonara*

Day Four: *Fear and Loathing in Hobart*

By 3 a.m. on Tuesday, three quarters of the 48 surviving Hobart boats had crossed Bass Strait and were near the northeastern tip of Tasmania. It was the last leg of the race. The winds had dropped to 25 knots out of the west-southwest and the skies were clearing. A second front was passing east along the south coast of Australia and was expected to generate winds of 35 knots later in the day off eastern Tasmania, the route of the race.

Earlier, Larry Ellison had given the order to tack his boat, *Sayonara,* west, to the coast of Tasmania. At the 3 a.m. position report to the fleet's radio-relay boat, *Sayonara* was in much calmer seas at the mouth of Storm Bay, which leads to the Derwent River and the finish line, 40 miles away. Rival maxi *Brindabella* remained approximately 25 miles astern of the American leader. Overnight, *Sayonara* had not gained the distance she had lost over the race record when Ellison tacked her to the Tasmanian coast Sunday night. Consequently, the chance of setting a new race record had vanished. *Sayonara* would have had to have crossed the finish line minutes after the 3 a.m. radio report for Ellison to win the 1996 race record from *Morning Glory* and his German business rival who owned the boat and the record. *Sayonara* still had some 40 miles and five hours to go.

Aspect Computing and *Midnight Rambler* continued to vie for the best finishes in their respective divisions. At the 3 a.m. radio sked, they were 25 miles off the northeast coast of Tasmania and out of the hellish conditions of Bass Strait. And to everyone's surprise, Ed Psaltis and the crew of *Midnight Rambler* were closing in on becoming the first small boat in a decade to win the Sydney to Hobart overall on handicap.

By Tuesday morning, the Australian Maritime Safety Authority's massive search and rescue was winding down. Fifty-seven crewmen had been plucked from the sea by rescue helicopters in 36 hours, most of whom had been spotted by nearly two dozen airplanes large and small. Additionally, every rescue boat AMSA could muster had been pressed into service, including the Australian Navy's fast frigate, *Newcastle*. While assembling the rescue fleet and assigning aircraft, ships and boats to search for the many stricken yachts, AMSA was also fielding 2,500 telephone calls from friends and relatives of the race's yachtsmen and from dozens of television, radio and press reporters.

On Tuesday morning, *Solo Globe Challenger* was one of the last stricken boats AMSA was tracking.

Tony Mowbray and his crew of eight on *Solo Globe Challenger* were in their third epic day Tuesday morning. They were continuing to Eden under a jury-rigged sail with a reduced crew after Sunday night's vicious knockdown and the rescue of three injured crewmen Monday morning. The wind and seas had abated overnight, and the crew celebrated with a few cold beers. To help keep the boat moving in the light winds would require more than the small sail jury-rigged on two spinnaker poles. The crew had begun working on the boat's stalled engine before dawn. At first light they got the engine started. Their immediate whoops and hollers over their success were drowned out by the engines of a P-3 Orion that began circling overhead.

The big aircraft dropped dye markers in the water near the yacht and a package, containing a hand-held radio, which was retrieved. Equipped with the radio, Mowbray was told by the Orion crew that the Navy missile frigate *Newcastle* was en route to the stricken yacht.

With the Orion overhead, *Newcastle* came into Mowbray's view minutes later and hailed the yacht on the hand-held emergency radio.

The warship launched a rescue boat and was prepared to take Mowbray and the rest of his crew aboard. Again, determined not to abandon *Solo Globe Challenger*, Mowbray sent two more crewmen to the warship. He remained aboard the stricken yacht with crewmen Bob Snape and Keith Malloy. With the yacht's engine running smoothly, they thought their chances of making Eden were good. Shortly after their rendezvous with the Royal Australian Navy frigate *Newcastle,* Mowbray encountered the fishing trawler *Rubicon*, which towed *Solo Globe Challenger* for 14 hours to the safety of Eden and dry land.

As *Sayonara* was closing in on the finish Tuesday, the Cruising Yacht Club of Australia was beginning to feel the pressure of press scrutiny and public concern. With the last of the air and sea rescues of Sydney to Hobart crew, press reports turned from rescue heroics to criticism of race organizers and the racers themselves.

Also Tuesday morning, the CYCA, the race's organizers, announced an internal investigation of the race, focusing on safety issues. The yacht club insisted that an independent investigation was unnecessary. Peter Bush, past commodore of the CYCA, was appointed to head the investigation. The bright and affable Bush, a veteran of 14 Sydney to Hobart races, was also known as Australia's dean of corporate damage control. In 1997, Bush took over planning the media strategy for an international food company involved in a high-profile extortion case. The company's management of that crisis became the textbook on how to survive a business-threatening episode.

The idea of an internal investigation was, typically, not greeted with enthusiasm by many who believed an independent investigation was called for. But a yacht club internal investigation under such circumstances was not unprecedented. Nineteen years earlier, the British yacht club that sponsored the fatal Fastnet race in which 15 sailors died investigated the event. The club's rigorous probe and its subsequent investigation report left no room for criticism. Also, the CYCA's investigation, while wide-ranging, was to focus on safety issues. Why and how six men died in the race and who, if anyone, was responsible was left to a New South Wales coroner's investigation.

The most heated public issue confronting the CYCA was the allegation that, given the weather forecast, the race should have been called off, postponed or the boats called back. Under the rules governing the race, the CYCA had the option to call off or "abandon" the race. But Bush maintained throughout that the decision to start and continue the race is best left to the skipper of each boat. And, he said, calling the boats back after the storm warning was issued was impractical.

"Unfortunately, once a race starts and the weather is not as predicted, yachts can be out there 40 to 100 miles, depending on the race. So it's not as simple as saying, 'Let's call off the race.' A good analogy is an auto race where you can put up a signal flag and within a few minutes you've got all the cars off the track," he said.

Australia Prime Minister John Howard agreed and gave the race and its organizers his backing on the last day of 1988.

"I'm not a yachtsman," Howard said. "I have to respect the views of people who are. The only principle that you can work by is that each skipper is in command of his own ship and he alone has to decide what that boat is going to do."

American expatriate Dan Tyler, the helicopter pilot instrumental in the *B.P. Naiad* rescue, chalked the controversy up to "tall poppy syndrome." He explained that the egalitarian nature of Australians is offended by conspicuous displays of wealth, such as huge yachts and private helicopters.

The CYCA's announcement of an internal investigation opened the floodgates of public and press sentiment that quickly polarized into two factions. On one side were members of the non-sailing public and Australia's daily press. On the other were sailors and yacht clubs. Some saw it as a class battle. Others saw the controversy purely as a media issue; the press using its bully pulpit to sell more newspapers. Undoubtedly, elements of both were involved — and more, as evidenced by these letters to the editor, from the *Sydney Morning Herald*.

Join in a conversation with yachties and you will invariably find them advocating the free enterprise spirit and the need for self-reliance in all areas of life.

Tune in to Australia's leading radio shock-jock, Stan Zemanek, any night of the week, or watch him on Foxtel's Beauty and the Beast as the media star slags off miscellaneous "boofheads" who have become dependent on the state.

Listen to a John Howard speech or interview these days and you are likely to hear reference to the concept of mutual obligation. Meaning that all members of society, from the poorest to the richest, have obligations to their fellow citizens.

And then watch as these fine sentiments are variously junked or fudged. All because of the Sydney to Hobart yacht race.

You did not need to be a weather junkie to know that conditions in this year's race would be treacherous. On the morning of the Boxing Day start, warnings to this effect were carried in the print and electronic media.

The Bureau of Meteorology has revealed that it issued a storm warning at 2:14 pm on December 26. That is just about one hour after the

1998 Sydney to Hobart had commenced. The fleet hit the storm with a vengeance some 24 hours later.

In spite of this advice, the Cruising Yacht Club of Australia (CYCA), which controls the Sydney to Hobart, took no action to discontinue the race. Subsequently the CYCA restated its policy that "a boat is solely responsible for deciding whether or not to start or continue racing." How convenient.

By Wednesday, December 30, the appalling toll was known. Six dead and numerous injured. There would have been many more casualties but for the enormous bravery of the men and women who undertook the necessary rescues. Crew included a 12-year-old boy and a Year 12 female student.

It is appropriate to sympathize with those who lost family, crew and friends. But it is timely to consider what lessons may be learnt from this tragedy.

To John Howard it is very much business as usual. While saying that he had been very upset by the deaths, the Prime Minister ruled out any "special inquiries." He believes that the coronial inquest and the CYCA's inquiry "will get to the bottom of anything that needs to be investigated." This although the CYCA will in effect be inquiring into itself.

Howard also declared: "I'm not a yachtsman; I have to respect the views of people who are and who understand the sea." Somewhere along the way the Coalition's attitude to sea rescues has altered. In late 1994 the French sailor Isabelle Autissier was rescued by the Australian Navy during the BOC Challenge around-the-world yacht race. Jocelyn Newman, who was then shadow minister for defense, commented that the Labor Government "should investigate whether the BOC, the organizers and the participants should not pay some of the costs of the operation."

The body of one of the Winston Churchill *crewmen washed from a life raft is removed from a Royal Australian Navy Sea King helicopter. Many in the 1998 race believe that without air sea rescue, few of the more than 50 crewman winched to safety would have survived the storm conditions.*

By the time the Coalition won office, however, this policy seemed to have changed. In January 1997 the British yachtsman Tony Bullimore had to be rescued at substantial cost and considerable risk to those involved. As Howard's Defense Minister, Ian McLachlan made no reference to the taxpayer's burden. Instead he expressed satisfaction that the mission was the best practical training that Navy personnel could hope for. Bullimore went on to sell his story at a high price. The men and women of the Australian Navy, who interrupted their leave to rescue him, received no such compensation.

In the October 1998 Federal election, the Liberal Party campaigned against what it alleged was Labor's policy to provide extra funding for the "elite arts." So there should be no problem in recording that ocean racing yachting is a sport for the well-off.

Richard Winning, skipper of the ill-fated Winston Churchill, is on record as maintaining that he looks on sailing "as a bit of recreation - gentleman's ocean racing." Needless to say, he was devastated by the loss of life in the Sydney to Hobart. Kevin Lacey, who was on board Innkeeper, told journalists that "for a while" the events of Sunday, December 27, were "a lot of fun." The skipper of ABN AMRO Challenge, Iain Murray, said that, until his rudder went, it "was all exciting stuff." Fair enough. But why should not gentlemen sailors having fun contribute to their rescues at sea, either by taking out special insurance or by making some sort of payment.

Not every yachtsman is wealthy. However, most are infinitely better endowed than their relatively poorly paid rescue workers, and the taxpayers who fund these services. In short, there is room here for a bit of mutual obligation.

Stan Zemanek is a case in point. In his recently released The Thoughts of Chairman Stan *(HarperCollins, 1998) he writes: "We give too many people too many options . . . if people have too many options, they'll accept the easy option . . ." Come Boxing Day and Chairman Stan was on board Titan Ford Foxtel in the Sydney to Hobart. He was quoted in* The Herald-Sun *of December 29 as commenting: "This is what sailing is all about; you go out there to do battle with the elements and you do battle against your competitors."*

Last Saturday ABC Radio PNN played an interview between Zemanek and David Lord about the 1998 Sydney to Hobart. Chairman Stan told Lord that in such a situation, "there's nothing you can do" and went on to blame the Bureau of Meteorology for (allegedly) not providing the "right sort of information." He said it was time to "make people [ie weather forecasters] accountable." No suggestion of mutual obligation here. Rather Chairman Stan elected to blame someone else for his own predicament.

Of course, sailors in distress should be rescued. However, there was a disturbing air of insouciance among some of those associated with the CYCA during and after the 1998 Sydney to Hobart. Almost universally, CYCA personnel ran a "no regrets" line.

One CYCA operative, Peter Bush, simply dismissed a suggestion by a reporter on ABC Radio's AM that the taxpayers had an interest in how the race was conducted. Team Jaguar's skipper, Martin James, rejected all criticism of the CYCA and described its administration of the race as an "icon." Ed Psaltis skippered the winner on handicap AFR Midnight Rambler (which he described as a "brand new toy"). Psaltis told ABC Radio that, when sailing, you are "there on your own." He neglected to add — until, on occasions, rescuers arrive at taxpayers' expense.

In short, like John Howard, the 1998 Sydney to Hobart winner forgot that mutual obligation applies to yachties as well as everyone else. In time, governments may act on this sound principle.

Gerard Henderson, *executive director of the Sydney Institute*

* * *

I would not be the only reader of the Herald who was struck by the irony of Leo Schofield's emergence as an antagonist to the moneyed elite of the yachting fraternity.

Mr. Schofield is very wrong to suggest that yachting is just a rich man's sport. While it is true that many of the larger and faster yachts are owned and funded by wealthy individuals, a look at the make-up of crews tells another story. In my experience you are more likely to find an ordinary working man or woman as a crewperson on a yacht than a highly salaried banker or lawyer, and even the second group would reject the values of a rich elite in favour of human virtues that are not related to material wealth and social standing.

It is true also that for every maxi that goes to Hobart there are a dozen smaller boats kept on the water through a hardworking owner's overtime or some sacrifice to comfort elsewhere for the sake of executing a passion. For every sailor that goes to Hobart there are hundreds from the dozens of sailing clubs around Sydney alone, mostly ordinary working men and women, who are inspired by the event and perhaps hope one day to crew on a Hobart racer.

I think most people in this country can appreciate one or more of the arts and be sensitive to the humanity and spirituality and sometimes courage involved in the creation of a great work of art. I believe this prevails to no less extent among the likes of the Hobart sailors, who if they have only one virtue it is the ability to cut to the core of those things that are worthwhile in a fellow human being, because so often their lives will depend on that knowledge. I know those men and women respect the doers in their sport, the arts or any field of endeavour and they have little time for the passive commentator.

Before we call for a "deposit to cover the cost of the rescue," as Mr. Schofield suggests, let's hear from the rescue helicopter pilots and their crews who have earned the right to speak on the tragic events of last week.

Michael Cahill, *Manly*

* * *

In the aftermath of the Sydney-to-Hobart yachting disaster, the media and press have been full of accolades for the relief operation with much said about the heroism of helicopter crews who went to the aid of those in distress under difficult conditions. I am sure those involved appreciated the recognition for their efforts; and I have no doubt it was well deserved.

A year ago, similar rhetoric flowed in regard to the efforts of bushfire-fighting helicopter crews across Australia. Late last year, the community heard about wonderful efforts by flood-relief crews including helicopter operators. As one who has seen both the civil helicopter industry and the defense forces go to the aid of the community so many times over the past two decades, I am proud of the humanitarian service that helicopter operators have provided and cynical about the depth of the public gratitude.

Will anything be heard of the value of helicopters in civil emergencies the next time an urban heliport is proposed to a local council? Will anyone remember the rescued survivors who described the sound of an approaching helicopter as "music to my ears" when complaining about the noise from helicopters flying along an access corridor?

Will the same politicians who managed to get their name in the paper last week by praising the rescue helicopter crews as "reluctant

heroes" and "angels of mercy" be talking about "blowflies from hell,"
"rich boys' toys," "trail bikes of the sky" or "an abomination against a
civilized society" (as opponents of a Sydney CBD heliport described
the helicopter industry) when opposing some item of necessary helicopter infrastructure in the future?

The helicopter industry has become accustomed to "foul-weather
friendship," and doesn't really care about the accolades, because that is
not what motivates it. But the public should be aware that the ability of the helicopter industry to respond to civil emergencies depends
upon the existence of a viable fleet. Without heliports and helicopter
routes, those will simply not be available when they are needed.

Daniel E. Tyler
President, Helicopter Association of Australia, Granville
[Tyler piloted the helicopter that winched
the crew of Business Post Naiad.]

Pilot Dan Tyler, a Nebraska farm boy now living in Australia, made
the tough decisions in the Business Post Naiad rescue.

* * *

The 1998 Sydney-to-Hobart yacht race will long be remembered as a race in which six yachtsmen lost their lives participating in the sport that they loved.

The weather conditions faced by the fleet as it entered Bass Strait were some of the worst experienced during the race's long history. That more lives and yachts were not lost is a testament to the efforts of the organizations and individuals that contributed so much to the rescue efforts. In many cases, individuals courageously risked their own lives saving or attempting to save the lives of yachtsmen and women or yachts and crews in danger.

I speak for all competitors, their families and indeed the sailing community as a whole in recognizing and thanking those brave men and women who gave so selflessly in rendering assistance to our sailors. Our heartfelt appreciation must also go to the families of those involved in rescue operations, as they too would have suffered enormous stress during rescue operations, worrying about the safety of their loved ones.

It is clear that enlightened Australians (sailors and non-sailors alike) understand that the Sydney-to-Hobart race, like so many other sporting endeavours which include an element of risk, must be allowed to continue. It is a privilege, available to all citizens of this country, to be able to participate in responsibly administered "adventure" sports and activities secure in the knowledge that our social infrastructure provides for highly trained and sophisticated search and rescue facilities to be available during times of "misadventure."

The assistance also provided by communities and businesses, particularly on the South Coast of NSW, to yachts that had withdrawn from the race, speaks volumes for their community spirit in assisting those in distress.

On behalf of all competitors, their families and the Cruising Yacht Club of Australia, I would like to express our gratitude to all those that contributed, for their efforts and sacrifices, during the extraordinary circumstances of the race.

Hugo Van Kretschmar
Commodore, Cruising Yacht Club of Australia, Darling Point

* * *

I was reading the letters page on Saturday (Herald, *January 2*). *Some readers' justification for the rescue operation of the Sydney-to-Hobart yacht race was that since we already have the infrastructure of the navy, army, and air force, and that they would be idle, they could thus be used for this purpose, at no great expense to the taxpayer except basically for fuel and personnel cost.*

Is this the same excuse we use to have this infrastructure for the reasons of war, because it only costs additional fuel or personnel?

Kimon Karitakis, *Ryde*

* * *

This year's Sydney-to-Hobart race, albeit a tragedy for those who lost their friends and family, should not be a trigger for knee-jerk reactions which so often follow these and exploited "controversial" events. Mr Henderson's suggestion ("Yachties are all at sea when it comes to their obligations", Herald) *that the racers and organizers should perhaps bear (or even insure for) the cost of rescuing is ludicrous.*

Should bushwalkers take out a premium before lacing up their boots? Maybe unfit-looking beachgoers should be stopped and told that they are likely to be rescued and hence must pay a toll before placing thong on sand.

Clearly, as a community we contribute to facilities and services that we may use less than others, if at all, but that is the very notion of a community and should Mr. Henderson or any other choose to participate in an activity that may result in their subsequent rescue then they may do so without fear of government retribution and, hopefully, sans media condemnation.

Daniel Shore, *Cronulla*

* * *

The media reporting of the Sydney-to-Hobart tragedy has brought to the surface some disturbing facts that hopefully the inquiry by Peter Bush will address. It would appear that anyone can join a crew for the race with little or no sailing experience — even children.

Take 12-year-old Travis Foley from Mudgee, for example. It was reported he was invited to join Aspect Computing after he impressed the skipper with his enthusiasm after a social cruise on the harbour earlier in the year. I shiver at the risk that this boy was placed in.

Then there was Melissa McCabe, who won her place on Team Jaguar through a high school essay competition. The perils of her "hell" experience were reported by her in graphic detail in The Herald *(January 2). The Team Jaguar crew had to be rescued after the yacht was dismasted in the storms.*

It's all very well to have a rating system for design and equipment requirements for yachts, as well as a rating system for blue water

16-year-old Melissa McCabe from Eden is welcomed home by her grand-mother, Joan Mould.

events, but the rating of vessels and events only goes half way in ensur-ing the safety of entrants. What is in place to ensure that the capabil-ities of skippers and crew are up to the task in front of them? I am per-plexed that such an international event and sport is self- policing and that skippers are taken largely on trust about safety equipment and crew skills.

The Sydney-to-Hobart race is rated as a Category 1 event earned through reputation - this year's and 1993, for example. Only round-the-world races encountering icebergs are rated more dangerous.

I suggest that there should be an accreditation system for each crew member based on his or her blue water experience. A minimum age for crewing - over 18 years seems rational - should also be considered. Event organizers such as the CYC should protect themselves by implementing a scrutineering system to check the seaworthiness of vessels and the maintenance of safety equipment.

Greg Sheldon, *Daleys Point*

* * *

I was enthralled and my heart uplifted by Philip Cornford's article "Deliverance" in News Review (Herald, January 2). It told the story of the ineffable heroism, strength and endurance of the men involved in the rescue of the 53 yachtsmen from eight disabled yachts.

In particular, the story of the men in Careflight One who risked their lives to pull out seven men from Business Post Naiad. The paramedic, Murray Traynor, went down the wire into a terrifying maelstrom of wind and water not once but seven times and each time a man's life was saved. He could not have done this without the efforts of his pilot, Dan Tyler, and the winchman, Graeme Fromberg, in coordinating the winch and controlling the bucking helicopter as it hovered just above the waves.

The names of these men and their deeds should be emblazoned in our hearts and minds and celebrated in song and story. They are the stuff of legend and the hope of humanity.

Ruth de Montfort, *Balgowlah Heights*

* * *

Congratulations to Ed Psaltis and Bob Thomas on their win in the race. I have competed against them on various boats over the years and know them to run a fine campaign. Ignore Mr. Henderson, who no doubt profits from the disaster by receiving fees for his drivel.

Congratulations also to my skipper, the 19-year-old Liz Wardley from Port Moresby, who had no hesitation in turning around when needed, to shadow a boat returning to safety after being damaged. It took us half an hour to get the nose around through the wind. A dangerous manoeuvre in itself.

The HF radio locked on rescue and search matters for hours. It was both surreal and very real and in the appalling conditions I thought of Flinders and Cook and the thousands who pioneered our country and saw it all before us.

My friend Jim Lawler is gone. Hail, Jim.

Carl Sriber, *Dixie Chicken, Rose Bay*

Public opinion about the race, its outcome and the rescue ran the gamut. But expressed or implied, almost all concerns about the Sydney to Hobart came down to matters of safety:

- Are the safety requirements and equipment adequate?
- Are skippers and their crews fully qualified for the hazards they face?
- Are the boats designed and built for heavy weather?
- Should the race organizers exert more control over the race from start to finish?

In response, skippers and crew had two major contentions:

- The captain or skipper of a boat makes the ultimate decision about starting, continuing and finishing the race.
- The 1998 Sydney to Hobart was simply another sailing race that called for its own tactics, sailing skills and decision making.

Unlike almost every other ocean race of similar distance, the Sydney to Hobart is classified among the most dangerous, at Category 1. Categories 0 to 5 outline construction, design and safety requirements for types of races. Round-the-world races, where icebergs may be a hazard, are Category 0; most inshore weekend regattas are Category 4. Categories 0, 1 and 2, according to their definition, provide standards for "races of long distance and well offshore, where boats must be self-sufficient for extended periods of time, capable of withstanding heavy storms, and prepared to meet serious emergencies without expectation of outside assistance."

Against that backdrop lies the yacht racer's dilemma: to be faster or safer?

Tony Mooney, technical manager of the Australian Yachting Federation, recalls checking safety equipment on a Sydney to Hobart boat in the earlier days of the race.

"We had this skipper who said, yes, sure, he had a first-aid box, as required . . . . It was found to contain a half-empty pack of Band-Aids and a bottle of scotch."

Today all race entrants must sign a safety equipment compliance form for hundreds of items ranging from lifebuoys to bilge pumps, torches to foghorns, whistles to weather broadcast receivers.

"The question, of course, is how far you go in the interests of safety," said Mooney. "You could end up requiring boats to take so much safety gear to Hobart they'd need to tow a caravan behind to carry it all."

There were also questions about the ability of the boats to withstand the storm conditions of Bass Strait. Many of the Hobart yachts, including *Sayonara*, were built on Farr designs. The Annapolis, Maryland-based company is a familiar name to sailors worldwide for its cruising and racing yacht designs. Several months after the Sydney to Hobart race, Farr Vice President Russell Bowler insisted that the Farr-designed yachts in the race were equal to the task. "Well handled, they can survive those conditions and others," he said. Bowler repeatedly stressed "well handled" as the primary ingredient that allows racing yachts to compete in almost all sea conditions.

Others were less optimistic about the light, fast design of many of the boats in the Hobart fleet. Geoffrey Gibson, whose brother, John, narrowly survived when *Winston Churchill* sank, was a vocal critic of the fast boats.

"Some of these boats are too light — just great big 18-footers, out of their element at sea," he said. An experienced sailor, himself, Gibson added, "I have walked around some of them, seen their vital parts, showy flash tarts of the sea, knife-blade rudders, and keels, exposed and unprotected; a disaster waiting to happen, to be snapped off, with consequences too terrible to contemplate. Too much sail, they ride on the water and not in it."

While the scrutiny of the Sydney to Hobart race continued to build, survivors, their family members and friends, and relatives of those who perished in the race were coming to grips with the storm's toll.

Tony Mowbray, his crew and his yacht *Solo Globe Challenger* endured the longest ordeal of the 1998 Hobart. Smashed by a rogue wave Sunday that disabled the boat and most of the crew of eight, Mowbray and two remaining crewmen finally reached dry land late Tuesday. During his two-and-a-half-day epic, Mowbray sent injured crew aboard helicopters and ships while steadfastly refusing to abandon his boat to the sea. The working-class skipper had put his life savings and more into the 44-footer, and he planned to sail around the world to raise money for an Australian children's hospital.

Tony Perkiss, crewman rescued from the yacht Solo Globe Challenge

But for those aboard *Solo Globe Challenger,* their harrowing ordeal was more than just an escape from death. It was life-changing.

For crewman David Cook, one of the crew rescued earlier who was reunited with his wife Michelle and five children shortly after his rescue, the experience was life-affirming.

"It's made me a hell of a lot wiser and I think I'm a lot stronger mentally. I have a different outlook on life," he said.

Despite his ordeal, Cook said he was willing to attempt the race again, but only if accompanied by the same crew.

"Most of the guys, except two, had never met before and after this I can count them as close friends," he said. "We've been through a hell of a lot together in such a short time. I'd only try it again with the same guys because I know I'd be in safe hands. The Sydney to Hobart is the pinnacle for open-ocean sailors. It is very trying for both boat and crew. It's also about the thrill of it all and not only getting to the finishing line but finishing well."

Mowbray, deeply shaken by the experience, said that coming face-to-face with his own mortality has changed his thinking.

"It's been a fairly emotional time for me," Mowbray said shortly after the race. "It's tipped me over the edge, the emotional trauma and physical carnage. I look at people who have died. It's just a horrendous situation. We've all reassessed our lives. I know my wife and my young kids are my priorities now.

"It possibly may be my last [Sydney to Hobart]," he said, adding, "That thinking may change as time goes by. Like childbirth, don't women forget the bad bits and do it all again?" Mowbray's plans for an around-the-world sailing trip in October to raise funds for a children's hospital have also been put on hold.

A week after the race, Mowbray and his two young children were at Marmong Cove Marina to see the once proud *Solo Globe Challenger* arrive home in Newcastle battered, disheveled and dismasted on a truck.

Mowbray said he plans to do the extensive repairs to the storm-damaged yacht and continue sailing.

"It's a passion that will be with me 'til the day I die," he said. "What I will do is be far more selective in where and how I do my sailing."

For the friends and relatives of Bruce Guy and Phil Skeggs, who died aboard *Business Post Naiad,* it was a time of grief.

On Monday, the surviving crewmen of *Business Post Naiad* were winched to safety. But rescue helicopter pilot Dan Tyler, unwilling to further risk the lives of his crew in the wild seas, had ordered that Guy and Skeggs be left aboard the battered yacht. The bodies were secured and a tracking device was placed aboard to assist in locating the yacht and recovering the bodies.

The Sydney-based police boat *Nemesis* reached *Business Post Naiad* on Tuesday as it drifted about 100 miles northeast of Eden. The forlorn and battered yacht was towed through the night to an isolated cannery wharf in the small port of Eden. Away from onlookers on a gray morning, the last day of 1998, a small party of police removed the body of Bruce Guy from inside the hull, and the body of drowned crewman Phil Skeggs from the tangled rigging on the deck.

Back in Launceston, Tasmania, Phil Skegg's home, when first told that *Business Post Naiad* was in trouble, his father Joseph Skeggs initially expressed confidence that his son would pull through.

"I wasn't really concerned because the boat was a first-class boat," Joseph Skeggs, a retired policeman, said. "They stuck strictly to the safety regulations and everything like that. It wasn't haphazard, everything was spot-on. The conditions could get pretty rough but [Phil] never worried about it.

"He knew what to do. I thought he'd be able to swim, and being a diver he'd know how to hold his breath under water, but it was pretty treacherous, and you've only got to get hit in the head and get tangled up in the line underneath and you're history in about half a minute, and it would be freezing cold.

"This chap that owned the boat was his mate and his neighbor, just lived over the back fence. He sort of liked it, the yachting. It's just one of those unfortunate things, there's nothing you can do about it, but just think about it," he said.

Phil Skeggs was the father of 6-year-old Joshua and 9-year-old Kirsty. His daughter had told her dad she didn't want him to compete in the Sydney to Hobart race because it would mean he would be away for Christmas.

Guy's grieving family said that they took consolation in the fact that he died doing what he loved best.

"Dad loved sailing," son Mark Guy said. "He loved the competition. He also loved a beer and a talk after the race. Dad simply loved life."

It was Tuesday morning during his live television interview that *Winston Churchill* skipper Richard Winning learned that three of his crew had drowned after they were thrown from a life raft. A shaken Winning, who was lifelong friends with two of the drowned men, questioned his decision to start the race with bad weather ahead.

"If I'd known this was going to happen, I wouldn't have left Sydney," he said. "I've sailed with [John Dean and Michael Bannister] since we've been teen-agers. They've both got young families. I won't do it again — I won't sail again."

The third victim, Jim Lawler, died after he was washed off his life raft when it was struck by a mountainous wave early Monday morning. Lawler and Bannister's bodies were found Tuesday morning. Dean's body was never recovered.

Winston Churchill crewman Paul Lumtin, who was winched to safety along with Winning, said his 24-hour survival odyssey was a life-altering experience.

"I think it has, in a word, changed my life," he said. "I have to find some sort of meaning for this. And I know that some good will come of it, and I know that I'll be a better man for it. And I know that for the rest of my life I'll be thankful to be alive."

While Winning had to undergo the shock of learning the awful truth on national television, the families of the three who died suffered a roller-coaster of emotions from hope to despair.

Shortly after Winning and those on his life raft were rescued Monday afternoon, *Winston Churchill's* second life raft was spotted and signals were exchanged between the raft and rescue aircraft. Unaware that her husband had been washed off the raft and lost the night before, Shirley Bannister opened a bottle of champagne when told that her husband's raft had been spotted. Married for 22 years, the Bannisters were days away from a trip to Paris. Only hours after the champagne was corked, Shirley Bannister learned that there were only two survivors on the raft, John Stanley and John Gibson.

Noble and graceful even in the depths of her grief, Shirley Bannister said: "I married for better or sailing. I could understand his love of sailing. He was a wonderful man. I'm going to miss him terribly."

John Dean's 15-year-old son, Peter, who was planning on sailing with his father in the 1999 Sydney to Hobart, said his father's ashes would be spread at sea, as his father had wished.

"At least it looks like he is going to get his wish," Peter said. "At least he died doing something he loved."

The agonizing vigil to learn the fate of loved ones was also endured by relatives of those on Richard Winning's life raft, which included 19-year-old Michael Rynan.

When news of Michael Rynan's plight reached them Sunday night, Michael's parents were devastated. John Rynan, the teen-ager's father, said it was impossible to hold out hope for long, knowing the magnitude of the storm in Bass Strait.

"Mate, I'd given him up. I'd given my son up for dead," he said.

After a sleepless, tortuous night, on Monday afternoon John Rynan sent his wife to a friend's house while he waited by the phone. The instruction to the friend was to "knock her out with a few stiff scotches." He felt she'd need a good night's sleep to deal with the death of her son.

But despair turned into elation when news came Monday night that Michael had been winched to safety from the life raft where he and three others had spent more than 24 hours after *Winston Churchill* was destroyed by a massive wave.

"Jeez I feel good," John Rynan said. "It is an unbelievable feeling. I am a sailor and a realist, and while I didn't talk about it, in the back of my mind I was preparing for the worst, especially as dusk was approaching."

Before returning home to his parents and his room decorated with posters of famous yachts and his scores of sailing trophies, Michael Rynan said his brush with death in the 1998 Hobart will not discourage him from sailing or trying the Hobart again.

"I've sailed all my life. It is my life. I would never give it up," he said.

Halfway around the world, in England, the mother of Glyn Charles, the Olympic yachtsman washed overboard from *Sword of Orion,* had held out hope until the search was called off Monday night.

" . . . It is some comfort that if he is dead, it happened while he was sailing rather than in a road accident or something like that," she said.

Mrs. Charles said her only son, who was in Australia training with other British yachtsmen for the 2000 Olympics in Sydney, was expected home for Christmas and only entered the Sydney to Hobart at the last minute. She spoke to him for the last time on Christmas Eve.

"He phoned to say he was setting off in a few hours. He felt it was an opportunity. I always said if something happened to Glyn at sea, I'd feel that he was doing what he loved," she said.

As relatives of the dead grieved, many others with friends and relatives in the race breathed sighs of relief as news finally got through that yachts had reached Eden or other safe harbors. As heated as the public and press

An injured crewman from Sayonara is helped from the yacht onto the Hobart Docks.

criticism was, it paled in comparison to the anger of friends and relatives of race participants who had great difficulty getting information from race organizers. The media saturation of the race was such that friends and relatives often knew that a particular boat was in trouble before rescue authorities knew. Frantic telephone calls to learn the fate of the crew were often met with misinformation or a busy signal.

The crew of *Ausmaid,* a South Australia yacht that took third place in line honors, told race investigators that families seeking information were given a "cold shoulder" or told "straight out lies."

The 10 crewmen of *Loki* were equally upset by the quality of information available to relatives during the race. The 44-foot Finnish yacht imported by Steve Ainsworth of Sydney earlier in the year was knocked down to 180 degrees and heavily damaged by a rogue wave during the storm.

Sailing in 60-knot winds and 35-foot seas, the giant wave broke before it hit the boat, filling its trisail with water and turning *Loki* parallel to the oncoming wave. The wave heeled the yacht over to 140 degrees, with its mast pointing at the trough. The wave was so huge that when it capsized the yacht, *Loki's* 70-foot mast did not reach the water at the bottom of the wave. The boat then slid down the massive face of the wave, landing on its port side with such force that it ripped the cabin floorboards loose. *Loki* remained upside down for two minutes before it righted, with minor crew injuries.

The *Australian Financial Review* incorrectly reported that Ainsworth was winched off the stricken yacht. After reading the report, Ainsworth's wife made a frantic call to the race sponsor and was told that the boat had retired to Eden. At the time, *Loki* had not retired and Ainsworth remained on board. With no other information forthcoming, she and relatives of *Loki's* other crewmen were left with nothing more than worry and fretful speculation about loved ones at the height of the disaster.

Fingers quickly began to point at Lew Carter, the volunteer radio operator aboard *Young Endeavour.* With an HF radio and a VHF radio on which to send and receive radio traffic, Carter used a single HF frequency for nearly all radio traffic. As a result, the HF frequency quickly became overburdened as the storm's damage to the racing fleet increased. As well, an emergency HF antenna had to be installed on *Young Endeavor* within hours after the start of the race. Proper antenna installation is critical for the long-range capability of HF radio, and the rush installation impaired the radio's range. Operating with an overburdened frequency and a limited broadcast range, Carter was criticized by some race competitors for not restricting radio traffic to emergency calls. Most, however, were far less critical of his procedures than was the final investigation report.

Said Ed Psaltis, the skipper of *AFR Midnight Rambler:* "The man who did the radio work on *Young Endeavour*, Lew Carter, did the most unbelievable job the way he handled it all. I think he may have caught a bit of flak about it. But everybody I've spoken to said that he did just the most sensational job."

Scott Gilbert, the sailing master aboard *Wild Thing,* which was forced out of the race with a broken mast, agreed. "I listened to all of it. There wasn't much else to do after we pulled out, and I just don't know what he could have done better to make things better. He was professional, he didn't get emotional, he had people wait their turn. And that's all you could ever do in that situation. If you just let a free-for-all you're never going to get anywhere.

"I don't know how any one operator could have done any better than he did under the circumstances. I think he deserves a medal. I really do. If anything, they may have to devise a system where, if there's a lot of boats in distress, they have another radio operator. Its simply too much for one person. Lew Carter was responsible for getting the position fixes on the radio skeds. That was his job.

"I think the people who are a bit dark about him are the ones who feel that they didn't receive the attention that they should have received quickly enough. In the heat of the moment how do you decide which boat is in more danger than the other boat?"

As the controversy about the race built, many of the yachtsmen were still racing. Aboard *Sayonara* a battered and exhausted crew had worked for hours to fix the boat's mainsail. At the first hint of dawn Tuesday, the 80-footer rounded Tasman Island and began the last leg of what has become known as "The Great Race." *Brindabella*, like *Sayonara*, could do no better than maintain her pace overnight. She was 30 miles astern of the leader.

For the first time in more than 24 hours, *Sayonara* was under full sail. At 6:45 a.m. *Sayonara* cleared Storm Bay, which had bedeviled Ellison in the 1995 Hobart when the winds died, nearly costing him line honors. With her sails gilded by the sunrise, *Sayonara* entered the still waters of the Derwent River, where she and her crew were greeted by a flotilla of well-wishers. Overhead, a media helicopter recorded the winner's arrival. At the head of the flotilla was a bagpiper in full regalia wafting his eerie notes into the dawn in the tradition of welcoming the line-honors winner.

"We'd come up the Derwent," Ellison said, "and it was a beautiful sunrise in Tasmania. It really was absolutely gorgeous. It was a strange, somber moment because at the finish of the Sydney-Hobart, there's a small boat that pulls up next to you with a gentleman who plays the bagpipes. And here is this gorgeous, eerie sunrise in Tasmania as you're coming up the Derwent — it was a bit of a surreal experience — and you hear the bagpipes and the colors and the hues in the sky are absolutely gorgeous. Gorgeous pinks and roses and blues and the sound of the bagpipes and this big, beautiful boat under full main and #1 jib ghosting slowly up the river. It gave us all a chance to reflect on how beautiful and fragile life is. We were very glad to be out of the storm, to have made it through the storm and just to have finished the race.

Sayonara *on the run up the Derwent River to the finish*

Overleaf: *Race winning maxi, Sayonara, sails into Hobart to a muted welcome.*

"It was a life-changing experience."

As ~~*Sayonara* crossed the finish line at 8:03 a.m., the resonating *boom!*~~
~~of an army cannon saluted her finish, five hours off the record. Ellison and~~
~~his crew had survived a hard chance.~~

Brindabella crossed the finish line in second place three hours later.

For seafarers, Constitution Dock is the center of the port city of
Hobart, Tasmania, Australia's second-oldest city after Sydney. From the
dock, a patchwork of green and red tin roofs mark the suburbs on the
pine-green flanks of Mount Wellington. Hobart's downtown area is just a
few blocks from the waterfront, which is dominated by well-preserved
stone warehouses, old pubs and a longstanding open-air market.

The traditional champagne and fireworks welcome at Constitution
Dock was canceled, and Australian flags flew at half-mast in honor of the
race's six fatalities. As *Sayonara* slid to the dock and tied up, her entire
crew lined the deck, straining to see loved ones among the crowd. For
many in Hobart, the end of the Sydney to Hobart marks the beginning
of the New Year's celebration. It had been so for more than 50 years. Not
in 1998. The battering to the boat and its crew was evident, and party-
goers stood mute as the 23 crew drifted toward loved ones for quiet, emotional reunions.

"It was not a usual celebration, to say the least," Ellison said. "The
flags were at half mast, and when we pulled up to the dock the guys on
board the boat saw their wives, their girlfriends. I'm not sure there was a
dry eye on board the boat. There were a lot of people just saying, 'I'm
sorry, I'm sorry for having gone. I'm sorry to make you worry, and I'm
glad to be alive.'"

Ellison told the crowd of several hundred spectators and news media
that he counted himself lucky to have finished the race, which he
ascribed to his decision to flee the storm and get to the Tasmanian coast
at the right time.

"We got in under the lee of Tasmania, otherwise I'm not sure the boat would have lasted," the American software billionaire said. "We were not focused on the race. We were focused on getting the boat finished. Here. In one piece."

New Zealander Chris Dickson, *Sayonara's* principal helmsman, echoed Ellison, and said the race ceased to matter by Sunday afternoon, at the height of the storm.

"I speak for the entire crew of *Sayonara*. We're thinking about the boats that are still out there. We're not thinking too much about how we've done," he said.

Then Ellison made the comment that continues to anger many Australians, sailors and non-sailors alike.

"Right now I'm not anxious to go back again, not if I live to be 1,000," he said. "It was by far the toughest race I've ever done in my life. It was horrible."

The comment immediately divided the crew of *Sayonara*. Some race veterans agreed with Ellison and announced that 1998 would be their last. Others, such as crewman Lachlan Murdoch, the son of international media mogul Rupert Murdoch, was quick to come to the Sydney to Hobart race's defense. While conceding that the race was his toughest challenge ever, Lachlan Murdoch said sailing will continue to be his passion.

"One of the lessons it does teach is that you never come back here unless you're totally prepared and you've got a professional crew," the younger Murdoch said.

George Snow, the owner and skipper of *Brindabella*, clearly upset by Ellison's rejection of Australia's yachting icon, reacted with a tight-lipped "his call." Snow's comment was undoubtedly leavened by the fact that Ellison had just edged him out — for the second time — in the Sydney to Hobart.

It was impossible to find a crewman on *Brindabella* who did not take the storm in stride. All called it "business as usual." And although unofficial crew spokesman Geoff Cropley stopped short of criticizing Ellison, he took issue with his methods.

"They're certainly good competition," said Cropley. "But I find it difficult how they can just fly in, get to Hobart and grab their kit bag and get on the next plane out and not hang around for lunch or a few drinks and reflect on the race. But that's the nature of professional sports. They're paid to do a job and they're very good at it and that's their living. They get paid for that event and then they're off to the next event. On *Brindabella* we're all mates, a bunch of guys who are good sailors. We pay our own way and have a good time."

Like Cropley, *Wild Thing's* Scott Gilbert agreed that the race was business as usual.

Bravado?

"I don't think it is bravado," Gilbert said. "I've done 11 Hobarts and I've seen stronger winds and I've seen bigger seas. But I think that certainly there's a period of time when, if you're in the wrong spot where the breeze builds quickly and the seas build quickly without a chance to expand, it's dangerous. There's just no distance between the waves and they just get so steep."

"Now there was a short period of time, four or five hours, I think, when the seas were really dangerous until the wind was consistently strong and the waves stretched out a bit. And that's where the problems were. It's not the height of the sea, it's the fact that the waves don't have any backs. I'm convinced that is the case. And I think that was the situation late Sunday afternoon in the '98 Hobart."

But for Ellison's rejection of the race, Gilbert pulled no punches.

"I think [big boats and professional crews] are great for the race," he said. "We attract international yachts, famous yachts that most people only ever get to read about. The big boats create a lot more media interest for the race, simply because they're there. And that's great for attract-ing sponsors, which makes the race bigger.

"What I really don't like is when someone gets to Hobart and says 'This is the worst bloody race I've ever been in and I'm never coming back.' That guy should get seriously kicked up the ass, because it's just not on. Regardless of what he thinks about it, it's not up to him to tell the world that the race is no good and that nobody should ever come and do it and that he'd never do it again. There are a lot of people who are pretty unhappy with his comments. I just think he needs a reality check. And when he went back to America and said the same thing after saying it after getting off the boat in Hobart — I just don't think it's the right thing to do."

At 3 p.m., the 50-footers *Ausmaid* and *Ragamuffin* rounded Tasman Island and began an unrelenting neck-and-neck duel up the Derwent River for third place. Four hours later, the South Australia yacht *Ausmaid* crossed the finish line. *Ragamuffin,* sailing out of Sydney, crossed the line exactly nine minutes later. With their handicaps, *Ausmaid* and *Ragamuffin* would later be named the 1998 Sydney to Hobart second- and third-place overall winners, respectively. On handicap, *Sayonara* took fifth place; *Brindabella* came in ninth.

In sharp contrast to the duel between *Sayonara* and *Brindabella,* there was congeniality between the skippers of *Ausmaid* and *Ragamuffin,* their close finish notwithstanding. Syd Fischer, the skipper of *Ragamuffin* and a veteran of 30 Sydney to Hobart races, said, "Congratulations to their crew and ours."

At the 2 p.m. radio sked, *Aspect Computing* and *Midnight Rambler* were off the south end of Tasmania's Maria Island, some 30 miles from Storm Bay and the last leg of the race.

As night closed in on the fourth day of the Sydney to Hobart, Ed Psaltis and the crew of *Midnight Rambler* were poised to become the first boat less than 40 feet to win the race on overall handicap in a decade. David Pescud of *Aspect Computing* and his crew were positioned for a single-digit finish, which would be the best-ever finish for the Sailors with disAbilities program. Crewman Cathy Josling had sent this email message to race organizers at "Telstra Control" only hours earlier.

> "It is 12:30 on Tuesday and we are approximately 45 miles from Tasman Island. We have our spinnaker up and are going around 9 knots. The wind is 12 knots and is coming from the northwest.
>
> "All is going really well — we are currently having gourmet toasted sandwiches, which the chefs are kidding us, are made with bread with a slight greenish tinge. They are joking, I'm sure? However the crew are questioning the missing pieces in the bread. Jack and Travis are the chefs and they are doing an excellent job.
>
> "On the serious side of things, the crew on watch are really working hard to get us there as quick as possible, trimming the kite with great concentration.
>
> "Jack had to take a trip up the mast recently to retrieve a spinnaker halyard which opened unexpectedly. The kite was swiftly recovered.
>
> "The boat is a little wet and smelly and some are looking forward to their first shower in Hobart.
>
> "We are waiting for the Tasmanian sunshine to greet us and we are already having bets on our ETA in Hobart — some optimists say 11:30 tonight and the pessimist says 9:30 Wednesday morning.
>
> "While the crew of Aspect Computing roll down the Tasmanian coast under spinnaker, their thoughts go back to two nights ago when the world was a different place. Their wishes, thoughts and hopes are with those seamen who are missing, and their loved ones."

Regards,
Cathy Josling for the yacht *Aspect Computing*

Aspect Computing *skipper David Pescud aboard the boat at the*
Cruising Yacht Club of Australia

"I was very happy to beat Sayonara on hand-icap. They were the best in the world and paid to do it. We were just the amateurs. So it was very satisfying to me to beat them."

—Ed Psaltis, skipper *Midnight Rambler*

Day Five: *The Finish of a Lifetime*

A t 5:04 Wednesday morning, Ed Psaltis and the crew of *Midnight Rambler* crossed the finish line, becoming the first boat of less than 40 feet to win the Sydney to Hobart overall in a decade. Psaltis, worn and haggard from the ordeal, had learned only a short time earlier of the extent of the storm's damage to the fleet and of the death of his father's close friend Jim Lawler, a crewman on ill-fated *Winston Churchill*.

Accustomed to finishing much farther back in the pack, Psaltis said, "It feels funny being the only boat in Constitution Dock" as *Midnight Rambler* took the first position in an otherwise empty dock. After a reunion with his wife, Sue, who had flown to Hobart out of concern for her husband, brother and brother-in-law, all who were on board, Psaltis told the press:

"We try to win every year, but it's a very, very tough race to win. It's like climbing Mount Everest. You need luck to win it.

"The loss of life is a terrible thing. We heard about it after the gale and we were just getting over the fact that we managed to survive it. We heard on the radio that there were boats lost and people in the water. And in these conditions that usually means that they're dead. It's a very sobering thing to hear.

"But what can you do? We just kept on and kept racing. But it's changed our opinion of what we've been through. Once it was just a gale that we survived. But now it's something else. Very sad."

In his downtown office 23 floors above Sydney Harbor four months later, Psaltis was still awed by his and his crew's accomplishment. Behind his desk hangs a large framed photograph of *Midnight Rambler* at the height of the storm in Bass Strait. Under a scrap of storm jib, the 35-footer hangs off the side of a steep wave, held only by its keel as Force 11 winds whip the sea into a white fury. What does the 1998 Hobart overall mean?

"It means a hell of a lot to me. It's something I've wanted to achieve for a long time. So it's a dream come true. It's very satisfying, deeply satisfying. I'll keep doing the Hobart but I don't think it will have the same feeling, obviously having won. It would be nice to win it again."

After 15 Hobarts, 39-year-old Ed Psaltis had accomplished what his father had set out to do. But in 20 Hobarts, the senior Psaltis had come close only once, never winning. Ed Psaltis said his overall win was particularly sweet, considering the competition.

"I don't have any grudge against Ellison or the maxis," he said. "They're in a different ballpark than me. I think it's great for the Hobart that we get an international field and flavor. As far as the boat itself, I was very happy to beat *Sayonara* on handicap. They were the best in the world and paid to do it. We were just the amateurs. So it was very satisfying to me to beat them."

Psaltis' accomplishment did not go unnoticed by his seagoing peers, many of whom were equally stunned by *Midnight Rambler's* win over much larger boats.

"I think it's fantastic, a remarkable bit of sailing," said Scott Gilbert, a Hobart veteran who has sailed the event several times in small boats.

"It's a lot harder in a smaller boat," he said. "For one thing, it takes longer in a smaller boat so you're in the bad conditions longer. And the

12-year-old Travis Foley, skipper David Pescud (center) and the rest of the crew of Aspect Computing celebrate their ninth place finish in the 1998 Sydney to Hobart.

motion of the boat is much more extreme. There are less people so you have to do more yourself, where if you're on a big boat with 20 people, nobody has to contribute a lot. On a small boat with six people, everyone has to contribute a lot. Otherwise it doesn't work.

"The guys in the small boats deserve a lot of credit for what they do. Without them you wouldn't have a race."

Aspect Computing, with skipper David Pescud and a crew of blind sailors, dyslexics and amputees beat *Midnight Rambler* across the finish line by 36 minutes. But, sailing in a different division than the smaller *Midnight Rambler, Aspect Computing* took first in two other divisions. Pescud and his crew were elated.

"Wow! Ninth across the line in the Hobart? In a 50-footer? With a bunch of weirdos? That's not bad," he said. "That's first in division and first in bluewater!

"It was the team, the crew. It really was. I left here thinking that I had six good sailors that I could rely on, and when the storm hit I found out that I had 12 good sailors. Everybody kept working, they just kept going.

"Somebody asked me where we go from here.

"Line honors."

Thirty-four more boats remained on the course. The last to finish, the Victorian yacht *Misty*, brought the curtain down on the 1998 Sydney to Hobart two days later, on January 1, 1999 at 6:39 p.m.

*"Oh Lord, thy sea is so vast,
and my ship is so small."*

—Richard Winning, skipper *Winston Churchill*

A Proper Sendoff for the Dead

On January 1, thousands of Tasmanian's long accustomed to raucous New Year's festivities instead stood in quiet ranks around Hobart's small harbor. The sun shone brightly on Constitution Dock at 2:30 p.m. and on the solemn group of 75 friends, relatives, fellow yachtsmen and clergy that had assembled to "farewell" the six men killed in the Sydney to Hobart race.

Against the amplified strains of Christopher Cross' *Sailing,* friends and relatives of the six who died spoke in choked voices and through sobs of their loss and their memories.

As aircraft streaked overhead — many of which participated in the Sydney to Hobart rescue — in salute, Monsignor Phillip Green, the leader of the memorial service, took the lectern.

"The fleet was ripped apart by the awesome power of nature. We who live by the sea and depend on it know with the yachties its beauty and its power," he said.

For each man who died, a relative or friend quietly cast a floral arrangement — a garland of white daisies surrounding a single red rose — on the waters of the harbor. As the wreaths grew in number and bobbed on the surface, many in the ceremony and the crowd were overcome.

With muted church bells ringing, Hugo van Kretschmar, commodore of the Cruising Yacht Club of Australia, offered:

"We will miss you always. We will remember you always. We will learn from the tragic circumstances of your passing. May the everlasting voyage you have now embarked on be blessed with calm seas and gentle breezes. May you never have to reef or change a headsail in the night. May your bunk always be warm and dry."

As the last wreath was set adrift by Richard Winning, the skipper of *Winston Churchill*, who lost three crew, he looked skyward and said:

"Oh Lord, thy sea is so vast, and my ship is so small."

Twenty-four hours later, in a unique tribute to those lost in the race, the combined Sydney to Hobart, Melbourne to Hobart and Tasmanian yachting fleets began the traditional King of the Derwent yacht race.

Slated for cancellation out of respect for the six who died, the race was allowed to go ahead after participants convinced yacht club officials that there was no more appropriate way to remember their fellow sailors.

"We're sailing for our mates," the yachtsmen said.

Chris Dicks sheds a tear as his crew reflects on lost fellow sailors.

Six wreaths commemorating the victims of the 1998 race bob in the water off Constitution Dock in Hobart.

"It's only a yacht race. It's not a race to the death."

—Peter Joubert, skipper *Kingurra*

Olympic City Epilogue: *The Investigation*

Almost immediately after the last boat crossed the finish line in the 1998 Sydney to Hobart race, the Cruising Yacht Club of Australia launched an investigation of the race. Seven investigators headed by Peter Bush, a former CYCA commodore, dissected the race component by component to learn what went wrong. The panel was comprised of sailors who all had vast ocean-racing experience, particularly in the Sydney to Hobart.

When completed four months later, the Australian press dismissed the 160-page report as a means for the CYCA to absolve itself of any blame and protect the continuity of the Sydney to Hobart race. But what the investigators learned is quickly becoming the international textbook of offshore racing safety, race qualification requirements and sea-rescue procedures. The Miami Yacht Club was the first to order a copy of the report, followed by dozens of others worldwide.

Because the storm that decimated the Hobart fleet sprang up with little warning, weather forecasting was a primary focus of the investigation. And the Bureau of Meteorology came in for harsh criticism. But, at least in the daily press, the Meteorology Bureau sought to blunt the criticism by issuing its own exhaustive report days before the CYCA report. Forecasters insisted they were not to blame for the yachting disaster.

Like all major yacht races worldwide since 1875, the Sydney to Hobart operated under the five fundamental Racing Rules of Sailing, first published by Britain's Royal Yachting Association. They are:

1. Competitors are required to render all possible assistance to any person or vessel in danger. They shall carry adequate life-saving equipment as required by the rules.
2. They shall compete in a sportsmanlike manner.
3. They will sail by the rules and accept the penalties imposed therein.
4. A boat is solely responsible for deciding whether or not to start or to continue racing.
5. Performance enhancing drugs are banned.

In such a race, the sponsoring yacht club may add requirements or rules, but it cannot change or delete the five principal Rules of Racing. The Sydney to Hobart is a Category 1 ocean race, which again is defined as: "A race of long distance and well off shore, where boats must be self-sufficient for extended periods of time, capable of withstanding heavy storms and prepared to meet serious emergencies without the expectation of outside assistance."

To make the Sydney to Hobart a race that any boat can win, various handicap classes are used. For example, Ed Psaltis' 35-foot *Midnight Rambler* cannot compete head-to-head with a boat such as 80-foot *Sayonara*, which has larger sails and goes much faster. For most handicaps, hull shape, rigging, length and other factors are used to calculate a handicap. The boat's handicap is used to calculate its race finishing time, a process similar to calculating a handicapped golf score: actual score minus handicap equals score.

Eligibility for the 1998 Sydney to Hobart race was limited to boats 30 feet and longer with a documented ability to right themselves from a 115-degree knockdown. Boats with a stability index of 110 degrees that had sailed in previous Sydney to Hobarts were "grandfathered" if they remained unmodified. All boats were required to have life vests and life rafts for all aboard. For the 1998 race, there were no standards outlining the type of life rafts boats must carry. But the rafts used had to be certified as operable every year. High-frequency radios, flares and fire extinguishers were required, as was an auxiliary engine. Half of the members of each crew were required to have competed in one Sydney to Hobart or similar race. Each boat had to be covered by $10 million in liability insurance.

When the fleet of 115 yachts set off on December 26, senior forecasters in the Meteorology Bureau's Sydney and Melbourne offices had been trying for days to come up with a definitive forecast for the race. Recent budgets cutbacks had left forecasters with essentially no weather instruments in Bass Strait. For current conditions, they depended almost entirely on weather data from the Esso Kingfish B oil platform in the strait, which is well-equipped for gathering weather data. To assemble a forecast, state meteorologists depended on regional and international computer models. The technology, which is in world-wide use, assimilates current weather data, primarily from satellite photographs, and provides likely forecasts. Meteorologists use the computer's forecast scenarios to arrive at their final conclusions — the weather forecast.

As in years past, the Meteorology Bureau extended special services to the CYCA for the 1998 Sydney to Hobart race. These services, for which the yacht club paid, included pre-race weather briefings and access to senior forecasters any time during the race.

The first official briefing was held at the CYCA two days before the race. At the briefing, according to the Bureau of Meteorology (BOM) report: "The general information provided during this briefing centered around weather conditions along the race course that could pose problems to competitors." The BOM briefing also pointed to other sources for weather information, and issued a couched warning that a low front was forming off Gabo Island.

By the time of that briefing, the only weather briefing skippers were required to attend, the BOM knew a severe low front was likely to form, but its forecasters did not know where. "The various computer models available to New South Wales forecasters at the time were not conclusive regarding the evolution of weather patterns for the race," the BOM report said. The forecast offered covered December 26 to 29. And, the report added, "the outlook is based on limited data and will have to be fine-tuned."

Private weather consultant Roger "Clouds" Badham, who has provided weather forecasts for Sydney to Hobart racing yachts and commercial shipping in Australia for 20 years, attended the December 24 BOM briefing at the yacht club.

"I have to say that on this occasion the stand of the briefing from the bureau's representative was very poor. For an approximately 20-minute period, nearly every weather feature that could possibly develop along the various sections of the race track was discussed. Most of this was quite superfluous to the task and only in the last few minutes were the actual forecast conditions addressed, and then the bureau's representative stated that as the models were presently disagreeing with outcome, he would only give the briefest of outlooks and that everyone would have to wait until the morning of the race. While the uncertain statement is true, there had been some consistency over the days leading up to the morning of the briefing. In my opinion, it would have been much more beneficial for the audience had he focused on the three most-likely outcomes as indicated by the models," Badham said in his post-race review of the 1998 Sydney to Hobart.

Cruising Yacht Club of Australia Commodore Hugo van Kretschmar (Left) and past CYCA Commodore Peter Bush, who headed the yacht club's race investigation, announce the probe and field questions from the press. Citing prudent seamanship, van Kretschmar was one of the first to pull out of the 1998 race and take shelter in the port of Eden. Bush initially said future Sydney to Hobart races may be canceled, but the investigation report did not recommend such a measure. Instead, the report recommended more stringent safety requirements, increased crew training and better weather forecasting as chief means to make the yachting classic safer.

At 4:29 a.m. on race day, the BOM issued its first race-day forecast, which it updated to a gale warning along the race course at 9:04, four hours before the Sydney to Hobart starting gun.

"On Boxing Day, 26 December, the first special race weather forecast was issued at 4:29 a.m. This was the first issue of the special forecasts that were faxed to the CYCA as well as to the *Young Endeavour*," according to the BOM report.

"The 9:04 a.m. issue of the race forecast updated the 4:29 a.m. issue by including a gale warning for waters south from Broken Bay. The warning, based on computer model output, was forecasting south to southwest winds with mean speeds in the 30 to 35 knots range with stronger gusts. Competitors were also warned that the strong to gale force SW/W winds would persist south of Jervis Bay over Sunday and would start to moderate over Monday evening," the report said.

This was the last forecast all of the Sydney to Hobart racers got before starting the event, and it has become controversial. The controversy stems from Badham's comments in his report that the BOM based its forecasts on stale information in a weather situation that changed by the hour.

"I believe that the timing of the official race forecasts is particularly pertinent. The BOM scheduled their race forecasts to be issued at 2 a.m. and 2 p.m. during the race period," Badham says in his report, which is part of the CYCA investigation report, "On most occasions the forecast was actually issued [between midnight and 1 a.m. and again between noon to 1 p.m.] local time. This is a particularly poor time for a number of reasons.

"Firstly, the numerical product that the forecasters use as a guidance is run twice daily at the BOM; namely at 11 a.m. and 11 p.m. local time. That is the time that the [computer] models are actually initialized and run. The product from these models becomes available at around 12:20 p.m. to 1 p.m. and 12:30 p.m. to 1 a.m.

"As such, it seems to me to be impossible that any of those forecasts could have used the latest available [computer model] guidance. There are no significant observations made at midnight local time so that detailed analysis is done at 9 p.m. and 3 a.m. local time.

"This means that the forecast issued at 2 a.m. is prepared on old observations and old analysis and old [computer model] guidance."

As the race began, the BOM finally got its computer models to agree that a dangerous storm was developing off Eden. The bureau issued the storm warning with winds of 45 to 55 knots to the CYCA, the radio-relay vessel *Young Endeavour* and to coastal radio stations an hour after the Sydney to Hobart race began.

Badham, who had provided detailed forecasts warning of the storm and its location to 20 yachts in the Sydney to Hobart, was critical of the BOM's tardiness in forecasting the storm.

"The general development and situation was well forecast by the [computer] models, but until December 26, there was a great deal of uncertainty about the actual location of the low-pressure system," he said in his report. Badham added that the lack of a marine weather station off the New South Wales coast, the most densely populated area of the country, impairs the accuracy of BOM reports. " . . . I frequently read coastal waters forecasts that are either wrong, poor and often at odds with their other forecasts. It is an area that requires addressing within the BOM to improve their product for sailors all around Australia."

Even with the storm warning issued, skippers and crew were not prepared for the stronger winds and much higher seas than were forecast. In questionnaires returned by nearly all 115 entrants, 90 percent of skippers said they inferred from the BOM forecast that wind and sea conditions would be "slightly stronger or slightly less strong than forecast."

The BOM report said skippers and navigators in the Sydney to Hobart fleet should have known better.

"It is known that wind gusts will cause temporary fluctuations about this *mean* and that maximum gusts of up to 40 percent above the forecast mean wind may be observed. Therefore with a forecast of 45 to 55 knots, regular gusts of around 70 knots were likely," the BOM report said.

Similarly, the BOM defended its prediction of wave heights accompanying the storm. "It should be noted that while forecasts and observations of waves are for the significant wave height [the average height of 33 percent of the highest waves], individual waves approaching twice that size can be expected to occur," the report said.

Badham, who had been restrained in his criticism of the BOM's weather forecasting, took off the gloves in his response: "I would suggest that the race forecasts for sea state were ultra-conservative. A wind speed of about 50 knots for 9 hours can theoretically produce a significant wave height of at least 9 to 10 meters, without taking into account shallowness, the 'in phase' development or the opposing currents. Using the old trusted [means] for calculating a developing sea under certain fetch and time constraints show that 10-meter seas should have been expected in Bass Strait. It would seem perhaps obvious that in future forecasts that the role of forecasting the Bass Strait section of the race be given to the Victorian [Meteorology Bureau] Office."

Eighty-two of the Sydney to Hobart yachts had a dedicated navigator aboard trained in forecasting techniques. Not a single one was aware of the BOM's assertion that wind gusts and wave heights could far exceed the forecasts. Crews of the other 33 boats were in the dark, too, according to the CYCA report.

Twenty-eight of the 1998 Sydney to Hobart yachts were singled out for special attention by CYCA investigators, most because they were knocked down, required rescue or had a crewman killed. *Bright Morning Star* was one of them.

Skipper Hugh Trehearne, a veteran ocean racer, reacted like many of the skippers interviewed about the weather forecasting for the Sydney to Hobart.

"At 2 p.m. on the 27th," Trehearne said, "we were taking 55 knots of wind across the bow. The [BOM] forecast must have been for a different sea than we were in."

Running under a deeply reefed mainsail in a constant 60-knot wind, *Bright Morning Star* was knocked down by a huge wave that put her mast in the water and injured three crewmen. After a treacherous overnight passage under bare poles and motor, Trehearne and his crew made it to the shelter of Eden Monday morning.

Brindabella crewmen told investigators that BOM forecaster Ken Batt's race-day weather briefing was a "circus" event that came across as "how to sail a Hobart [race]" rather than a weather briefing. They recommended meteorology consultant Roger Badham's inclusion in future pre-race weather briefings. And like many, the crew of the second-place finisher expressed disappointment with the CYCA's Internet Web site. The Web site was jammed during the race by skippers, crew, relatives and friends desperate to get weather updates and news of their friends and loved ones. In many cases, erroneous information was given to relatives, causing them further anxiety. *Brindabella's* crew summed it up for investigators: "Web site sucks."

The skipper and senior crewman of the 40-year-old ketch *Canon Maris* told yacht club investigator Greg Halls that the BOM's pre-race weather briefing "was too flippant, and the weather bureau should have a more professional approach."

Sydney Skipper Ian Kiernan and Richard "Sightie" Hammond are considered two of Australian yacht racing's senior statesmen. Hammond, sailing his 40th Sydney to Hobart in 1998, told investigator Halls that at the height of the December storm he "had never seen current or sea conditions of such confusion and magnitude in 39 previous Sydney-Hobarts."

As they neared Bass Strait early Sunday, *Canon Maris* was close reaching with a #4 jib and a reefed mizzen in 35- to 50-foot seas, with westerly winds of 60 knots. Extensive sail damage forced Kiernan and his crew of six out of the race Sunday afternoon.

Victorian yacht *Jubilation*, with a crew of experienced ocean racers that averaged 58 years old, survived the weather the old-fashioned way — by knowing what the barometer was telling them. Crewmen told lead CYCA investigator Peter Bush that the boat's navigator had been plotting weather patterns for three months prior to the race and correctly predicted the track of the storm. But, they added, "You did not need a weather forecast if you watched the barometer."

As agreed upon before the race, *Jubilation* was steered to shelter before the height of the storm, and the crew rode the worst of the storm out at anchor. At 4 a.m. Monday, they resumed racing for Hobart under a quadruple-reefed mainsail and a #4 jib in rough but manageable seas. *Jubilation* crossed the finish line at 1:52 p.m. on the last day of 1998 and took third place in her division.

Similarly, Tasmanian skipper John Bennetto of the yacht *Mirabooka*, depended on his own knowledge and seamanship from 38 previous Hobarts to see his boat through to a 21st-place finish. "I take notice of the forecasts but I don't treat them as gospel," he said after the race. "In my opinion, modern society relies too much on technology."

Bennetto said *Mirabooka* went into "safety mode" early in the 1998 Sydney to Hobart and sailed an easterly "outside" course to avoid the worst of the storm. Forecasts were received three times a day, but Bennetto said he watched the barometer and relied on his own weather experience, especially when his barometer "dropped like a stone" on Sunday.

Sailing in such conditions as the 1998 Sydney to Hobart, he said, is like driving a twisting mountain road after dark.

"Every corner in the road brings a new problem in the way the seas are uneven. No textbook tells you how to drive or how to sail," he said.

A Sydney to Hobart skipper and finisher in 1984, 1993 and 1998, years when 60 percent of the boats have been forced to retire, Bennetto dismissed the forecasting controversy of the 1998 event.

"In 1997, we were heading toward Eden and 40-knot winds were forecast and they didn't come," he said. "Later the gauge hit over 60 knots but we were prepared for the squall even though it was harder and later than forecast. I didn't go and belly-ache to the weather bureau."

Not so the crew of *Midnight Special,* who were all winched aboard helicopters after the yacht was rolled and dismasted. They were especially critical of the BOM's pre-race weather briefing, calling it "a farce, a comical approach to serious information" in the CYCA investigation report.

The eight veteran crew of *New Horizons,* a 36-foot Victorian sloop, said the BOM "under-forecast" the storm. And, according to CYCA investigator Roger Hickman, "Had they heard of other vessels' situations, they may well have turned back earlier, as they felt they sailed blissfully into these abhorrent conditions."

New Horizons was knocked down three times by huge waves, once near midnight on Sunday, and again at dawn on Monday. After the second knockdown, which injured half of the crew, the yacht was headed for the shelter of Eden. Within an hour, things got worse.

According to Hickman: "The on-watch, who were still harnessed in shortened tethers, heard and saw a massive roller coming through. The helmsman put the helm hard down, swung the boat through some 90 degrees and met the wave about head-on. By this stage, the vessel was in the white water and simply slid down the front of the wave. The speed climbed enormously, and the boat vibrated as if it was surfing backwards down the face of the wave. The boat was then engulfed with white and green water, rolled heavily and came out the other side."

A police boat met the cold and injured crew off Eden late Monday and towed *New Horizons* to port.

Sword of Orion skipper Rob Kothe, whose boat was destroyed and his British helmsman Glyn Charles drowned, left it with the ominous rhetorical question: "How can you get something upwind in 80 knots of wind?"

While focusing on weather forecasting, the CYCA investigation report also scrutinized the yacht club's own procedures as the race organizer. The report identified serious flaws chiefly in required safety equipment, pre-race documentation of boat safety standards, communications with yachts during the race, the lack of an emergency-management plan and its ability to quickly contact next of kin.

Within its wide scope, the investigation looked at such large issues as the alleged predisposition of lighter, faster boats to get knocked down in storm conditions. It concluded that no boat that met the design criteria for the Sydney to Hobart was more or less prone to knockdown. But investigators failed to address the fact that many of the lighter, faster boats could not be slowed down adequately in the storm's high winds, even under bare poles. In several instances, yachts that could not be slowed sustained hull and rigging damage from launching off steep waves and broachings. Such situations may have been preventable in a boat of older design that pushes through the water rather than skimming across its surface.

Smaller matters were also examined. For example, the probe identified the danger of lashing a broken spinnaker pole down the middle of the foredeck, which was the practice of several boats. The result during a capsizing is that crew cannot escape the boat through the forward deck hatch, which is typically located on a boat's centerline.

Storage batteries that use liquid rather than gel became a hazard to several boats that capsized and the acidic, acrid fumes from the batteries filled the cabin, the report said. Certain bulky life vests worn on deck during high winds and waves endangered more crewman than they helped. Nylon webbing used on some boats for "rat line," to which safety lines were attached, was found to stretch too much and be useless, if not dangerous.

Life vests with built-in safety harnesses were found to be dangerous, as in the case of *Kingurra* crewman John Campbell, who was wearing one when he slipped out of it and was cast adrift wearing only long underwear.

Kingurra's skipper Peter Joubert was one of the few in the race who were openly critical of race organizers.

"The race organizers weren't properly in touch with what was going on out there," Joubert said after several weeks in the hospital. "It's only a yacht race. It's not a race to the death."

In its report, the CYCA announced a host of changes for the 55th Sydney to Hobart in 1999, on the eve of the new century, when Sydney will host its first Olympic games in 2000.

Race organizers are expecting the largest number of yachts ever. The decision to race or continue racing remains with the boat.

Sword of Orion *skipper Rob Kothe, whose boat was destroyed and his British helmsman Glyn Charles was drowned. Kothe broke with racing protocol during the second day of the race and reported 70 knot winds and huge seas to the entire fleet. The CYCA's investigation report recommended that such reports should be mandatory in future races.* Sword of Orion *was heading for shelter when it was struck by a huge wave that washed Charles overboard. Despite a massive search for nearly three days, the 33-year-old's body was never found.*

Chronology of Events

The following chronology of the race was taken from the CYCA Report of the 1998 Sydney Hobart Race Review Committee May 1999. The report was established using a number of sources including the RRV Radio Log, notes from the CYCA situation room in Sydney and Hobart and encompasses the time period 26 December (1300 hours) until 29 December 1998 (1700 hours). Details in this chronology may not be completely accurate.

note: SKED is a shortened term meaning schedule.

DATE	TIME	EVENT
26/12/98	1300	Race start
	2000	**Sked 1**
	2126	ABN Amro reports rudder damage, retires
	2236	Sledgehammer reports broken steering cable, retires
	2330	Challenge Again Man Overboard (MOB)
	2337	Sydney reports rudder damage, retires
	2346	Challenge Again retrieved MOB, all ok
	2348	Alexander of Creswell offers assistance re ABN, is advised all under control
27/12/98	**0300**	**Sked 2**
	0515	King Billy taking water, retires
	0532	Innkeeper lost life raft overboard
	0602	Allusive reports problem keel, heading towards land for repair
	0615	Wild Thing rig damage, retires
	0650	Marchioness rig damage, retires
	1000	Team Jaguar dismasted, motoring back to Eden
	1013	Assassin via Allusive retires
	1035	Tartan heading to Eden for shelter
	1102	Red Jacket retires
	1141	Innkeeper sail damage, retires
	1235	Doctel Rager reports severe weather ahead, winds 50-60 knots, gusts 70+knots
	1250	Secret Mens Business, Wild One & She's Apples II also advise of severe weather
	1329	Secret Mens Business heading to Eden for shelter
	1332	Wild One heading to Eden for shelter
	1334	Henry Kendall heading to Eden for shelter
	1335	Sea Jay heading to Eden for shelter
	1336	She's Apples II heading to Eden for shelter
	1346	Indian Pacific heading to Eden for shelter
	1400	**Sked 3**; Sword of Orion advises fleet of extreme winds of 50-70 knots, gusting up to 80 knots

DATE	TIME	EVENT
27/12/98	1400	(contd.) ahead; Elysion Blue, Maglieri Wines, Wide Load, Kickatinalong retire; Team Jaguar's engine disabled (rope around propeller) after knockdown; Polaris & Bobsled seeking shelter
	1415	VC Offshore Stand Aside (VCOS) rolls 360°, Miintinta retires for Eden
	1515 (approx.)	Siena hears VCOS' Mayday via ABC helicopter and stands by VCOS
	1525	AMSA records 3 EPIRBs (Team Jaguar, merchant ship & trawler)
	1527	Dixie Chicken going to stand by Outlaw
	1530	Cyclone retires
	1535	Rapscallion heading to Eden, not retiring
	1600	Solo Globe Challenger (SGC) knockdown & dismasted; helicopter lifts injured crewman off VCOS; Team Jaguar requesting assistance, crew ok
	1623	Pippin reports SGC knocked down and dismasted, crew ok, standing by
	1635	Canon Maris retires, heading to Sydney
	1638	Challenge Again heading to Gabo Island
	1640	Not Negotiable heading to Eden for shelter
	1644	Sword of Orion heading to Eden, 38°18'S,150°17'E
	1650	Sword of Orion roll-over 360°, dismasted, MOB, May Day, EPIRB activated on deck, lost sight of MOB 5-7 minutes later
	1655	RRV broadcasts reminder to the skippers that the responsibility/decision to continue racing rests with them.
	1700	AMSA declares May Day for general area, winds of 60 knots and multiple incidents; Team Jaguar advised commercial tow available through "Moira Elizabeth" ETA 6 hrs; Winston Churchill knock down, hull damage, sinking
	1702	Chutzpah heading to Eden, all ok

DATE	TIME	EVENT
27/12/98	1711	Bin Rouge retires, heading north
	1712	Impeccable heading to Eden, not retiring, all ok
	1713	Inner Circle seeking shelter Gabo Island
	1720	Business Post Naiad (BPN) rolled 360° and dismasted, 5 crew on desk washed overboard and recovered, deck breached, engine started and course set in northerlydirection, May Day sent & EPIRB activated; Hawk V retires, 2 injured crewman
	1721	Winston Churchill May Day, boat taking water, 9 crew are getting into life raft, yacht sinks minutes later
	1737	Hi Flyer heading to Eden, injured crew member, not retiring
	1738	Midnight Special heading to Gabo Island
	1745	Forzado retires
	1746	Unipro retires to Eden
	1748	Loki reports smashed window, takes on water
	1749	Yendys advises of May Day from BPN, message that BPN had rolled over with major hull damage,its position 38°05'S,150°32'E, was attempting to steer 174°
	1755	Southerly heading to Sydney, all ok
	1800	Siena relieved of rendering assistance to VCOS by SAR authorities and retires due to injured crew member; Ruff N Tumble retires; Zeus II dismasted, retires
	1810	Adagio retires, heading to Bermagui
	1815	BPN 43 miles from Disaster Bay, 38°03'S, 150°32'E, steering 300°, 5.4 knots; Sword of Orion sights yacht, fires flares
	1820	Relish IV retires, all ok; crew of VCOS airlifted; Anitpodes heading to Eden, not retiring
	1825	Jack Guy heading to Jervis Bay or Sydney
	1830	Kingurra reports May Day, MOB (John Campbell) no life jacket, 38°00'S,150°47'E,

DATE	TIME	EVENT
27/12/98	1830	(contd.) deployed EPIRB, boat was knocked down
	1907	Liquid Asset returning to Eden, not retiring, all ok
	1910	Kingurra MOB recovered by police en route Malacoota: Pippin released from rendering assistance to SGC and continues racing; Outlaw structural damage, Dixie Chicken standing by; Secret Mens Business crew injury, drop off at Eden and continue racing; Trust Bank Hummingbird retires to Eden
	1915	BPN via Yendys, BPN at 37°59'S, 150°31'E steering 299°, 6 knots
	1920	B52 rolled 360° and dismasted, activated EPIRB; Sword of Orion MOB, helicopter en route, 38°14'S,150°24'E; Margaret Rintoul II, 38°15'S, 150°22'E reports red flare sighted at 1845 hours
	1930	Sagacious & Hummingbird retire
	1940	Zeus II via emergency aerial heading to Eden
	1958	Tilting at Windmills advises BPN steering 295° at 5 knots, 37°56'S, 150°31'E
	2000	Midnight Special rolled 360° and dismasted, EPIRB deployed; Solandra dismasted, reported by merchant ship "Patsy Ann", 37°45'S, 150°38'E motoring to Eden; Hi Flyer retires; Sword of Orion hears SAR aircraft overhead
	2006	Jubilation sheltering in Eden, not retiring
	2010	Rapscallion dropping off injured crew in Eden; Loki no motor 38°02'S, 150°37'E, steering 075°
	2015	Gundy Grey knock down, life raft inflated & washed away, injured crew, retires to Eden
	2016	Dixie Chicken retires
	2030	Ocean Design retires
	2045	BPN concerned about fuel contamination; Sword of Orion heard SAR helicopter, gives position, EPIRB placed in water
	2049	Miintinta's engine overheats and stops

DATE	TIME	EVENT
27/12/98	2055	Bright Morning Star retires to Eden
	2106	Terra Firma retires to Eden
	2112	Team Jaguar asked to release flares so "Moira Elizabeth" can identify
	2119	Inner Circle reports position of red flare 37°37'S, 150°33'E
	2130	Alexander of Creswell & Solandra (lost rig) retire; Challenge Again & Inner Circle sheltering at Gabo Island; merchant ship "Patsy Ann" departing to area of Winston Churchill
	2136	Kendell, Southerly, Wild Thing & Impeccable report sighting of red flares
	2200	Miintinta taking water, trawler from Eden to rescue
	2201	Ocean Road sheltering in Eden
	2210	Team Jaguar 37°41'S, 150°32'E activates red flare for "Moira Elizabeth"; Sea King helicopter returning to site of Sword of Orion
	2218	"Moira Elizabeth" activates red flare for Team Jaguar
	2224	"Moira Elizabeth" was offered to be released by RRV, takes decision to stay
	2235	Hawk V retires
	2300	Midnight Special activates EPIRB
	2300	BPN rolled through 360° for second time, inverted for 4-6 minutes
	2302	Team Jaguar sees 2 red flares at 280°, distance one mile; "Moira Elizabeth" about 9 miles away, sees nothing, expects rendezvous 2 hours
	2310	Miintinta last report, 36°56'S, 150°37'E, flooding
	2322	Bacardi reports helicopter in company with Sword of Orion; Sword of Orion taking water, another helicopter searching area for MOB
	2325	RRV in search pattern for Winston Churchill
	2356	Team Jaguar activates red flare for "Moira Elizabeth" 37°31'S, 150°43'E
	2359	Inner Circle reports sighting of red flare

DATE	TIME	EVENT
28/12/98	0000	Helicopter dispatched to search for Winston Churchill
	0003	Tenacious 37°34'S, 150°18'E knockdown, no motor, all ok, heading to Eden
	0005	Boomaroo sheltering near Eden, continuing race
	0036	Impeccable retires, anchored in Eden
	0050	"Moira Elizabeth" fires red flare for Team Jaguar to sight, flare sighted
	0109	"Moira Elizabeth" 4 miles from Team Jaguar
	0215	"Moira Elizabeth" preparing to take Team Jaguar under tow
	0250	Sword of Orion hears SAR helicopter, gives position, EPIRB placed in water
	0300	Sked 4
	0305	Vessels asked to deactivate beacons if not in imminent danger by RRV
	0315	3 people winched off Sword of Orion, balance will be picked up by daylight; Midnight Special fires flares
	0500	Miintinta towed by fishing boat "Josephine Jean", still taking water; Sword of Orion, 6 remaining crew being lifted; Midnight Special rolled 360° again during helicopter rescue, 5 crew airlifted en route Merimbula
	0555	Team Jaguar under tow, 43 miles to Eden, all ok
	0557	Miintinta crew transfers to trawler via life raft
	0600	4 crew airlifted off Midnight Special en route Malacoota, boat abandoned
	0610	RCC - confirmation 6 crew airlifted from Sword of Orion
	0645	Adagio motoring to Bermagui
	0705	Outlaw 36°52'S,151°42'E damaged, engine problems, heading to Eden, crew ok, requesting stand by
	0710	Zeus II dismasted 36°45'S, 151°23'E, engine problems, jury rig to conserve fuel

DATE	TIME	EVENT
28/12/98	0738	Miintinta, tow line broke, yacht abandoned
	0800	She's Apples II damaged steering, returns to Eden for repairs; 3 crew airlifted off SGC
	0841	BPN 7 crew winched off, 2 dead crew remaining on boat, BPN 37°22'S,150°42'E
	0846	97 no steering 37°58'S,151°02'E
	0859	"Moira Elizabeth" towing Team Jaguar, 37°06'S, 150°21'E, ETA 1230-1300 hours in Eden
	0924	Antuka retires, motoring to Eden
	1000	Atara sends distress email accidentally
	1005	Veto instructed by RRV to light flare following 2 missed Skeds
	1017	Relish entering Eden, injured crewman, requests ambulance
	1020	Sea Jay retires to Eden
	1030	Fudge relays Atara's message to RRV, apologises for mishap
	1039	She's Apples II departing Eden to Hobart — racing
	1049	Kendell departing Eden to Hobart — racing
	1050	SCG no communications, adrift 151°53'E, Navy asked to attend scene
	1103	Lady Penrhyn retires in Eden
	1106	Chutzpah retires to Eden
	1115	Search pattern for Winston Churchill established by AMSA
	1118	Wild Thing ETA Eden 0600 hours
	1203	Loki retires to Bermagui, no motor
	1215	Challenge Again departing Eden to Hobart — racing
	1243	Breakaway departing Eden to Hobart — racing
	1245	Bin Rouge departing Eden to Hobart — racing
	1246	Tenacious retires to Eden
	1324	She II departing Eden to Hobart — racing
	1335	Vagrant entering Eden, retired, one injured crew

DATE	TIME	EVENT
28/12/98	1400	Sked 5
	1645	"Tug Rubicon" departs Eden to tow SGC
	1825	Bin Rouge rudder problems
	2130	Search terminated for MOB for Sword of Orion, search for Winston Churchill's crew ongoing
	2230	Helicopter finds 2 crew from Winston Churchill, advised 3 others swept from life raft at 0500 hours
	2325	Bin Rouge retired in Eden
29/12/98	0125	New Horizons 37°01'S,151°07'E, no engine, no radio, 4 crew injured
	0156	Secuité/PAN PAN from Race Control Centre for yachts to look out for 3 MOB from Winston Churchill 37°18'S,150°40'E
	0201	Waitangi II via Avanti lost radio, everything ok
	0305	Veto missed Sked 3 (and Sked 2), asked to activate EPIRB by RRV
	0400	P3 aircraft dispatched to search area for Veto, "Tug Rubicon" and "HMAS Newcastle" searching area for SGC
	0810	Tartan departing Eden to Hobart — racing
	0830	Phone call from owner of Veto, dismasted, no radio, all ok, at Batemans Bay
	0859	Mike Bannister's body (Winston Churchill's MOB) found
	1000	SGC 2 crew taken on board of "HMAS Newcastle", 3 crew remaining on board of SGC, motoring to Bermagui
	1700	Search for Winston Churchill's 2 missing MOB abandoned

Photo Credits